CREATIVE FIREPOWER!

Grow Faster with New ProActive Tactics in Advertising and Public Relations.

Robert T. Haller

Leister and Sons Publishing Company
New York

Contents

In memory of Louis Martin, who inspired me to forge ahead; and whose indomitable spirit helped make this book a reality.

Preface

We just completed a client meeting with venture capitalists. My client, Kash Gobindram, president of Kash 'N Gold, Ltd., had decided to take his company public. My agency had doubled his business in just six months. We doubled it again this year. And, we'll do it again next year, maybe better. Not bad for a rapidly emerging growth company . . . with great aspirations.

That's how this book got started.

Kash and I were talking on a Friday evening, discussing how we could make both of our companies grow faster. Normally in the agency business, we say: "We'll grow as you grow!" And we will.

However, Kash said to me: "Bob, you need to write a book. You need notoriety. You need to be famous. You need visibility. Look what it did for David Ogilvy, Ken Roman and Jane Maas, Al Ries and Jack Trout. You're a great strategic and tactical planner. You have killer instincts. Tell the world what you did for us. Besides, I've never seen my name in a book."

And so it started. Should I or shouldn't I?

I had many brainstorming sessions with my partners,

Bob Muller and Charlotte Haller, and close associates, Bill Taylor, Bob Button, Mel Ross and an old publishing pro, Louis Martin. We spent weeks creating alternative titles and positioning statements until we reached a final decision. We would focus on new opportunities in advertising and public relations. They would be ProActive and marketing-driven. All the way!

Then I read the new book by Herb Schmertz, Mobil Oil's scrappy vice president of public affairs: "Good-bye To The Low Profile."

That was it. I knew it was my turn at bat.

Besides, how could I disappoint a client. So, here we go.

If anybody has any doubt about who the Godfather of this book is, you can blame my good friend, Kash.

ONE

The ProActive Challenge

Half measures don't win. There is no substitute for victory. Or success.

Strategic planning and brilliant tactics are the keys to winning big battles. While superiority of numbers and firepower win on the battlefield, you must *outsmart* your competition *decisively* to win in the marketplace.

What we are going to talk about is total victory and maximum, cohesive force. New ProActive tactics . . . not the kind found on a high intensity battlefield, but the kind applied to a highly competitive and volatile marketplace. Where you and I do business every day.

We do *not* believe in the theory of minimum force and gradual escalation. That concept killed over 55,000 Americans and lost the Vietnam War, a tragedy that still haunts our nation. This same concept has killed many brands and corporate dreams.

We do *not* tiptoe into the water to see how far it takes us or buy a ticket half-way across the Atlantic. It's still a long, long swim to safety . . . if you make it. Odds are, you won't.

We believe in doing things right . . the first time! In concept, execution and follow-through.

We believe in ProActive marketing. Take the initiative and keep it. Look at the flip-side of every problem and search for alternative opportunities. Develop the best solution and exploit it to the fullest. Create new strategies and hard-hitting tactics. Pursue the objective relentlessly . . . and then some.

We believe in achieving nothing short of victory. In winning BIG!

BIG dreams reap BIG rewards. Isn't that what business is all about?

We are mission-oriented. We make things happen. When you think ProActive, you *act first* and take a *pre-emptive* leadership position. Make the other guy react.

Use a multi-dimensional planning approach. Think total marketing communications from the outset. Strategy isn't thought up. It's thought out. Corporate and brand positioning must be sharply honed. They must be on target.

I have worked at major blue chip advertising agencies — Ogilvy & Mather, BBDO, McCaffrey & McCall and Interpublic. My staff understands and uses all of the planning disciplines that major agencies use. However, we do one *critical* thing different. We combine advertising *and* public relations, using a dynamic, marketing-driven, synergistic technique called ProActive communications that gets results.

To focus effectively on a client's business, one should wear two hats, agency *and* client. Having worked on the client side as an advertising manager at two major companies, I think like a client. I look at every buck spent as if it were coming out of my own pockets.

Statistical planners sometimes lose their perspective when crunching numbers. They are *not* just numbers, a million here and two hundred thousand there. It's money. Real money. Planners can get so swept up in analyzing cost efficiencies, they sometimes lose sight of the true value of the dollar. If they counted the numbers out in singles like a cashier, many expenditures would be planned at lower and more cost effective spending levels.

I frequently have heard art directors and production managers at the big agencies rationalize high costs, saying: "But that's what it costs. You've got to pay the going price for quality, even if you go over budget. If you don't buy first-class, you end up with schlock."

And I say: "Nonsense! Let's take the increases out of *your* salary." It's amazing how quickly an art director and production manager will quickly find other resources at lower negotiated prices. This applies to both print and television, where the high cost of production has almost become obscene.

Our staff has been able to reduce art, photography and production expenditures by more than 50 percent, delivering the same quality and consistency of product. Our secret — there are two price levels in town. One for the major agencies and one for everyone else. We use different resources than the major agencies and negotiate prices far more effectively. And we deliver as promised.

This is one of the reasons why so many companies have started in-house agencies. Yes, you can reduce production costs and recapture media commissions. But the price is heavy. What you lose is agency objectivity, talent and the big Madison Avenue look. And in most cases, the BIG IDEA, which can have a *negative* effect on your bottom line.

Not all agencies are alike. People *do* make the difference. For years, agencies have tried to integrate advertising and public relations functions into a holistic marketing matrix. It has *not* worked for many reasons.

Advertising and public relations people are adversaries

to a certain degree. Both compete for *their* share of the same corporate budget. Both are somewhat mistrustful of each other and their techniques. Both are intuitively afraid that the other may screw-up the program and cause irreparable damage to *their* part of the business. Both are excellent practitioners of their own craft.

At the corporate level, the public relations director wants to report directly to the CEO, not to the marketing director. There are good reasons to support this juxtaposition. A good public relations director must have the CEO's *ear* . . . and be an extension of presidential and board of directors' policy. In dealing with the press and editors, there is a strong division between *church and state.* Between editorial departments and those advertising people, who may contaminate the morals and objectivity of the purists if you let them. (Ad agencies can bring advertising pressure to bear, if you're not careful.) Since many public relations people are former journalists and would prefer to work as journalists if the salaries were only higher, they retain the same *purist* thinking.

"We'll publicize your advertising," they say. "We'll publicize your products. We *know* what editors want." And so they preach, as *guardians* of the true faith.

But, do they know? Really know?

As marketing practitioners, we are image makers. We create quality images for corporations and their brands. Every communication has an impact on your corporate and brand image — external with the media, the public and stockholders, government, financial and community relations; internal with labor and employee relations.

You can't divorce public relations from marketing nor allow a "holier-than-thou" attitude to prevail during marketing planning sessions. There is a need to create a better understanding within the public relations profession and train people how to use the public relations tools available to achieve corporate and brand sales goals. Fortunately, having spent ten years as an appliance retailer where I used public relations as an *effective* tactical marketing tool, I automatically think *both* ways . . . advertising *and* public relations.

Stephen B. Elliott, the former corporate director of advertising for the W.R. Grace Company, said in an interview that he thinks *both* ways, too. Steve started off as a journalist and learned his craft at the J. Walter Thompson advertising agency, one of the industry giants. Steve spearheaded the corporate advertising advocacy campaign for W.R. Grace, marketing a corporate point of view to help his company grow.

Herb Schmertz, Mobil Oil's vice president of public affairs, has also marketed his company's objectives, introducing new op-ed advertising techniques as an aggressive tactical marketing tool. As a former labor negotiator, Herb learned his craft well, using ProActive marketing tactics. He knows instinctively when to push, when to pull back, when to compromise . . . how to achieve objectives where everyone keeps *face*. And how to build friendly alliances, even with former adversaries.

It all gets down to objectives, attitude, motivation, positive thinking, forward planning and multi-dimensional *smarts*. Advertising *and* public relations can pay off handsomely, if employed as cohesive, ProActive tactical marketing tools.

That's what this book is all about.

TWO

One Step Ahead

Everything is marketing-driven.

ProActive advertising and public relations can sell your corporate image, products and services . . . as they have never been sold before. If you unleash this new dynamic force, your company can leapfrog ahead of competition.

There are twenty principles to consider.

1. *Take a fresh look at your business.* Throw out all of the sacred cows. Emancipate yourself from being held captive to the way you've done things for years. Constrain office politics and rise above them, ensuring that all key executives and players do the same thing. Streamline analytical and decision-making procedures, even your organizational structure, so you can take advantage of new ProActive opportunities as they arise.

2. *Focus on attitude.* Capture the "Can-do" spirit of the entrepreneur. Build and create and innovate in everything you do. Develop the intuitive energies, positive thinking and work ethos that make great things happen. Be willing to take calculated risks that pay off BIG. Motivate your corporate, group and individual managers. Then, harness that energy to achieve your goals.

3. *Recruit people smarter than yourself.* Look for super-achievers; high energy and talented people who thrive on challenge. People who dare to be different. They can be team players or loners, all sharing a common bond as adventure-seekers, who can rise to any occasion and get results; people who have an innate burning desire to succeed; people who place the thrill of competition above all else. The *doers* of this world who take great pride in accomplishment, in climbing new mountains, in forging new records. In winning! Turn them loose and let them fly. Guide this vitality in the right direction and watch your business GROW.

4. *Lead by example.* For ProActive communications to function effectively, leadership must start at the top and funnel down. The full cooperation of senior management is essential, not as reflections of what the CEO may be thinking, but as decisive actions that accomplish specific goals. Management must be dedicated to this principle and set high standards for all subordinates to follow. ProActive planning must become The Order of the Day, every day. Everybody must participate, both in spirit and in fact. No deviations. No procrastination, No rationalization. No waiting it out. No playing it safe.

You cannot afford to pay lip service to ProActive communications and expect it to work. It requires total commitment, total involvement and allocation of sufficient resources. It means going beyond the core mission and forcefully influencing your socioeconomic and technical environment . . . to improve corporate performance and growth . . . to exercise corporate responsibility . . . to act as a good corporate citizen, which ensures economic survival. And, to have perseverance to see it through.

5. *Be objective.* Instill in your staff the discipline of true candor in all of their thinking. If your people do their homework properly, ProActive plans can be built on a

strong foundation of facts rather than supposition. In most business dealings, no one sets out deliberately to be dishonest. It is a human trait to be subjective; to defend your judgments, good or bad, justifying them with a broad array of facts and rationalizations; possibly trying to guard your flanks and rear.

The system can work against you. How many times have brand managers charged ahead unwisely with a new product introduction, going for the long shot? Since this may be their only chance to have a winner, they plunge ahead taking unnecessary risks. Objectivity can limit potential failures if career safeguards are built into the system to protect the jobs of your subordinates, who must survive with the "go, no-go" decisions of corporate life. It is a thorny problem that only ProActive management can solve. Some of the "go for broke" misjudgments that affect your bottom line can be prevented through greater emphasis on objectivity.

True objectivity can provide a strong factual base to make sound business decisions that reduce the risk and assure controlled growth, propelling your company forward.

6. *Learn from experience.* We are great believers in the concept of *lessons learned.* Project reviews are planned after every operation and campaign are completed. What did we do right? What did we do wrong? What could we do better? We play the Devil's Advocate and let the chips fall where they may. Nobody's job is in jeopardy. This type of exercise usually leads to higher levels of performance. It requires positive thinking and a great amount of tact to strip away defensive mechanisms and rationalizations. The results: more effective fine-tuning of a successful campaign or creation of a bold new concept to help a company forge ahead.

Many of us in the creative world can go to the greatest show on Broadway and tell how it could have been done better. It happened to me when I saw *Fiddler on the Roof* and *42nd Street*, which were both long-running, profit-making shows. But who is to say that the scale from 1 to 10 must top-out at 10? Why erect outer limits that discourage higher levels of performance?

When you believe in the *pursuit of excellence*, it doesn't matter how good you are or how great a job you accomplish, there is always room for improvement. Who's to say that you can't get a 15 or a 20?

During World War II, the U.S. Navy Seabees had a marvelous slogan: "The difficult we do right away. The impossible takes just a little bit longer!"

7. *Hire an outside agency.* Many companies, products and services have foundered because of internal politics, lack of objectivity and an absence of ProActive thinking. Failure can be the result of poor planning discipline, not doing homework properly, not reading the market or competition correctly, not anticipating or adjusting to change quickly enough — poor judgments that could be avoided.

That's why companies need outside agencies for advertising and public relations. Agencies provide professional talent, objectivity and diagnostic findings that are the cornerstones to successful campaigns; no different than using consulting attorneys or physicians for legal and medical matters. Agencies can avoid internal company politics and tell it like it is. Straight from the shoulder, diplomatically and persuasively. Brainstorming sessions can reach the core of a problem, backed-up by facts, sometimes intuitive *gut* feelings from years of experience. There is no substitute for third-party thinking. However, an agency is not the decision-maker. You are! It is your company, your money. An agency can only recommend.

Work closely with your agency as partners, keep them totally informed and involved; motivate them to think of your business as their own.

8. *Think product at all times.* In ProActive planning, approach every assignment like it is a unique product entity, whatever its nature. When planning a brand strategy for a new product or line extension, tangible or intangible, think *product* and visualize it as a competitive product, distinctly different from other products in the marketplace. When marketing a new service or reinforcing an established service, visualize it as a *product*, competitive with other service products. When it is a corporate image campaign, visualize the company as a corporate *product*, competitive with other corporate products. And when promoting a corporate advocacy issue, visualize the issue as a *product* competitive with the counter-issue.

The *product* is what you have to sell. The marketing fundamentals and planning disciplines are similar. They encompass a review of the industry, category and competition, product features and benefits, price and value, distribution and service and target audiences.

9. *Create a unique product positioning.* By looking at every entity as a *product*, the first task is to think about its *positioning* . . . or need for *repositioning* in its category or industry. David Ogilvy, one of the great pioneers in the advertising field, once said that how you position your product is probably the most important marketing decision a company can make. And he was right.

For years, Madison Avenue greats have developed different theories about how to position your product effectively in the marketplace . . . to compete for your *share of mind* as well as *share of market.* Rosser Reeves, former chairman of the Ted Bates Agency, called the concept the USP, for Unique Selling Proposition. At Interpublic, it was called the Unique Persuasion Proposition. Al Ries and Jack Trout of Trout & Ries Advertising lay claim to creating the term *positioning* in 1969. Whatever its name or whoever authored it or whether it is called marketing positioning, product positioning or positioning, the concept continues to be the foundation for formulating sound marketing strategy. Essentially, *positioning* creates that one singular concept that has the greatest capacity to persuade . . . to *sell* your products and services in a competitive marketplace in the greatest volume . . . to carve-out a major *share of market* for your product and capture the largest *share of mind* from the defined target audience.

The simple test: think of a product category. What brand comes to mind? First, second and third? For personal computers, you might say IBM first, Apple second, NEC third, or possibly another brand. The challenge is to be in the top box in the battle for *share of mind.*

For corporate image and issue advertising, you want to create the one singular concept that has the greatest capacity to persuade . . . to *sell* your corporate image and advocacy issues in the marketplace of ideas . . . to all of your target audiences, influentials and constituencies.

10. Focus on the BIG IDEA. Defining a correct positioning is only the start. It must be *focused* on the middle of the target's bull's-eye. You cannot place enough emphasis on focus. It is so easy to wander, to stray slightly off-course from a precise trajectory. It takes discipline and training to keep a steady eye on the critical center of the bull's-eye. The key to ProActive planning is to find the right *trigger*, the right *leverage point* to overcome resistance and force maximum positive response from your target audience. Your product's tone-of-voice must be in harmony with the needs of your audience, serving-up what *they* believe they need; not what *you* think they need.

This is the BIG IDEA. It is that one persuasive idea . . . the *emotional trigger* . . . that unleashes the full sales potential of your product.

Creating the BIG IDEA is an art, not a science. While research can point you in the right direction, the creative juices will ultimately take over. Intuitive thinking and judgment prevail. It usually results from a lonely copywriter and art director struggling over a typewriter and layout board, rather than a decision by committee. The BIG IDEA can come at anytime. At the office, while driving, when taking a shower or waking-up at 3:00 o'clock in the morning. Some of my best concepts come just before I get out of bed, having a chance to think quietly about ideas generating overnight in my sub-conscious. Other times, the idea comes right out-of-the-blue, hitchhiking on some unrelated theme. You learn to live with these creative manifestations, knowing that they will penetrate the void and somehow surface in a flash of pure brilliance.

11. *Create a personality for your product.* Every product should have a *distinct personality*, a character of its very own. When people think of a brand, service or corporation, they should be able to create a mental image of it; a mental picture that they can almost touch and feel and talk to. It is not too different from describing the features, background and activities of a close friend or aquaintance to another person. A friend's personality and features are usually sharp in your mind and relatively easy to describe. Try to create this same type of brand or corporate personality that sets you apart from your competition. The personality must be attention-getting and memorable. This should result in increased awareness, preference and sales.

12. *Build interaction into your campaign.* Involve the target audience mentally, emotionally and physically. Tempt them to do what you want them to do . . . to buy your goods and services . . . to buy now, not later . . . or never. To perceive your company favorably . . . to agree with your public relations programs and support your corporate point-of-view, taking whatever actions you propose.

Use direct response and telemarketing techniques to sell your products and establish a dialogue with customers and prospects. Send them literature and follow-up promotional mailings. Cross-sell other marketing programs.

13. *Beat the power curve* The theory behind ProActive planning is to *act first* and force your competition to react to your operations, not the other way around. This can only be accomplished through systematic planning . . . thinking ahead to anticipate problems and opportunities *before* they happen. Agendize and prioritize so you can stay ahead of the competitive power curve, rather than fall behind it. Position your company for change and growth by setting a leadership pace within your industry. Act decisively and control your company's destiny. Develop sound strategies and bold tactics that generate momentum, build bigger markets and keep the competition off-balance to achieve your goals.

Many companies spend too much time watching competition and reacting to it. There never is enough time for forward planning. Everyone is too busy putting out fires or beating the bushes for more sales or reacting to unexpected problems that need to be solved immediately.

We live in dramatic times. The marketplace is volatile with no let-up in sight. Rapidly changing technology and competitive pressures, domestic and international, will propel your company into the 21st Century with lightning speed. Rising population and demographic shifts, changing life-styles and buying patterns, increased consumer demands, rising expectations and many other factors will force companies to develop new ProActive marketing strategies and tactics.

How do you stay ahead of the power curve? Better yet, how do you catch-up so you can get one step ahead?

14. *Plan on a multi-dimensional track.* You need to plan and operate on two separate tracks that are time phased with milestones for critical actions and accountability. The first track is *business as usual*, planning ahead for next season and next year, conducting on-going operations, putting-out brush fires that continue to erupt; achieving your sales projections and shipping the goods.

Simultaneously, you need to establish a ProActive planning task force to *leapfrog ahead* of day-to-day business to overcome the daily pressures of reactive planning. If the workloads and travel schedules of your key executives are too heavy, you may need to back them up with professional administrative support so they can delegate work and free themselves up for foward planning. An alternative is to hire a strategic planner for each operating division. He should be familiar with your business and coordinate with key executives, gaining their input and recommendations. A second alternative is to hire an outside management consultant, who can help restructure your company and write the required ProActive strategic plan.

15. *Develop a ProActive situation analysis.* ProActive planning requires a methodical *environmental* situation analysis of all the marketing, economic, sociological, technical and geopolitical factors that may affect your business. No current issues should be overlooked, since their impact could have broad ramifications in the future. They should be reviewed on a trend basis to keep sharp adjustments in perspective. Market dynamics need to be evaluated, defining technological and competitive threats; consumer, trade and labor demands; problems and opportunities; socioeconomic pressures and perceived competitive weakness, which you can exploit fully. Conversely, you want to detect adverse trends, shifts in social behavior and corporate vulnerabilities that can be used against your company.

Greater emphasis needs to be placed on innovation and research and development. New products, not just line extensions or "me-too" products, but truly new products that will create new and bigger markets that your company can dominate. If your company is overburdened with the goal of achieving short-term profits, your inability to generate additional funds for innovation and marketing may restrict future company growth. This limitation may require a new infusion of capital and resources. You may want to consider selective trade-offs in stock to attract new investment capital and the right ProActive planners who can make your company grow faster.

As you update the ProActive situation analysis, assumptions should be developed, which are based on conditions and activities that you can forecast for the future. These assumptions should recognize controllable conditions and those beyond your control. Estimated levels of sales, costs, expenses and profit goals should be projected by time frame. Competitive resistance and counter-force tactics should be anticipated. These assumptions should encompass your corporate mission, objectives, resources, capabilities and operating procedures. Risk assessment should also be estimated.

16. *Make your strategic plan actionable.* Fact-finding and recording of historical information are essential to strategic planning. After the situation analysis is completed, a shortfall can occur when strategic objectives and tactics need to be formulated. Most marketing professionals find this task challenging and formidable.

When writing the marketing plan, your objectives should be specific, realistic, attainable and measurable. They should be targeted on those market segments that afford the greatest growth potential and return on investment. Modeling and charting are helpful analytical tools that can provide new insights in strategic planning.

Scenarios need to be designed for each objective, describing alternative tactics and courses of action. Your company's resources, capabilities, operational readiness and shortfalls are plugged-in to determine their impact.

An investment spending program should be developed to evaluate the effect that increased advertising and promotion spending will have on sales, market share, distribution and profitability. This should be planned on more than one expenditure level, possibly using a high and low spending plan, forecasting on both an aggressive and a conservative basis.

The alternative plans should be evaluated to determine the best course of action.

17. *Test and test again.* Once you have determined the best course of action or the best alternative courses of action, a test market program should be planned prior to a regional rollout or national expansion. Sufficient time and research funds will be required. While testing is expensive, it can save your company a large amount of money by reducing the risk of failure. It provides the opportunity to evaluate your product and marketing program under realistic, competitive marketing conditions and to make whatever improvements are necessary so that your product has the best fighting chance when you go national.

Experience has proven that test markets should be selected in sets of three for each major variable to be tested. Control markets should be established as a base. Three test markets are selected to prevent the problem of how to analyze findings when one market is up and the other market is down because of unexpected market conditions. The third market can be your tie-breaker.

Advertising, sales promotion and public relations should be employed at the same or varying weights that you plan to use when you go national. While media costs vary from market to market, you will be testing the media mix, media weight, impression delivery and content of your advertising and promotion.

If you load up the test market with higher levels of advertising and promotion than you plan to use when you go national, you may be successful in the test markets, but fail when you go national. That is why everything should be representative and tested at relative weights.

Some companies prefer to load up a market to ensure success, recognizing that competition may counter-attack with higher than normal expenditures to kill your product while it is still in the test market stage. This is a contingency that should be planned, allocating additional counter-attack funds that can be projected nationally. Excessive loading can distort your final evaluation. There are many research techniques that can be used throughout the ProActive planning and implementation process. The key is to keep testing . . . to improve and fine-tune every element in the marketing mix.

18. *Feedback can be your Sunday punch.* It is almost like instant replay in professional football, where you can spot a weakness in the opponent's defense, take advantage of it and put big points on the scoreboard. You can also verify an official's questionable call or prove him wrong. During the testing and evaluation stages, monitoring systems assure timely and accurate reporting of essential information. During national expansion and implementation, feedback reports are critical to success.

Especially during the growth and maturity stages, you can capitalize on local market opportunities and exploit them to the fullest. A *systematic* feedback reporting system needs to inform top management of the rapidly changing conditions in major and smaller markets, where new competitive products are being tested and evaluated.

When key executives and field representatives understand their role in ProActive planning and the true purpose of feedback reports, they become your company's "eyes and ears" — their observations and insights can help determine the future course of events.

With lap computers and modems now available at relatively low prices, you may want to consider issuing them to your field reps for quick and easy feedback reports. Your ProActive planners should design a brevity code to communicate essential information quickly. The feedback system should be planned on a continuing cycle.

19. *Give it a sense of importance.* The daily pressures of business can often overwhelm the best intentions of management. Slippage can occur and your ProActive planning process can be slowly downgraded to a less important role. ProActive planning must be kept in the forefront at all times. It must have the CEO's mandate . . . that this will be the prevailing management technique for everyone.

One good way to motivate your people is to instill in them a *sense of purpose* in what they are doing. The "why we do it" can be just as important as "how we do it" or, "how we can do it better." Thus, the need to give it a *sense of urgency* . . . to plan and execute quickly, so your company can stay one step ahead.

20. *Seize the initiative.* Good timing is critical to success. The ability to seize the initiative and make smart ProActive judgments, while working with imperfect data, can be the difference between success and failure; between outstanding results or a lackluster performance.

The marketplace is littered with companies and products that have failed because they were too far behind the power curve. But were they really? Did they really understand the market dynamics and the needs of their customers? Did they generate demand for a new product that the consumer wanted or did they try to sell a product that didn't really satisfy a perceived consumer need? Did they bring their product to market when consumers were buying or did they delay too long and catch the market on the downswing? Did they react to competition and follow the leader with another "me-too" product? Or, did they tiptoe into the market with too little and too late?

The *window of opportunity* may be open for only a short period of time. Companies that want to charge ahead need to open their eyes and their minds . . . to *see beyond* what they know. To use ProActive planning so they can act decisively at the right moment. To take the high ground while opportunity beckons!

THREE

Combined Arms

Let's mobilize your resources and deploy maximum firepower upfront where it really counts. Let's energize that firepower into *creative firepower*, concentrate it against the best targets of opportunity and fire away. To role play for a minute, try to think of yourself like a military commander. He *combines* his infantry, armor, artillery, air and sea power to achieve maximum shock action, firepower and mobility. He uses every ProActive tactic at his disposal: frontal assaults and flanking attacks; airborne, airmobile and amphibious assaults; close air ground support and air strikes to penetrate deep into the enemy rear; to interfere, interrupt, interdict and neutralize; to dislodge, bypass and capture. He attacks aggressively in overwhelming force to seize the objectives and pursue the enemy until victory is won. He never lets up!

CEOs of small and medium size growth companies are similar to military commanders in many respects. They are action-oriented, have many of the same instincts and believe in many of the same principles . . . in teamwork, in unity of purpose and integration of effort. They *combine* advertising, sales promotion and public relations into a cohesive unified force, where all of the required disciplines are linked firmly together to achieve their sales goals. They all seem to share the same "Can do" entrepreneural spirit — always in-charge, directing the action, keeping their finger on the pulse of every part of their business. Always moving ahead . . . in the spirit of the offense.

Dynamic growth companies are never allowed to get fat. They are usually run lean and mean. They can't afford the expense of carrying large, unwieldy, executive staffs; nor do they want them. It slows down the action!

The CEO is boss. What he says goes! In many cases, he acts as his own marketing director. Having the best understanding of the company's core mission, the CEO sets corporate policy and objectives. He also makes the critical strategic decisions and oversees their implementation.

The late Vince Lombardi, the football coach of the Green Bay Packers and dean of coaches, once said: "Execution is everything!" I couldn't agree more. You can have the greatest playbook and players in the country, but if you don't get the right teamwork, if your players don't run the right patterns or blocking assignments correctly, your team won't score many touchdowns.

Execution *is* everything.

The marketing director is the key player, the one who can make it happen. He must be an astute strategic planner and a master tactician, charged with the responsibility to expand sales and distribution. Everything comes into play . . . product development, merchandising, pricing, packaging, and more.

He needs to energize his marketing communications, which include national, local and co-op advertising, print and broadcast; sales promotion and point-of-purchase displays; sales contests, incentive programs and premiums; trade shows and special events; catalogs, sales literature and direct mail; and when there is time, public relations.

There are never enough people to accomplish all of the tasks. The time demands are incredible . Nothing seems to be prioritized. Everything is needed *yesterday*. The factory never delivers the product on time. Shipments are always late. There never seems to be enough time to do it right, but always enough time to do it over. And somehow it gets done. When the boss motivates his troops to higher levels of performance, everyone marches to the same drummer's beat. When the boss says we will use public relations to sell our product, the staff falls into line. When the boss thinks ProActive, everyone thinks ProActive, too.

The enthusiasm that one finds in ProActive growth companies is contagious. The same principles can be adapted by larger controlled-growth companies and by many of the conglomerates.

An example of a hard-driving, ProActive CEO for a growth company is Robert Pliskin, president of Seiko Time Corporation. I first met Bob when he was the president of Longines Wittnauer Watch Company. Bob had been hired as CEO after a three-year series of sales declines. He was determined to turn it around. And he did with our help, using ProActive marketing strategy and tactics.

Pliskin was his own marketing director, working closely with his advertising agency, Ogilvy & Mather. David Scott, Chris Moore and I were assigned to the account as trouble-shooters . . . to stop the sales decline and save the account. We didn't know it at the time, but a letter firing the agency had already been drafted. But Bob, being fairminded and patient, gave us a last shot.

Under David Scott's leadership, it turned out to be our best shot. We used to refer to David, behind his back, of course, as "The Wiz." I've always had great respect for him . . . as one of General George Patton's tank commanders in North Africa during the early days of World War II, when the Allies were getting mauled; and also as an outstanding creative director. Chris was David's protege, fresh out of Princeton, who developed into a talented copy chief. We repositioned Longines as the premier Swiss watch, the one watch you'd want to give or receive as a gift. Everything else was second best. Tactically, we used TV for the first time, creating "I was hoping for a Longines" campaign. Disappointment was used as the *emotional leverage point* to break through viewer apathy. The commercial was an instant success with immediate sales increases. Within a year, research showed that we had *doubled* our levels of advertising awareness, brand awareness and brand preference, good sales indicators.

This was the first of four Longines success stories.

During the 1970s, new technology created havoc in the watch industry, which had enjoyed slow, but controlled growth up to that time. Digital watches roared onto the scene, capturing everyone's fascination. Everybody got into the act. High tech companies like Texas Instrument and Fairchild Instrument, consumer product companies like Gillette, plus all the big watch companies launched new products. The LED, soon followed by the LCD, were instant hits, until severe price cutting and service problems overwhelmed the watch industry.

Pliskin had the *sixth sense* to predict there would be no winners in the emerging digital price wars. He presented a new challenge to us: to rise above the price wars and promote the top of the Longines line; to highlight solid 14K gold watches, a market segment where competition was inactive. Our agency response was to create the Longines Golden Wings Collection. We promoted it on TV, using the successful "I was hoping for a Longines" theme; and in national magazines and newspapers.

About this time, Pliskin asked me to try to get publicity for his company and his product line; publicity that would help increase sales.

Most advertising agencies shy away from this type of a request, because it diverts dollars from the advertising budget to public relations. However, with my background in public affairs, I realized we could enhance Longines' credibility by getting national prominence in the newspapers, which could be merchandised to the trade, showing jewelers what editors were saying about Longines.

I jumped at the opportunity and turned the agency team loose. Jackie Kilgour, who handled O&M publicity at that time, arranged for Bob to be interviewed by Phil Dougherty for his column in the *New York Times*. Jackie pulled out all the stops, using the luxurious tenth floor conference room and serving Irish tea, which she knew Phil liked. The results: a great 1½ column story in the *New York Times*. Pliskin was delighted. His phone didn't stop ringing. Calls came in from all over the country, ordering more goods and opening new accounts.

Our campaign achieved national publicity when it was spoofed on network TV — on the Johnny Carson, David Letterman and Archie Bunker shows. Longines merchandised the publicity back to the trade, showing the jeweler how we were pre-selling their customers, reinforcing our role as the jeweler's watch company.

Pliskin had made it into the big time. Now, he got serious about public relations and asked me to recommend a public relations agency that could help him market his product on a continuous basis, which we arranged.

The digital watch business finally crashed and many newcomers to the watch industry got out of the business. Every company got hurt, manufacturer and jeweler alike. Some did not survive. While most of the watch companies dumped their LED lines, including Longines, our gold sales flourished during that two-year period, increasing dramatically from $250,000 to $14,000,000!

This was our second success in three years. Sales for Longines continued to rise under Pliskin's stewardship.

Anticipating new opportunities in another high potential market segment, we repositioned Wittnauer, a secondary brand whose styling had been improved, as a fine Swiss-styled watch that can be purchased at popular, affordable prices. The creative leverage point capitalized on Longines' prestigious image and Swiss styling, since Wittnauer was a product of the Longines Wittnauer Watch Company. Prospects were encouraged to demand the best . . . at their price range. A new awareness campaign was launched on TV: "I want a Wittnauer!" And sales began to climb.

At the end of five years, we had *doubled* sales for Longines and Wittnauer watches, helping increase sales from $25 million to over $50 million; our third success story.

We had a fourth success, which has never been written about until now. Pliskin's new publicity agency, which we helped recruit, arranged a major story in the *Chicago Tribune*, which was read by Mr. Hidiaka Moriya, then president of Hattori, North America.

We helped make Pliskin so successful . . . that he got a better job! Bob Pliskin is now president of Seiko Time, the largest watch company in the country.

I suspect Bob believed in the old adage: "If you can't beat them, join them!" And he did.

Pliskin went on to run a tight ship at Seiko, making waves whenever the marketing needs required it. He continues to use ProActive marketing strategy and tactics.

When an agency gets a new assignment, it should look at it from every perspective. It should discipline itself to be open-minded and not prejudge until it learns more about the client's business. Does the solution require advertising or public relations or sales promotion or special events or direct marketing or some combination?

Clients are concerned about the growth of their business, and rightfully so. Some look for a quick fix, a quick turnaround. Others look for faster controlled growth. They may not be happy with the creative work they are getting and want better results. They want to put a halt to rising production and media costs.

Clients want smarter, more experienced executives to work on their accounts, not the juniors parading through their halls. They want top management involvement, since that's what they pay for, and they want to reduce risk and eliminate failure.

They look for new creative ideas to solve difficult marketing problems. That's what our business is all about. They want to have a better understanding of how the agency business works. And they want the reassurance that their agency will love them, protect them, nurture them and make their business grow.

What they don't ask for, but really need are new ProActive marketing tactics that offer greater control and flexibilty, better impact and interaction, improved targeting and deeper market penetration.

The business schools and MBA programs are part of the problem, especially since the advent of the personal computer and Lotus 1-2-3 spread sheets. The schools have been grinding out mathematical *wunderkind*, many of whom have no real conception of what makes business work. They lack street smarts and realistic experience. They have been trained to run numbers many different ways, to use them to support a concept or to shoot it full of holes. They have a special jargon, converse in demographics, probability curves, Nielsen ratings, cpms, GRPs . . . and they call it efficiency.

I've seen weeks of study go into developing a proposal based on delivering optimum efficiency. It was efficient, yet totally ineffective. It didn't sell a damn thing!

When an agency talks cost effectiveness, this means fiscal responsibility. They should produce quality work at lower-negotiated prices. Media plans should be negotiated and executed the same way.

When an agency talks efficiency, this means doing things

right. When they talk effectiveness, this means doing the right things . . . at the right time . . . for the right reasons. And foremost in everyone's minds . . . to never lose sight of the ultimate goal. To *sell!* To get results. And to make a *profit.*

When public relations is combined with advertising, as part of our marketing mix, strong inroads can be made in the battle for *share of mind* that cannot be achieved by using advertising alone.

For example, when a product is promoted *editorially* as a major news or feature story in a national magazine or newspaper or on TV or radio, you establish credibility, believability, interest and interaction between the audience and your company. Just the fact that your *product* appeared as editorial in national media enhances its credibility far in excess of what can be achieved through advertising. When public relations and advertising combine, they become a powerful and formidable weapons system.

There is a big difference between press agentry and marketing-oriented publicity. The press agent usually has tunnel vision . . . to get his client's name, company and product into print. That's his job. And that's just about as far as his thinking goes. Any story is a good story. Just as long as it appears.

Right?

Wrong!

A ProActive marketing-oriented publicist is sensitive to your company's marketing objectives . . . to your corporate image . . . to how you want people to perceive your product . . . and to the action you'd like to see them take.

We've worked with press agents before, the good and the bad. The Calamity Janes and Unpredictable Dans will sell you on their media contacts and the mystique of getting media placements. They ask you to trust them and give them carte blanche. But buyer beware! Yes, you may get press coverage, but it could be all wrong. It could create the wrong image, using sensationalism instead of a marketing-oriented public information program.

There is no great mystery in working effectively with the press — both print and broadcast. These are the skills of our craft, and they are labor-intensive. Planning and pre-production are essential to creating a good story. Check, double check and then check again. Once your story or newscast becomes a happening, you can get tremendous mileage out of it. Media coverage can be managed to your advantage. Large stories can be reprinted along with their media logos for distribution to key accounts, prospects, influentials and other editors, who may now be encouraged to write *their* story, using a different editorial slant. Smaller stories can be ganged-up as a montage. These stories can be reprinted as inserts for sales and press kits and sales presentations.

When TV and radio placements are arranged, you may want to shoot behind-the-scenes photo coverage, making a special event out of the interview, talk show or newscast. Promotional mailers can be designed, using the photos and captions, telling what happened in exciting terms. The product is always the hero. And you could be, too.

This is basic marketing-oriented public relations, and it really reinforces the idea of progress and success.

A ProActive marketing publicist is constantly battling for limited media space and time. The guy who gets there first with the best story usually gets the action. In dealing with the trade press and a few consumer magazines, it helps when you're advertising in the same publication. While publishers insist on separation of *church and state*, they are not going to bite the hand that feeds them. You may have to do some hand holding, but *quid pro quo* deals can be arranged, where advertisers will get preferential treatment and publicity coverage. Your story has to stand on its own two legs, but if it is newsworthy, it will appear with prominence. The challenge is to achieve editorial continuity, not just isolated one-shot efforts.

As advertisers, you can obtain *free* advertising coverage as part of media merchandising promotions. Most media allow one to two percent of the advertiser's media budget to be used as a promotional allowance. This can result in free radio spots, outdoor posters, special media mailings to customer lists and other opportunities. If you ask, you get. Not all of the time, but lots of the time.

It doesn't cost to ask!

To assure continuity, friendly media relations should be maintained on an *on-going* basis, not just when you want to get a story published. The public relations and journalism professions are small industries. Everyone knows everyone else. It's a people business and you're only as good as your reputation. Burn someone just once in this business and you go down in flames . . . forever. People don't forget, especially editors. Since so much business is conducted over the telephone, you've got to be trusted and reliable, especially when working under the pressure of tight deadlines, a way of life in our business. Information must be accurate, complete, timely and responsive to editorial inquiries. You should also know how to work with confidential and sensitive information and know how to protect your sources.

As a colonel and public affairs officer in the U.S. Army Reserve, I am Pentagon-trained and have a *top secret* security clearance. There is a certain awareness and finesse involved when working with sensitive and classified information. In some cases, the information is on "close hold" and cannot be released at all. In other cases, limited information can be released in accordance with security guidelines, disseminating it on a relatively low visibility basis. Where security is not involved and the principle of "full disclosure" applies, stories can be disseminated for broadscale, high visibility use.

When you manage ProActive communications for companies in aerospace, defense and high tech industries, you've got to worry about the threat of technological transfer — of another country stealing your high tech secrets. Effective low visibility programs can be created that target on specific influentials to achieve short-term goals. You must learn the nuances and know how to work within this sensitive environment. Not everyone does.

In consumer products and services, confidentiality is just as important. You must know how to protect "inside" information and know how to market and package your programs effectively to the press.

This is where *creative firepower* comes in. Public relations is just as competitive as advertising, perhaps more so. You not only fight for *share of mind*, but also for *share of linage* and *share of airtime*. Since your batting average is only as good as your last story, you've got to be on top of the news, constantly searching for product twists that are newsworthy. How well you develop feature stories and package them to the press can make the crucial difference.

We have developed unique ProActive capabilities that are marketing-driven to generate greater media visibility and interaction. Advertising and public relations are interwoven where one supports the other. Combined, they provide greater control and maximum flexibility.

These new ProActive concepts, success stories and marketing opportunities that appear in the next chapters could be your bridge to tomorrow.

As we say in the infantry: "Follow me!"

FOUR

Creative Firepower

It was in mid-March, 1985 when our client, Stan Reiff, general manager of E.S.C. Electronics, called to tell me he was changing jobs. Stan is a well-known, highly knowledgeable, dynamic, marketing professional.

"Bob," he said. "I'm going over as marketing director. They're going to let me pick my own agency. You're a condition of employment," he joked, light-heartedly. "Do you want the business?"

When you have a growth agency, this is a telephone call you cherish. Getting new business is very competitive. You never know where a lead will come from. The best new business comes from referrals . . . from people who know you, know the kind of work you do . . . and know you always deliver as promised. Once you land a new account, you work hard to do the best creative job, since success breeds success.

With Stan moving on to greener pastures and having confidence in our agency, the decision was easy. "Absolutely!" I responded, hoping that he had gone over to AT&T, Panasonic, Sony, NEC or one of the other heavy hitters where the big bucks were.

"What's the name of the company?" I asked.

"Kash 'N Gold," Stan responded, enthusiastically. Stan is one of the sweet guys in this business who everyone loves. He's big, about 6 feet four inches and over 250 pounds. He doesn't have to be a tough guy. If he ever sat on you, you'd never get up. So he just keeps on selling and selling.

"Cash and what?" I asked.

"Gold." Stan answered, spelling it out. "G.O.L.D."

"What do they make?"

"Novelty phones," he explained. "Now Bob, we've only got six weeks to prepare for the consumer electronics show in Chicago. We need a brand name, a logo, two line catalogs and sell sheets, advertising, promotion and publicity."

That's how it all started.

We used ProActive marketing tactics from day one, integrating all of our communications activities. Based upon our unique cross-training in advertising and public relations, we developed new effective techniques that are still not quite understood in our industry.

These ProActive tactics were responsible for taking a relatively unknown company into the big time . . . from a *No Name* company into a *Big Name* . . . in six short months. We harnessed this momentum and propelled it forward, continuing to *double* sales as we charged ahead.

We met the president, Kash Gobindram, at our first meeting. Kash is a young, ambitious, somewhat reticent Sindhi Indian, who immigrated to the United States from Indonesia when he was 18. His father, a self-made millionaire, lives in Singapore and is well-known throughout the Far East.

After graduating from college in California, Kash decided to make the United States his home. He started an import-export company in New York in 1982, importing long-range telephones to sell in Latin America and Third World countries.

Recognizing new opportunities that unfolded from deregulation of the telephone industry, Kash decided there was real growth potential in this industry if he could develop his own *niche* in the marketplace.

On one of his buying trips to the Far East, Kash discovered some new novelty phones. He knew instinctively they could be marketed successfully in the United States. Utilizing his father's financial resources and manufacturing contacts, Kash focused on the novelty phone business as his marketing niche.

Stan Reiff was hired primarily to expand distribution nationally, using a mass merchandiser concept . . . selling to department stores in major cities across the country. Initially, Kash looked at Stan more as a national sales manager rather than marketing director, but Stan's responsibilities now include all marketing activities.

During our first meeting, Stan showed us the first of many novelty phones that we needed to promote. It was a gold metallic look-alike of the Porsche sportscar. "It's a quality product," Stan explained. "It's not anything like the disposable novelty phones that played havoc with the industry several years ago. We want to feature it at the CES Show. We don't have a license to name it the Porsche, so come back with a brand name. Quick!"

I enjoy creating new brand names. It's not easy, but once you hit on the right one, you know you're home free. Some copywriters go off in a corner and write lots of names, hoping that one or two will be approved.

We work this way, too. We've also developed different techniques, like those I started at Ogilvy & Mather.

At O&M, Roger Butler, a senior copywriter, and I were assigned to the American Express account to act as troubleshooters for *Space Bank*, a new product concept that centralized hotel and travel reservations for business travelers. American Express had wanted a new brand name, and we had gone through five copywriters. They had all struck-out. I can still recall walking into Roger's office, unobserved . . . and watching him struggle through the mental process that we all go through.

I'm sure Roger had been given a copy of the marketing objectives, strategy, positioning statement and probably a ten-point list of criteria for name development.

Roger sat at his desk with an 8½" x 11" yellow notepad at his fingertips; another pad with ideas buried beneath it. He'd think of a name and jot it down on the center of the page. He'd flip the page and stare out the window. Another idea would come. He'd jot that idea down on the next sheet of paper. And so it went. Sheet after sheet.

I asked: " Roger, why do you use all of that paper? It's so wasteful. Why don't you write all of the names down on one or two sheets of paper? We can spot the good ones."

His answer was simple and direct, just like the copy he wrote. "I want to give each name its own sense of importance. I want to look at it, think about it, visualize it. Ask for it by name. You can't do that when the name is ganged-up with other names and lost in the crowd."

When you're assigned to an account as a trouble-shooter, it's because others have failed. Your job is to save the account. So we usually pull out all the stops. In this case, I wanted to hedge our bets, so I went to the director of our computer department and asked if there was a way to design a computer program to develop a bank of brand names. Together, we developed a list of about 100 stem words, prefixes and suffixes, based on the established criteria and Roger's efforts. The computer spewed out a final list of names that looked like a telephone book.

We staged our presentation for the American Express people, who lined the large conference room table on one side; flanked by an equal number of O&Mers on the other side. Roger presented the new names he liked best.

As expected, the people at American Express really didn't know what they wanted. "No," they said. "It's still not there. We need more names."

It was my turn, and time for a little showmanship. I had prepared four 18" x 24" flipcharts of the objectives, strategy, positioning and the criteria for name development. I discussed the problem, the need for more brand names and how we had used computer programming. As I did this, I took the top sheet of the computer printout that I had placed on one end of the twelve-foot long conference table, and slowly opened the huge accordian fold, walking the length of the table, saying: "We have developed names . . . and names . . . and more names."

I stopped at the far end of the room and turned to the audience, and said in a low, modulated tone of voice: "Gentlemen, we have over *twenty thousand* brand names and mutations for your review!"

The impression had been made. Our client went back to American Express Plaza and came to grips with the marketing decisions that had to be made.

Computer programming can be helpful in brand name generation. The preparatory work that precedes it is nerve racking. Most copywriters hate it. Computers don't dream up names. They combine, sort and list words and phrases, merging and purging at great speed, in combinations you never think of. You only get back what you put into it.

With this background, I started to develop alternative brand names for Kash 'N Gold, using my word processor, but knowing I could switch to computer name generation, if necessary.

The criteria for name development was simple. Consumer electronics is a volatile and highly competitive industry. Retailers think in terms of products and lines of products. What's new? What's in? What's hot? What looks like a winner?

Our client promoted a full product line, not just a single

item. The brand name had to be all-encompassing. It had to
connote novelty phones in a memorable way. And we didn't
want to take ourselves too seriously.

I developed a list of 50 brand name candidates, zeroing-
in on three finalists. My partner and senior art director, Bob
Muller and I walked over to Kash 'N Gold, discussing
which one we liked the best. When you have the capability
to create quickly, sometimes you move too fast.
Bob and I had keyed on the Porsche. We had created a
great name for it and any other automotive look-alikes they
designed. It satisfied the criteria of being a winner. It was a
natural for CES. .

However, Stan showed us the rest of the line that had
just arrived in-country, the Banana Phone, Cucumber
Phone, Toucan Bird Phone and other zany products.

The second choice on our list was TeleMania, which
everyone thought was right on-target. It created a sense of
excitement and provided the energy, momentum and
memorability that was needed. What started out as a
brand name became a formal division of the company in
less than a year.

The TeleMania brand name was featured prominently
in all communications. The corporate name was de-
emphasized because it did not connote a quality image. A
great amount of thinking went into the development of our
marketing plan and objectives, which outlined a brand
strategy. First, we planned to emphasize the brand, rather
than sell the features and benefits of specific phones. While
we planned to promote specific items, they would be
subordinated to the brand name, which would act as a
catalyst to sell the entire line.

Second, we planned to segment the industry and build a
new market segment for novelty phones, focusing on the
highly lucrative gift market that we segmented even further.
Our products would sell at suggested retail prices under
$69 . . . to assure a high turnover rate for the retailer.

The company achieved this objective by developing an *outside, inside* pricing strategy. Instead of starting with cost plus mark-up, it started out with the suggested retail price point. Then, it worked backwards, directing its resources to manufacture quality products at that specific cost. In this manner, it was able to control prices and offer higher mark-ups to the retailer.

The decision was made to design *exclusive* products. When Kash started his company, he imported what he was able to find on the shelf in the Far East. Despite factory commitments not to do so, he discovered that while he was advertising a new market segment and generating interest in novelty phones, his factory resources were selling similar products to his competitors, who were knocking-off his brand and taking a free ride on his coattails. To eliminate this problem, Kash now designs his own molds, which cost approximately $40,000 to $50,000 per mold. This tactic ensures legal protection and international proprietary rights. If someone attempts to infringe on TeleMania's patents or trademarks, he can expect swift legal action.

The requirements for product design went far beyond exclusivity. The new products had to be unique and exciting, and have "obvious mass appeal." How that combination is created must remain a closely guarded secret.

The company pays close attention to engineering and quality control to assure the shipment of quality products. Its rate of return of defective goods remains at less than one percent and that is no mean feat. To promote the quality attribute, we created a One Year Limited Warranty for all products, while the industry standard remained at 90 days. This warranty was expanded to five years in 1986.

The third marketing objective forged a *pre-emptive*, leadership position in the telecommunications industry. We started thinking as leaders from the first day. While we still were relatively unknown, we had the inner confidence to know we had a hot line. We knew we would be winners.

We thought like champions. Acted like champions. And quickly became champions.

Kash set the path for his company at our first meeting. "I'm going to change the course of history in the telecommunications industry," he said, confidently. We all smiled agreeably, hoping secretly that we would just have a successful CES show in June. If we had a good show, we'd have a good Christmas season. Kash's comments sounded like a challenge. A little motivational rhetoric never hurt. But Kash really believed it. Deep down in his soul, he knew he was going to be Number One. And we charged ahead, thinking like leaders, never looking back!

The fourth marketing objective achieved *mass market* distribution. To sell our products in all channels of distribution and in all types of outlets. There was a consensus that since the line was so broad, there would be something for everybody. And that's exactly how Stan and his reps achieved national distribution.

The fifth, and last objective, was to be *innovative* . . . in product design, packaging, advertising, promotion, display and publicity. Innovation became the way of life . . . our springboard to success!

I can't recall how many times Bob Muller and I ran back and forth to the client's office; and how many times the client came to ours. We worked with a great sense of urgency. My partner is one of those low key, versatile artists who can think on a multi-dimensional level. Although I'm the marketing and copy chief, there are times when you can't determine who is the art director and who is the copywriter. Bob and I are a finely honed team. We know when to inspire each other, when to criticize and when to agree, always focusing on the center of the bull's-eye.

Charlotte Haller, one of our account executives, was also involved in our product reviews. Charlotte is a smart, personable, creative person, whose charm and good humor keep us moving on a straight path. She brings a woman's insight and shopper's point of view to our planning, invaluable when dealing with consumer products.

We had placed TeleMania prototypes around our conference room. They were zany, colorful phones. I'm not sure how Bob hit on it, but he came charging into my office, exclaiming: "I've got it! I've got the line."

And he did.

"Crazy phones for classy people!"

We had the name, and the positioning, and Bob went back to his drawing board to develop the famous TeleMania logo — with the smiling "M" and what later became known as the "Happy Face," a caricature of a telephone receiver in bright magenta color with a human tongue sticking-out at you good humoredly.

We charged across town to show everything to the client. They loved it. We were off and running.

The first TeleMania half-page ad featured the 928ME for Porsche-lovers. In it, we promoted a dealer contest, offering an all-expense paid holiday for two to Monaco, plus a free Porsche 928 rental for one week. The ad directed readers to visit the TeleMania booth at CES.

We had our first meeting with the sales reps at the show. Stan and I winged it. No notes. No audio visual aids. That was to come later. We shot from the hip, full of enthusiasm, asking for their support and total commitment.

TeleMania was a hit from the moment CES opened. Everyone became a quick believer. All our words of encouragement came home to roost. Buyers from many major stores in the country came to see us. We worked round the clock, talking and showing product. If you've ever worked a trade show, you know how it all becomes a blur. People. And more people. Questions and answers. Sell, baby, sell. Write orders. Big ones. Hand out those sales kits. Nobody walks by without getting a TeleMania "Happy Face" button pinned on them. You're on a roll. Keep it hot. Keeping on selling.

We put our publicity program into high gear, too. When we arrived at CES, I went directly to the Press Center and handed over 300 press kits, which were distributed to reporters, photographers and TV crews. Getting trade publicity was critical, since our primary goal was to achieve maximum visibility and sell our products to as many retail chains as possible. When you're the new guy on the block, you have one advantage. You're new. While you're peddling your wares, the magazines are doing the same thing . . . trying to seduce you into advertising exclusively with their magazine. If the magic is right, it can become a mutual admiration society. If you handle yourself professionally, you can be assured of some press coverage.

The disadvantage of being new is great. You're fighting for limited space against the heavy hitters. It seems unfair. The big guys get the headlines and most of the linage, because they are so well established. The little guy, who needs visibility to survive, goes pleading . . . hat in hand with hope and prayer. The big guys dominate the show with gala press parties, big dinners and entertainment soirees that you can't compete against. It's like power football. If the other team keeps possession of the ball and keeps running at you . . . three yards and four yards each carry, they score the first downs and all the points. They run out the clock. You hardly get a chance to score.

You can compete, but it is difficult. The best way to get news is to create it. If you've got a "me-too" product or you approach the press like amateurs, forget it.

We were successful, because we played it straight. We went out of our way to make friends, stopping at the media booths every day, talking to the publishers and media reps, inviting them to our booth and hospitality suite.

They could see firsthand the excitement created at the booth and the retailer traffic. Despite the intense selling activity, Kash and Stan spent time with everyone I brought by. If I saw photographers wandering the aisles or a TV crew in the vicinity, I persuaded them to come by our booth. If I couldn't do it myself, I got one of our models, a former *Playboy* centerfold, to do the enticing. We had zany, colorful products that made great photos and copy.

It doesn't hurt to play the role of the underdog, especially when the magazines sense you could be the next season's big winner. Elaine Forey, the smart, dynamic, no-nonsense publisher of *Mart* magazine, gave us a lot of support, featuring our products in a big way. Elaine is a fine writer in her own right. If she wasn't convinced that TeleMania had a winning line and a strong marketing program to back it up, I don't think we would have been featured so prominently. My job was to inform, to generate enthusiasm and win her support. I can't speak highly enough of this fine publisher.

Another media pro Stan and I have known for many years is Bernie Schneyer, the president of *Dealerscope*, who can wheel and deal as well as any media pro I know. He has done wonders for his magazine, earning everyone's respect. He gave us a lot of help, including a co-op merchandising deal in *Forbes, Playboy* and *Venture* magazines.

I talked to all of the trade magazines, finding my way to hidden press rooms to talk to editors. Everyone promised support. Some were short on delivery.

I kept track of editorial linage at the show and afterwards. We made our policy clear. If the magazines gave us the publicity we required, we'd advertise in their publications. If the product line wasn't publicized regularly, they could forget about TeleMania as an advertiser. Kash and Stan supported this media policy.

Not all magazines believed us. *Consumer Electronics*, one of the largest in the field, gave us lip service and minimum coverage. We dropped them from our schedule and have not used them. Because of the duplication of readership in the field, we didn't miss them. They did give TeleMania some recent publicity and may work their way back into the advertising schedule.

Immediately after CES, we launched our new *advertorial* campaign, a highly effective technique in which our agency specializes. We ran our first paid *advertorial* in *Dealerscope* in July. It consisted of a horizontal half-page, four-color ad promoting the Porsche, which appeared on the bottom of the page. The top portion of the page was editorial, using the same format, headline and caption treatment, type face and type size, as other editorial in the magazine. The only difference was that I wrote every word of the copy in the editorial, saying what I wanted to say the way I wanted to say it. It was written in a journalistic style, rather than as advertising copy. We designed the layout at the agency, setting copy on our typesetting equipment so it looked just right, and shipped it camera-ready to the publication for printing. We added this disclaimer: *"Advertorial,"* on the top of the page in 9-point type.

The headline read: "TeleMania: The Talk of CES." We ran a large, two-column caption: "Kash 'N Gold proved to be one of the summer show's main attention getters." If retailers read nothing else, we had hit a grand slam home run!

I quoted Stan, whom I described as a 20-year veteran of the electronics industry, saying: "It was the best show I've ever seen." The show provided a great start for our dealer contest, which ran for six months.

This ProActive *advertorial* tactic provides total control and flexibility. It achieves the dramatic impact of a full-page conventional editorial and ad, presented in their most credible and persuasive form. Two cardinal rules to follow: first, the *advertorial* must be newsworthy; second, never run the same *advertorial* twice. While display ads can be repeated more than once, *advertorials* lose their credibility if they are repeated. It's like reading old news.

The *advertorial* disclaimer does not appear to be a problem. Readers don't seem to pay attention to it, either missing the disclaimer or thinking it applies to the ad; or, they just don't care one way or another.

In August, the second ad promoted Zip the Chimp and the TeleMania Banana Phone. Zippy was marvelous at the photography session. Accompanied by his trainer, Zippy arrived on roller skates, wearing a cowboy hat, T-shirt and pants, and beaming the widest grin you'll ever see. We were able to get more out of Zippy in a one-hour shoot than you can get out of most human models. He kept us in constant laughter. Photos captured that fun and excitement, showing Zippy holding a half-peeled banana in one hand and the TeleMania Banana Phone in the other. The headline read: "Crazy Phones for Classy People!"

We combined the Zippy half-page, four-color horizontal ad with our second *advertorial* in the August issue of *Mart* magazine. We designed the headline to have the same graphic look as other editorial matter in the publication and negotiated preferred position, running it as the lead-in page to the telecommunications section of the magazine. The headline said, boldly: "TeleMania: A Sure-Winner!"

Our primary selling points were getting across quickly. TeleMania was a hot line. We pumped up the heavy buyer traffic and enthusiasm at the show and promoted our One Year Limited Warranty, an industry first. We went public with Kash's philosophy, quoting him: "Our company plans to change the course of history within the telephone industry. TeleMania will pursue a leadership role in the novelty phone business."

Photos and captions of other products were featured — the exclusive 928ME for Porsche-lovers, the exotic Toucan Bird from the Amazon and the Crazy Cucumber Phone. The last paragraph of the story listed the company's address and telephone number.

The impact of a full-page was excellent, especially since *Mart* is a tabloid publication measuring 11 x 14½ inches. Reprints were made of the full-page *advertorial*. They were distributed to the sales reps, who showed them to key accounts, selling right off the page, writing orders. They were also used for direct mail — to prospects and media influentials. Anyone we wanted to impress.

During the CES show, the company showed a prototype of a duck phone that was hand-painted to look like a real Oregon mallard. From the moment I saw it, I knew it was a winner. It was placed on a bottom shelf at the exhibit and dealers kept reaching down to get it. We'd put it back and someone else would come by, looking at it. Stan had a pocket full of orders before he left the show.

We named the product "Quacky" and modified our theme line in our advertising to read: "Quacky Phones for Classy People!" Bob Muller came up with a great eye-catching visual, photographing the duck on an elegant silver serving platter, garnished with bibb lettuce, cherry tomatoes and lemon slices. The copy told the retailer that here was another BIG volume, high profit, sales winner that was served on a silver platter. "Stock 'em in. Watch 'em fly off your shelves." And so they did. The company sold over 80,000 units during the first year.

We planned to run the Quacky Phone as the bottom half of our third *advertorial*, a full-page scheduled for *Leisure Time Electronics* in September. However, what started out as a carefully orchestrated plan quickly turned sour and became a major fiasco.

It is amazing how people in the communications business fail to communicate with one another. The left hand does not tell the right hand what it is doing.

Our agency was in daily contact with the magazine rep and publisher, advising them that an *advertorial* was coming. An early layout of the ad was shown to them. Since the ad was prepared camera-ready, we wanted to use the same typeface the publication was using. Our production manager called the media rep and asked for specific guidance. She contacted her production people and called back, providing the specific typeface and point size.

The editorial segment of the new *advertorial* read:

"TeleMania's Key To Success: New Products That Turn Over Fast." We used two cross-heads: "Hot Price Points" and "Unique Products." Conforming to the publication's request, a disclaimer, "Advertisement" was centered in 11-point caps at the top of the page. The full-page ad with the Quacky Phone as an integral part was shipped to the magazine prior to its deadline.

During this time, our agency had been having running discussions with *Leisure Time* about the lack of publicity they had given TeleMania. When Kash and Stan met with the publishers to iron-out this problem, they had a bomb dropped on them.

They were advised that *Leisure Time's* editor-in-chief had pulled the editorial part of our *advertorial* during the press run, without asking our permission, and had run the half-page, four-color Quacky Phone ad in their September issue. They were apologetic and said that amends would be made. I was out-of-town when this meeting was held, but I was quickly informed upon my return. Very quickly.

In my 30 years in this business, I have never had a magazine mutilate an ad. If the *advertorial* was not acceptable, the entire ad should have been rejected. A magazine does not have the right to cut apart an ad and run a fraction of it. The damage was serious, since TeleMania had now lost some visibility and momentum.

Evidentally, there was an executive suite battle going on, because the publisher departed after this fiasco. The editor-in-chief claimed he hadn't been informed by the advertising department. During the press run, he saw our ad coming by in the same editorial typeface that he was using. He said it did not conform to his magazine's policy about *advertorials* or to the American Society of Magazine Editors guidelines, and that's why he pulled it. One of the ASME guidelines states that type used in *advertorials* should be distinctly *different* from the publication's normal editorial typeface.

This is a small industry. Mistakes do occur. People are

usually forgiving and nobody needs to fall on his sword when problems occur. There is always a middle ground where everyone can walk away as friends. Magazines can only stay in business by building positive relationships with their advertisers. One thing is certain. The same problem is never allowed to occur a second time.

We talked with the new publisher of *Leisure Time* and negotiated a *free* make-good a four-page, four-color insert for their December issue, preceding the CES winter show. In retrospect, TeleMania lost a little momentum in September, but came out well ahead in December.

While our agency negotiated the make-good with *Leisure Time*, we moved quickly and offered the same full-page *advertorial* to *Mart* for their October issue. We coordinated with them and reformatted the typeface to look *exactly* like *Mart's* typeface. We changed the size of the disclaimer, reducing it to 6-point type, placing it unobtrusively alongside a photo of Zip the Chimp on the top right hand side of the page. We ran reprints and merchandised the ad to the trade.

Each one of our *advertorials* focused on a different marketing strategy, stressing fun, excitement and progress, reinforcing the concept that TeleMania had a hot line that turned-over fast. A fourth *advertorial* in the campaign was created for *HFD* to promote quality distribution, which was expanding rapidly in all classes of trade. Recognizing that Stan was well known throughout the industry, we convinced him that he should be the hero in this *advertorial*.

The headline shouted in big bold type: "TeleMania boosts retailer sales with hot selling line of novelty phones for gift market." We shot a double-column photo of Stan, doing what came naturally — talking on the phone, taking new orders. We quoted Stan from a real-life occurrence at Times Square Stores. It read: "Our products are so hot, we sell through before local ads even run!"

The copy talked about our vertical marketing strategy,

which featured a broad line with something for everybody . . . decorator pieces that tickle your funny bone. We never lost sight of our sense of humor.

The editorial format gave us a chance to report the latest news: Sales were good. Turnover was fast. Profit margins were high. We had our finger on the hot button.

To underscore the quality distribution, we listed examples of the key accounts by name and store type: department stores, like Rich's, Jordan Marsh and A&S; mass merchandisers and promotional stores like Caldor's, Alexanders and TSS; a major gift store chain like Spencer Gifts; catalog showrooms like Brendles and direct marketing like Sharper Image. Since these leading outlets considered TeleMania a real money-maker, other major stores would follow their lead. And they did.

While we were developing the *advertorial* campaign, our public relations arm was busy, too. We had arranged with Bob Freeman, our good buddy in *HFD*'s front office, to have Manning Greenberg, a senior editor, interview Stan for a major story. It was originally planned to precede our September 30th *advertorial*, but didn't appear until December 9th; another reason why you can't always depend on free publicity.

When Stan's *HFD advertorial* broke, TeleMania had another instant sales success. Buyers recognized Stan and called in, placing large orders. A recurring comment: "That was a great story *they* wrote about you."

A humorous incident occurred at *HFD* when our *advertorial* appeared. Bob Freeman had forgotten that Manning's story had been rescheduled. When our *advertorial* crossed his desk, he was so pleased with its appearance that he called up Manning to congratulate him for his best-designed and written editorial. When Manning told Bob that he hadn't written the story yet, Bob called me up, a little red-faced, but as magnanimous as ever, complimenting us and laughing about giving credit to the wrong guy. He also called Stan to congratulate him. Kash 'N Gold *doubled* its business during that six-month period. During the Christmas season all the TeleMania people were in a full court press, selling goods, opening-up new accounts, taking reorders and making sure shipments went out on time. Co-op advertising was executed with major stores like Bloomingdales, John Wanamaker, Woodward & Lothrop, Rich's, Jordan Marsh, Fortunoff, and Caldor's, participating in their magazine supplements and flyers.

During the early evening hours, we planned for the next CES show in Las Vegas in January. We planned two more *advertorials* for the pre-show December issues; one for *HFD* and the other for *Mart*. Both stories captured a sense of excitement and success. They were combined with a new half-page, four-color teaser ad, announcing twelve new best sellers, and telling a secret: the TeleMania Corvette Phone was here!

We came to CES with banners flying high. The *HFD advertorial* had the audacity to say: "TeleMania: Wow!"

The caption for Stan's photo read: "This year our sales were phenomenal. But you ain't seen nuthin' yet!"

Never forgetting to show the merchandise, photos highlighted three of the best sellers. We were coming to Las Vegas, telling all the buyers that TeleMania was the hottest game in town!

Elaine Forey, God bless her, served up a Christmas present, the inside backcover in *Mart's* pre-show issue at no premium cost. This endeared her to us forever. Another advertiser had canceled-out, making the space available. These are the fringe benefits of good media relations.

In return, Elaine asked us in her own subtle way to change the typeface in our *advertorial* so it would *differ* slightly from the publication's. How could we say no?

We took a different editorial tack in *Mart*, featuring Kash in a double-column photo and writing the story in a statesmanlike, presidential tone-of-voice. Since humility is not one of our strengths, our headline proudly proclaimed: "TeleMania: Big Success Story!" If buyers hadn't gotten the message yet, they did now.

It was important to defuse any negative image about the company being too aggressive or a threat to traditional telephone companies. Kash said succinctly in this *advertorial*: "We've created a new market with unlimited horizons. So everybody wins!"

Exclusivity, uniqueness and excitement in product design became the hallmarks of the TeleMania Collection. In this article, Kash talked about expansion and growth, how he planned to control the exclusivity of new products by owning the molds. He also talked about CFI — in *his* ad with *his* money, saying: "I attribute 40% of our growth to the outstanding job of CFI. They accomplished what no other agency could deliver. Their creative concepts, their style, their finesse and sense of humor, their strong marketing capability, their total involvement in our business. Our ads look like a million dollars. That's what it takes to be successful. That's what it takes to be a winner."

These are the small triumphs that cement a strong client-agency partnership. That's what makes it all worthwhile.

We made reprints of the two *advertorial*s from *HFD* and *Mart* along with the four-page insert from *Leisure Time* and distributed them in both our CES sales and press kits.

The TeleMania booth at Las Vegas was another winner. The new red Corvette Phone was the big product for the show. The company constructed a Corvette look-alike out of plywood and mounted it on a pole that revolved. It was an excellent attention-getter. We all walked on stage, sporting brand new red Corvette racing jackets.

Three models were hired, two of them in colorful costumes; one dressed as a gorilla, since the CES people would not allow us to bring Zip the Chimp or any live animal; and the second, as a hugh yellow banana to promote the Banana Phone. Our models were magnets. Everytime they went for coffee or soda, which was often, they brought onlookers back to our booth. They were also great subjects for photographers and TV crews looking for something *different* to shoot.

We worked with the press in Las Vegas much as we had in Chicago. Except this time we weren't the new guys on the block. TeleMania was a proven entity. Buyers from all the major chains and specialty shops came looking for us.

The seventh *advertorial* ran in *Dealerscope's* post-show February issue, featuring the new red Corvette Phone as the "American Dream." We had fun with our theme, modifying it to say: "Racy Phones for Classy People!"

The headline in the editorial segment summed it all up: "TeleMania Hits the Jackpot at CES '86!"

The two-column subhead quoted Stan, saying: "CES exceeded our wildest expectations!" Try to get editors to use that kind of language on your behalf.

During the first year of business, we placed product publicity in leading national magazines: *Woman's Day, Seventeen, New York, Forbes, Venture, Robb Report, VW Porsche, New Home*; in leading newspapers: *The New York Times, USA Today, Chicago Tribune, San Francisco Chronical, Star* and *Village Voice*. For TV, the *Johnny Carson Show, David Letterman Show, Live at 5* and the *Today Show* on NBC; the *CBS Morning Show, Eyewitness News,* the *Afternoon Show* and *Newswatch 6* on CBS; and *PM Magazine, AM Los Angeles* and *5 PM News* on ABC.

Trade publicity was planned to be consistent and featured new products in *HFD, Mart, Dealerscope, Leisure Time Electronics, Consumer Electronics* and *Potentials In Marketing.* Bernie Schneyer twisted his editor's arm to get the TeleMania Dollar Phone featured on the front cover of *Dealerscope.* Talk about visibility.

It takes time to generate product publicity. You can't turn it on and off like a water spigot. You have to maintain a constant flow of communications with the editors, serving up creative ideas that tickle *their* fancy. If your timing is right, friendly persuasion can fit your product into stories they may be planning. You must have new products ready to meet editorial deadlines, which could be well in advance of your factory production schedule. Many good media opportunities are lost because new products are not available when editors need them.

When we launched the TeleMania publicity campaign, we called to pitch new products and feature stories to the editors. Now, they call us.

This momentum carried TeleMania into the next CES Show. We introduced the new Teddy Phone, a cute Papabear and a Teddybear, and Quacky II, the new two-piece duck that quacks when the ringer goes off. The news in our eighth *advertorial*, a CES post-show issue of *HFD* said it all: "TeleMania: All Sold-Out!"

These ProActive tactics paid-off for TeleMania. They will continue to pay off as Kash 'N Gold grows. Perhaps, Kash misspelled his corporate name. At the rate they're going, it should be spelled: "Cash and Gold!"

If you turn on *your* creative firepower and use ProActive tactics, it can only result in one thing.

Opportunity for growth.

TeleMania: The Talk of CES

IN ONLY its second season at the Consumer Electronics Show, Kash 'N Gold Ltd. proved to be one of the Summer show's main attention getters with its unique national line of affordable, novelty, premium and fashion telephones and a Dealer Contest for a dazzling week for two in Monaco.

Kash 'N Gold had tripled its booth space to promote its new TeleMania line, featuring metallic finish sports car phones for Porsche and Ferrari lovers, and popular novelty phones such as the Exotic Toucan bird, sea shells, a banana, a cucumber and even a duck decoy—a complete line which carries a one year limited warranty.

"It was the best show I've ever seen," says Kash 'N Gold Marketing Director Stanley Reiff, a 20 year veteran of the electronics industry. "The show also provided a great

start for our dealers contest, which will run for six months."

The Grand Prize in the TeleMania Dealer Contest will be an all expense paid week for two at an exciting resort in Monaco, the free rental of a Porsche 928 for the week, $200

in casino chips and a TeleMania 928 ME Car Phone. Second and third prizes include TeleMania Sports Racing Jackets and the TeleMania Car Phones. The drawing for the contest, which ends Dec. 2 will be held in New York. Dealers may

contact Kash 'N Gold at 130 W. 25th St., N.Y., NY 10001 or phone (212) 929-6969 for more information.

TeleMania prides itself in offering attractive, often humorous, gifts that excite the mass market, products that appeal to varying

Kash 'N Gold Ltd. proved to be one of the summer show's main attention getters

tastes and trends, Reiff says. "These fully-functional telephones, priced to sell in volume at under $50 and with designer packaging, are especially popular with quality department stores, mass merchants and premium industries."

TELECOMMUNICATIONS

TeleMania: A Sure-winner!

One of the most talked-about companies at the CE Show was Kash 'N Gold, Ltd. which introduced its hot selling TeleMania line of novelty, gift and fashion phones for the mass market. For the first time, buyers were presented with a complete line of quality phones that are priced to sell in volume from $19.95 to $49.95 – all under the new TeleMania national brand. To back-up their quality claim, TeleMania is offering a One-Year Limited Warranty – an industry first.

"It's a whole new ballgame," said Stan Reiff, Kash 'N Gold's Marketing Director. "The June CE Show was the best I've ever had in over 20 years in the business. We had tremendous buyer traffic and enthusiasm throughout the show from leading department stores to mass merchants. Everyone. After they saw our TeleMania line, their purchase commitments confirmed that we have a big winner. We're looking forward to a record-breaking selling season."

TeleMania's complete line includes a wide variety of products –

from exclusive metallic sports-cars for all Porsche-lovers and Ferrari-lovers, to colorful Banana and Cucumber Phones for the kitchen; to the exotic Toucan Bird Phone and Polaris Seashell Phones; to UFOs, Key Phones and futuristic Avante Garde Fashion Phones. All in a wide spectrum of colors.

Go wacko with Crazy Cucumber! Or Pick a Pickle! Zany ideas for the kitchen or patio.

"Our company plans to change the course of history within the telephone industry," commented Kash Gobindram, K&G's President. "TeleMania will pursue a leadership role in the novelty phone

business – in product design, in features and functions, in packaging, advertising and display. High quality products and quick turnaround in-house service will be maintained at the highest level to assure success."

Exclusive design for Porsche-lovers. 928ME in gold, silver and copper metallic finish.

The company plans to develop new line extensions for its current product line as well as new product groups. "We will only create exclusive designs to be marketed under our TeleMania brandname," pointed-out Theo Basch, Vice President, talking about new prototypes. "Creativity is the key factor that sets

Go wild with the exotic, colorful Toucan Bird from the Amazon. Marvelous gift idea.

us apart from competition. We will only design high interest items that have mass appeal. Our growth potential is limited only by our imagination and the needs of the market."

TeleMania's packaging, advertising and display are attractive, attention getting and humorous. Their distinctive new logo and themeline: "CRAZY PHONES FOR CLASSY PEOPLE!" will be an integral part of their national campaign. Using award-winning Zip the Chimp in their current advertising and promotion has all the excitement of another creative triumph. As TeleMania's headline says: "Go Bananas! With Banana-Mania. And watch 'em peel off your shelves."

For more information, contact Stan Reiff, Marketing Director, Kash 'N Gold, Ltd., 130 West 25th Street, New York, NY 10001 or call (212) 929-6969.

TeleMania boosts retailer sales with hot selling line of novelty phones for gift market

NEW YORK—Continuing its aggressive national introduction of TeleMania novelty phones, Kash 'N Gold is forging ahead with a comprehensive marketing program. According to Stan Reiff, Vice President, Marketing, the reorders are pouring in.

"Turnover is the name of the game," Reiff stated. "I've been in consumer electronics for over 20 years, and I've never had a line turn this fast. Our products are so hot, we sell through before local ads even run."

Kash 'N Gold has positioned TeleMania as the industry leader in novelty phones for the gift, fashion and premium markets. They know who they are, what they are and where they're going. TeleMania has created a new niche in the gift market with high sales potential.

"There is a definite need for our type of quality merchandise," Reiff explained. "We're targeting on every consumer that has a sense of humor. Our line is a fun line. You see it in our brandname TeleMania. In our slogan: 'Crazy Phones for Classy People!' In our unique packaging. In everything we do. Fun phones – that's how we want the consumer and industry to view us.

"Our products are so hot, we sell through before local ads even run!"
—*Stanley Reiff, VP Marketing*

"Our TeleMania line is so broad and diversified that we have something for everybody. We will continue to design exclusive new products that are attention-getting, colorful and conversation pieces.

"We use a vertical marketing strategy. Car phones for Porsche-lovers. The Banana, Cucumber, Toucan Bird and Quacky Duck Phones. All decorator pieces that tickle your funny bone. Plus many more. A complete line.

"We back every product with a One Year Limited Warranty, to stress the quality of our line."

Reiff stated that TeleMania is not in competition with other telephone brands. "We're not a primary phone nor do we plan to get into the more features, more memory battle. TeleMania is a second, add-on phone. A fun phone that you want to buy as a gift or for yourself. We want to be the comic relief for any room in America."

According to many retailer reports, TeleMania phones are creating excitement on the selling floor with real stopping power. Sales are good. Turnover is fast. Profit margins are high. Return per square foot is excellent.

With hot price points from $19.95 to $49.95, the TeleMania Collection fits into all classes of trade without any conflict. Key accounts include major department stores like Rich's, Jordan Marsh and A&S; mass merchandisers, Caldors and Zayre, promotion stores, Alexanders and

Go bananas!
With TeleMania's
new Banana Phone.

TSS; gift stores, Spencer Gifts; catalog showrooms, Brendles; direct marketing, Sharper Image; plus a host of specialty stores.

TeleMania looks like a real money-maker. For more information, contact Stan Reiff, VP Marketing, Kash 'N Gold, Ltd., 130 West 25th Street, New York, NY 10001 or call COLLECT (212) 929-6969.

QUACKY PHONES FOR CLASSY PEOPLE!

New! Another BIG volume, high profit sales winner served on a silver platter. Exclusive Quack Phone that looks just like a decoy--from the TeleMania™ Collection of hot selling novelty phones. A "must" gift for hunters, sportsmen and wildlife-lovers. A decorator's delight. Stock 'em in. Watch 'em fly off your shelves. Only **$39.95***

Kash 'N Gold, Ltd., 130 West 25th Street
New York, NY 10001 • TLX 299053 KASH UR
For information, call (212) 929-6969 Collect

* Mfg suggested retail price

FIVE

No Fault
Corporate Image

Many companies never achieve their true growth
potential because of vague or distorted corporate images.
Your corporate reputation is one of your most valuable
assets and should be treated with the same reverence and
attention you devote to your products and services. It can
lead to bigger profits.

ProActive tactics put muscle power into your corporate
advertising and public relations campaigns. The tactics
must be marketing-driven, integrating all of your corporate
communications to help *sell* a corporate viewpoint. A strong
corporate image can make the crucial difference and be a
tie-breaker in dealing with all of your publics — consumers,
suppliers, distributors, media influentials, employees,
investors, activist groups, government officials, labor
unions and others.

A corporate image is constructed from the ground up,
much like a building with a solid foundation. If it isn't built
properly, cracks and crevices can quickly develop, causing a
nightmare of expensive repairs and maintenance costs.

A great deal of lip service is paid to corporate image. It
requires a long-term investment and constant attention.

Some companies have developed effective corporate advertising campaigns. Some employ campaigns that are neither consistent nor effective. Others run no corporate campaigns at all, but rely on their product and operating divisions to carry the ball. Still others ignore opportunities altogether, suffering a corporate image by default.

To create a corporate image that works effectively, the attitude of a company must be reviewed at the highest management level; leadership, management policy, allocation of resources must start with the CEO and funnel down — with no deviations. No bright, aggressive corporate advertising manager or public relations director can force it up from below. It must start at the top, and management must work at it continuously.

As soon as a corporate mission is defined, objectives can be developed to reflect the desired corporate image, the perception others have. This perception can be powerful. Marketing research should define how your company is viewed by specific target audiences. Objectivity is important, since you need to know the hard truth in terms of perception. The last thing you want to do is invest in a corporate advertising campaign where the blind lead the blind.

Qualitative and quantitative research should precede corporate campaign development, focusing on what advertising should say to defined target audiences.

If there are any perceived internal or external corporate problems with any of the publics that surface in your research, they should be addressed and corrected *prior* to starting a campaign. Credibility and believability are the cornerstones of corporate image. Ads must be truthful, supported by facts. They cannot be built on puffery, bias or deception. Lest they boomerang, causing serious negative results that can take years to overcome.

Concept testing of alternative themes can help improve the effectiveness of your campaign.

The key to building a strong ProActive corporate image is to employ all of the proven disciplines we use every day to market consumer products. Although semantics may differ, these same principles can be applied to any corporate situation, problem or conflict. If harnessed properly, they can be applied to your corporate campaign to assure both short and long-term success.

Corporate *positioning* should define your company's mission in terms of importance and uniqueness. Your company's *qualities* must be perceived as distinctly *different* from competitors in your industry. Your operating divisions should be positioned as distinct products, defining their personalities and identities in clear, concise terms. Specific target audiences should also be defined. However, be careful you don't fall into the trap of becoming a corporate clone. Not every company should be positioned as the high tech wonder of the future. A warm, human approach can work wonders. Create a positioning that can be yours only. One that can be used for years.

Your corporate tone of voice is important. You do not want to sound like a preacher or talk in grandiose corporate platitudes. While we can make a strong argument in favor of the effectiveness of long copy ads, people really don't like to read. TV has taught us that. They want everything fast and simple. Hit them with strong graphics and emotional appeals that clearly distinguish your company from everyone else. Talk to people in terms of *their* self-interest. "How will this information affect me?" Speak conversationally, one-on-one. Just as you speak to your best friend. Remember, consumers are not interested in your problems. They are only interested in how your company will *benefit* them.

Corporate advertising should carry its own weight and be accountable for achieving quantifiable goals that can be measured. Your corporate advertising budget should be linked to corporate marketing strategy and increased performance. You don't have to reinvent the wheel to determine if corporate advertising works. There are many studies available to prove this point. What you should test is the attainment of specific communication goals, including shifts in awareness, corporate image characteristics, attitude change and persuasion.

Two questions to ask yourself: "Is the new campaign distinctly different from competition?" and "Will the new campaign penetrate all of the advertising clutter and communicate my corporate identity effectively?"

Think ProActive and great progress can happen.

One example of a successful image change shows how a stymied growth company can turn into a profit-maker. In 1979, Allegheny Airlines had a serious image problem. Although Allegheny was the sixth largest national airline for passengers, research revealed the public perceived Allegheny as a small regional airline that served the Allegheny Mountain area. The public also had a simplistic view of big airlines as good and small airlines as bad.

Allegheny changed its name to USAir, created a new logo, painted its planes a different color with its new identity and revised all of its advertising and promotion. A new image was born.

The new name, USAir, had the sound of a large national airline, overcoming its previous image. By the next year, according to published reports, Allegheny had increased sales 34 percent and profits 73 percent.

Another example of a jumbled image was RCA, which had experienced frequent top management turnover, and failure with its videodisc player and sale of C.I.T., its financial unit. Investor confidence had slipped and Wall Street had a Missouri complex of: "Show me!"

New management decided to reposition the company. Qualitative research was conducted among portfolio managers and securities analysts. The results indicated that investors did not understand the full depth of RCA as a diversified company, including the leadership role RCA had in the aerospace and defense industries, satellite communications and video technology.

During the research, perceptive insights were developed, indicating an inner confidence that RCA had bottomed-out and a turnaround was in sight. This idea created a new marketing strategy, repositioning RCA, using nostalgia and momentum as the emotional leverage points.

The new campaign featured Nipper, the well-known RCA mascot logo. The headlines captured the inner confidence in RCA that was expressed during the research. They were: "Who said you can't teach an old dog new tricks?" and "Why RCA is one of a kind." The first Nipper ad promoted RCA's pioneering role in technology, showing the old dog watching rock video with his paw on the TV's remote control. The second ad promoted RCA's three core businesses and their achievements.

The use of Nipper, RCA's fox terrier logo, reinforced the perception of RCA as a company that can be trusted with long term stability. The level of consumer perception of the terrier's association with RCA was high.

The corporate campaign was placed in leading national business and life-style publications, including *The Wall Street Journal, The New York Times Magazine, Financier, Sports Illustrated* and *Smithsonian.*

Tracking studies were conducted, and according to published reports, dramatic increases were noted in unaided awareness of RCA as a communications, electronics and entertainment company. While increases varied at high levels for portfolio managers and investors, gains in image and product attributes were impressive.

RCA was recently acquired by General Electric, the company that spawned it more than half a century ago. It does look as if old dogs can learn new tricks.

New corporate campaigns can be created at varying

rates of speed. If the creative team works on judgment alone, the task can take as little as one to three weeks to develop alternative concepts. If research is required, six to eight weeks may be added before you see the first proposals. It depends upon how streamlined your agency's planning is and how quickly your creative team works. Their availability is also important, especially in the larger shops, since they may be committed to other projects and your campaign has to wait in line or get serviced by juniors.

Of all the campaigns I have worked on, the one that took the longest to create and get approved is the one that has run the longest. We called it the "Matsushita Miracle." No pun intended. It took over a year to get approved. The campaign is still running, strong and healthy, ten years later.

I was supervising the Panasonic account at Ogilvy & Mather, when our account team was asked to create a new corporate campaign for the parent company, Matsushita Electric. Russ Johnson, the marketing communications director and vice president of Panasonic, who has retired, had grown up with the company and understood the psychology of how the Japanese people do business in America. Together with Frank Novak, who was one of his smart, down-to-earth deputies, Russ guided us through a maze of meetings. "It's going to take time," he warned, patiently, during our first meeting. "It will be difficult. There will be many management meetings, up and down, before it goes to Osaka, the parent headquarters for approval. Everybody on the committee will participate, stating their opinions, pro and con. When a decision is reached, everyone will join forces harmoniously and execute the decision, since they will have made their contribution to it. That's the Japanese way. Then it will take more time once it gets to Osaka. The decision-making procedure will be repeated. More time will be needed for coordination, back and forth."

As I look back on some of those meetings, it often seemed

as a futile exercise. Our creative director was Dick Evans, a brilliant, street-wise copywriter, who started out in direct response where every ad must pay out in dollars and cents. Dick supervised a group of talented, undisciplined writers and producers, who seemed to do their best thinking when playing one-on-one Nerf basketball outside Dick's office. Understanding the nature of corporate advertising, we shot straight for the bull's-eye — Mr. Konosuke Matsushita, the founder of the company. His philosophy helped build an empire and has been copied by other Japanese companies. Russ had provided us with a limited edition book, translated from Japanese into English, giving us a better knowledge of the man and company.

I have always had great respect for the Japanese people. I joined the U.S.Navy when I was 17 years old and spent 2 1/2 years as an aircrewman flying in and out of Japan's Haneda airport during the Korean War. The Japanese people were still rebuilding their country from the ravages of World War II. I can recall seeing vast areas that had been demolished by B-29 bomber raids. Yet, the Japanese people did not sit back on their haunches, waiting for someone to help. They pulled themselves up by their own bootstraps, working long, arduous hours. Using bamboo, wood slabs, rope and metal from empty beer cans to rebuild entire cities. They labored quietly with dignity, respect and pride, tempered by their own brand of humility.

I got my first taste of being a merchant on the Ginza, Tokyo's Fifth Avenue. I'd buy Japanese cigarette lighters, binoculars, silk pajamas and kimonos at very low prices, fly them back to Guam, my home base, and sell them at handsome profits to my rock-happy, island-based buddies. Talk about mark-up. Would you believe 1,400 percent?

More than 20 years passed before I had the opportunity to work on the Pansonic account. The Japanese people had paid their dues and what they have accomplished is indeed a miracle.

Today, they design and engineer quality high tech products that are not only superior to competition, but products that respond to rising consumer demand. They tread lightly, keeping a low profile, as they penetrate one U.S. industry after another. They have built new markets, suggesting that there is plenty of business for everyone. They understand the power of advertising and investment spending. They believe in research and development, both at the factory and in the field.

The Japanese engineers and marketing personnel with whom we worked were selected from among Matsushita's top five percent. They went on the road, conducting personal surveys, talking directly to dealers and consumers all across the country. They listened and took copious notes, working their traditional twelve-hour day, six days a week. While it was not sophisticated research, it got down to the grass roots. They learned our culture, made friends with dealers in every major city in the U.S. and went back to Japan with many new product ideas consumers wanted — if only someone would listen. And listen, they did.

This concept of listening and Matsushita's unique management philosophy became the focus of our new campaign. The first ad's headline read: "The Matushita Miracle: How to build $4.6 billion in sales from a $50 start."

By 1985, total sales had increased to $24.9 billion!

Our campaign linked this unique management philosophy to their four major brands: Panasonic, Technics, Quasar and National.

Our leverage point zeroed-in on their corporate difference, and we flagged it in a cross-head: "Profit is not the goal." Body copy went on to explain that business could not operate without resources from society. Profit should not be the primary goal of business. The goal should be to contribute to society in return for using its resources:

"First, by producing unique products that please consumers in quality and price;

"Second, by paying taxes to government and dividends to shareholders;

"Third, by continually improving products and technology to assure future contributions to society."

The copy emphasized that a business cannot do any of these things unless it earns a reasonable profit, the major social responsibility of any business enterprise.

Our second cross-head focused on another unique concept: "First we build people," which emphasized personal growth, dedication, self-development and self-esteem. While this philosophy may sound familiar today because of extensive press coverage during recent years, it was new when we created the campaign. We had the foresight to target on a unique corporate quality that was different from all competitors.

Graphically, we recommended painting a fine portrait of Mr. Konosuke Matsushita, featuring it as a full-page in color, facing a page of copy. As Russ had cautioned, we had touched on a highly sensitive issue. Just the idea of using the founder's picture in an ad required many client discussions and committee meetings. Mr. Konosuke Matsushita was a great man, revered by his employees — almost a diety. The decision was finally made to approve the agency recommendation and forward it to Osaka for review and comments. Months elapsed before we finally received approval to proceed.

Since Mr. Konosuke Matsushita could not come to the United States for the photography to be used as subject matter by the artist, a good photo of the founder was forwarded to us. The final artwork was impressive. It went through the same review procedures at Panasonic and Osaka before final approval came for production.

Since we were preparing a continuity campaign, we prepared a second ad, featuring Mr. Masaharu Matsushita, son-in-law of the founder and president of the company. Now he is chairman of the board. We were able to schedule photography at Panasonic during one of Mr. Masaharu Matsushita's trips to the U.S. Dick Kline, the art director, and I supervised the photography along with Frank Novak. It was a VIP scenario with everything pre-planned to the last detail, allocating two hours for makeup and photography. The photo session went smoothly. Mr. Matsushita was very cooperative, presenting a most dignified, statesmanlike appearance. Our artist prepared a second painting, which went through the same review and approval stages.

In this ad, we continued to stress the company's unique philosophy, focusing on how Matsushita listens to employees and dealers, emphasizing "to contribute to society, you must listen to society."

Other prototype ads were created for the campaign. They featured high quality, high tech products and services that would meet future consumer needs.

The campaign was launched successfully 18 months later in *Time* and *Fortune* magazines. Once started, it provided a strong consumer environment for the four major brands, which continues to this day.

About this time, Ogilvy & Mather parted company with Panasonic because the account was not profitable enough. An effort was made to negotiate a fee arrangement, based on agency costs, overhead and profit ratio. Panasonic did not want to terminate its standard agency commission arrangement, and the agency resigned the business.

I pleaded with top agency management not to make a hasty decision, based upon the slow start-up and marginal billings for three other labor-intensive campaigns we had been working on. Unlike the Japanese companies that can see far beyond the next quarter and think long-term, O&Ms short-term thinking lost a good account.

While O&M management may have thought it had made a smart business decision, one might suggest that big agencies can become enamored with their own sense of self-importance, which can often border on arrogance.

Resigning Panasonic was a dumb decision! Today, one of the growth divisions I worked on is the Panasonic Industrial Company, marketing business information systems and video equipment. It is a major account. And the corporate campaign, retaining our format, lives on. My only regret is that I lost contact with my friends at Panasonic. I still cheer them on from the sidelines. I look forward to working with other Japanese companies.

There are two other long-running corporate campaigns that should be mentioned. The first is TRW, the conglomerate resulting from the merger of Thompson Products and Ramo Woolridge. The current campaign was created over 12 years ago when the corporation realized that investors and the public did not know what kind of company it was. The company needed to establish a clear identity.

The company had four major businesses: aerospace, automotive, electronics and aircraft. Their communications objectives needed to stress high quality products for their customer base, a profitable growth company for the financial community, a great place to work for employees, a good corporate citizen for community relations, and a good investment for shareholders.

While these objectives are fairly common, the challenge was to bring the different businesses together under one umbrella, where maximum flexibility could be maintained. The advertising campaign used print and TV to focus on new ideas and innovation in a high tech society, reinforced by a corporate identity slogan that has been burned into the public's consciousness: "From a company called TRW."

Giants like TRW need the flexibility to be perceived as different types of companies, depending upon the economic state of their industry. This had to be accomplished without endangering TRW's other customer bases. For example, when aerospace was hot, TRW wanted to be associated with aerospace. When aerospace and automotive both cooled down, the company wanted to be perceived as a superior electronics company on the cutting edge. TRW's positioning provides this flexibility.

TRW's corporate identity program has linked the TRW logo with all of their operating divisions and products. In 1974, only 34 percent of the public could identify the company. Today, more than 75 percent are familiar with TRW and two-thirds have favorable opinions about the company.

The second long-running campaign is that of GTE from Stamford, Connecticut, which launched its "Gee . . . No, GTE" campaign in 1978. Using TV and print, the company's advertising featured high interest GTE products and services, focusing on high technology, advanced communications and the information business.

Still concentrating on corporate identity, the campaign focus shifted last year. Marketing objectives pointed to greater sales opportunities in the telecommunications industry. Research showed that business customers were more interested in solutions than in high technology. Thus, the new campaign emphasized: "How GTE can make your business work better." A toll-free 800 telephone number was added to create interaction with their customers. The GTE slogan was retained.

This repositioning and fine-tuning within GTE's corporate campaign demonstrated the campaign's overall strength and staying power. If you can create the right corporate image that is flexible and can withstand the test of time, you can accelerate your company's growth . . . and leapfrog ahead of the competition.

Twelve opportunities to remember:

1. Think ProActive!
2. Sell your corporate message like a product.
3. Go for high impact and importance.
4. Search for the unique quality that sets you apart.
5. Target on a clearly defined audience.
6. Focus on the emotional leverage point.
7. Hit 'em with dynamic graphics, less copy.
8. Keep your message simple.
9. Stress benefits and audience self-interest.
10. Plan a continuity campaign.
11. Use a response device to stimulate action.
12. Look for new media options where you have greater control and flexibility.

Twelve pitfalls to avoid:

1. Don't try to achieve too many objectives.
2. Don't select the wrong target.
3. Don't choose the wrong attribute for your image.
4. Don't bore your audience with your problems.
5. Don't write or edit by committee.
6. Don't be afraid to show warmth and humanity.
7. Don't distort the facts or hide the truth.
8. Don't become a captive to your subjective ideas.
9. Don't look for a quick fix and immediate results.
10. Don't put all your eggs in one media basket.
11. Don't let the TV networks push you around.
12. Don't over-react to short-term crisis management.

SIX

Advertorials on a Fast Track

We have found that the ProActive *advertorial* technique can achieve impact and credibility at consumer and trade levels. It can add new vitality and character to your corporate image, especially if you are seeking a high visibility profile. It can satisfy other marketing objectives, too. It can introduce a new product, reposition a brand, reinforce a brand strategy and focus sharp attention on special events and area development. It can increase consumer and trade preference for your products and provide the foundation for a strong merchandising program.

It is not surprising to see *advertorials* executed in different ways. As specialists in the *advertorial* technique, CFI uses a paid *advertorial* in its *purest* form, where we have *total control*. We combine two distinct forms — an editorial and a small space ad, integrating them into a full-page ad. It is written like a reporter's interview, *not* as advertising copy, and it is marketing-driven. When executed properly, the editorial segment of our *advertorial* captures the reader's attention and interest, while he is in a receptive reading mood. He usually reads our copy all the way through without realizing it is an ad. Then he reads our display ad, absorbing its full impact. It doesn't matter what he reads first. Each segment of the paid *advertorial* reinforces the other. The impact of a full-page is impressive.

We negotiate with each magazine and comply with its guidelines. We use a small disclaimer in the upper portion of the ad, reading "advertisement." We set a type font different from the publication's *only* when it insists upon it. If not, we want our *advertorials* to look like editorial text, so we can talk directly to our audience, one-on-one.

We make no pretensions about how and why we use this ProActive marketing-driven technique. Does it build sales and profits? You bet it does. How long will we continue to use it? Just as long as it works.

Trade magazines give us the necessary control and flexibility. In consumer electronics, *HFD, Mart* and *Dealerscope* have been cooperative. *Dealerscope* will provide staff editors to write the copy, if an advertiser does not have the capability. In the jewelry field, *National Jeweler* provides a similar service. Our type of *advertorial* has excellent potential in other trade categories — travel, drug, food, fashion, industrial and high tech. If a company wants to impress its customers, this is a good way to do it.

Advertorials have other *faces* in which CFI has experience. One of the most controversial trends in consumer magazines today is an *advertorial* that is *not* an *advertorial*. It is an *advertising supplement*, consisting of anywhere from four to 48 pages. The supplement is bound into the magazine as an integral part of the editorial text. It provides advertisers with a unique opportunity to run ads in special magazine sections that offer a highly compatible editorial environment. It also provides magazine publishers with a new way to generate additional sales revenue, accounting for $113 million in 1986. Because the advertising sections are not written by editorial staffs, they have gotten a lot of flack from the editorial community.

The theme of an advertising section will focus on a

special interest or technology, running the full gamut from computers, office equipment and telecommunications, to area economic development, tourism and travel to insurance, health, food, sports and fashion. If the section is sponsored by one company or country, the advertiser has reasonable control over copy content of the editorial matter. If it is multi-sponsored, advertisers go along for the ride, having little control over copy content. The high cost of publishing special sections encourages advertisers to participate in multi-sponsored sections, where they can run their regular display ads adjacent to or facing editorial matter. The ads can be full-page or fractional pages.

The advantages to the advertiser are obvious. The single editorial theme can provide the right selling environment for corporate or product advertising, especially when the editorial promotes your company and brands. The supplements provide dynamic reader impact and serve as a vehicle to generate reader action. Reader response bingo cards, listing each advertiser, have become an integral part of the supplement, providing an advertiser with new prospect names and a measurement tool to evaluate the effectiveness of their ads.

Experienced corporate advertisers find the themed sections a *unique* way to step out of the clutter of magazine display advertising. Instead of fighting for preferred position in a magazine, they can now select advertising sections that talk about *their* product category in more favorable, positive terms. First-time and low-budget advertisers also find the special issues attractive, running fractional page ads that are cost effective. While a 15 percent premium is usually charged to cover the additional cost of producing an advertising section, it does not seem to deter its growing acceptance.

Advertisers also find that the single topic themes of the advertising sections provide longer shelf-life for their ads, since readers keep them on-hand for reference.

Some editors are concerned that the editorial purity of their publications is being threatened. They see the *advertorials* as an attempt to deceive their readers into believing that these sections are editorial text and written by the same writers. They insist that editorial matter must provide a bona fide service to their readers. They're afraid their readers may now find the advertising section interruptive, give it a passing glance and jump ahead to another page; or worse, switch to another magazine.

They are also concerned about the *quality* of the editorial in the advertising sections. Since many of the sections are written by outside writers and freelancers, I wonder if the quality is really in question or is there a perceived threat to the editor's livelihood? Editors do not have a franchise on good writing. In some cases publishers are hiring some of the best freelance writers, who bring product expertise to the supplement that cannot be matched by the staff writers.

Some editors' concerns are well-founded. Advertisers and agencies can intrude into the editorial domain, which up to this time has been sacrosanct. There is validity to the editors' argument that the *advertorial* concept *blurs* the distinction between ads and editorial. When readers cannot see a clear difference between what is an ad and what is not, they could become skeptical and apathetic, questioning the credibility of the publication. It will be up to the publishers to assure that their *advertorial* writers maintain the highest editorial quality. Anything less will affect the publication's bottom line.

Editors have found strange allies in advertising agency creative chiefs, who oppose the *advertorial* technique, but for different reasons. Most agencies do not like writing one-shot promotions. It can muck-up an established campaign and siphon-off dollars from the budget. When agency creative people and media buyers drag their heels, it becomes difficult for a media sales rep to push the *advertorial* program through. That's why most advertising sections are sold directly to advertisers to gain their approval first. Once the agency people know the client wants to do it, they become cooperative.

As specialists in the *advertorial* technique, our staff doesn't have this problem. We are always on the lookout for new creative and media concepts and will present them to our clients, taking along the media reps if it will help.

We are hard-nosed, however, when it comes to demanding a *quality* product. We recognize the importance of using well-known writers, who are celebrities and experts in their own fields. It adds to reader-interest and the effectiveness of the promotion.

The editorial segments must be informative and newsworthy. The writing must be crisp, clear and accurate. The tone of voice must be compatible with the magazine. If there is too much huff and puff and goody-two-shoes, readers will see through it and abandon ship.

In area economic development, for example, an advertising section can create a quality showcase for a country wanting to put its best foot forward to attract new business. When you think ProActive, you promote from strength. You need to position or reposition your country, focusing on its new achievements and its security and stability, its growth opportunity; how its enlightenment is enhancing human rights and the education of its people. How its history, culture and tourist attractions can be featured to attract new visitors from the U.S., Europe and the Far East.

Our staff has close contacts with some of the best freelance magazine writers and award-winning photo-graphers, who can be assigned to prepare special advertising sections. The sponsoring country can share some of the costs by getting banks, hotels, airlines and multi-national companies to participate, since everyone benefits from it. The advertising supplement now becomes the vehicle for a major marketing program with unlimited merchandising possibilities.

Most consumer magazines follow the guidelines for special advertising sections established by the American Society of Magazine Editors. It is interesting to see how business and consumer magazines promote their advertising supplements to advertisers and their agencies. They use slick media promotion pieces to emphasize the high impact of the editorial content and target audience delivery. They promote the merchandising value, consisting of reader response cards, free reprints and bonus circulation. When the supplements are reprinted, the magazine's logo is usually on the cover. This can be a very effective sales promotion tool, when merchandising the supplement to the trade. A display ad that appears in a supplement in the right editorial environment is far more impressive than just showing an ad with the standard guideline: "As appeared in . . .

The magazines differ when they address the problem of authorship. *Business Week* sells the virtues of the specific supplement, but does not mention that it is not written by staff personnel nor do they identify the writers. *Fortune* and *INC.* go to great lengths to recruit outstanding authors and writers in their fields of expertise to research and write their advertising sections. Their names and backgrounds are promoted boldly in sales promotion literature. *Forbes* maintains a different composure, offering a single sponsor the flexibility to use one of their staff writers or a qualified financial writer whom the magazine staff recommends. *People* uses staff writers from their sales development department.

The editorial graphics for special advertising supplements also differ from magazine to magazine. *People's* format, which is photo-heavy and text-light, is drastically different from those of *Fortune* and *Time*, which are just the opposite. Every publication develops a personality for its supplements, compatible with the rest of the magazine.

Almost every major magazine has gotten into the act. *Reader's Digest, Business Week* and *Forbes* set the pace. *Newsweek* and *Cosmopolitan* paired-up with two trade magazines, *Digital Retailing* and *Dealerscope*, to promote computers and consumer electronic products to their audiences. *Sports Illustrated* did the same thing with *Infoworld. Time, McCall's* and *Woman's Day* have used former editors to write the specialty sections rather than use freelancers or promotional writers. *Better Homes & Gardens* has run drug, toiletry and cookbook promotions, which are displayed prominently in supermarkets along with manufacturers cents-off coupons included in the shrink-wrap. Even *Field & Stream* is fishing in new waters, developing its first 48-page "Guide to Huntingwear" in its efforts to attract new advertisers.

How effective are the magazine advertising sections?

According to *Fortune*, advertising sections increase sales for their advertisers. On the average, 22 percent more inquiries are generated when an ad appears in the section than when it simply runs in the issue; 53 percent took favorable action when literature was requested; 33 percent discussed the product with associates or decided to investigate further; 15 percent purchased or recommended the purchase of the product featured in the literature. The effectiveness was validated by other research, indicating high rates of recall, interest and intent to buy.

Some of the nation's leading newspapers like *The New York Times, The Wall Street Journal* and *USA Today* have been selling advertising sections for years, promoting business development, tourism and new technologies. The advertising sections are written by the promotion departments and free-lancers. The copy is slugged: "Advertisement."

Advertorials have still another *face.*

They provide an answer to one of the greatest dilemmas facing corporate America.

How can a corporation fight back when it is smeared by

a TV broadcaster or newspaper reporter who wants to sensationalize the news? What ProActive tactics can an advertiser use to overcome the inaccuracies, distortion and over-simplification that can devastate your corporate image and bottom line? Must an advertiser absorb all of the punishment or is there a way to respond decisively? Another form of *advertorial*, the op-ed ad, was perfected by Mobil Oil in the '70s for this purpose. It is also called *issue* or *advocacy* advertising. Mobil's op-ed ad campaign became the pace-setter for the entire industry. If you like controversy, you will like *advocacy* advertising and creative confrontation: Batten-down the hatches and full speed ahead!

SEVEN

Advocacy
Versus Adversary

The day of the low corporate profile may be gone forever.

Advocacy or issue advertising has exploded onto the scene, forging a bold new dimension in corporate advertising and public relations. It is here to stay.

If you think ProActive, your company needs to be more than just a good corporate citizen. It needs to influence its environment — economically, sociologically, technically, logistically and politically. There is no reason why a corporation must be the "fall guy" to a hostile anti-business press and negative public opinion.

A good corporate citizen should be seen and heard. Your company should try to shape the dynamic forces that affect its existence, positive and negative. The goal is to achieve real growth and reasonable profits.

A good corporate citizen should participate in a vigorous two-way dialogue in an open, uncensored forum to share its ideas and to influence public opinion.

Advocacy advertising provides this public forum.

It provides a company with the opportunity to enhance its visibility and corporate identity. Will this impact on your corporate image? You bet it will!

Let's define advocacy or issue advertising. It communicates a corporation's point of view on a public issue that may affect a company's business, environment or country. It enables a corporation to present its side of a controversial issue to the American people.

Advocacy advertising differs from image advertising, since it does not promote a product or service. While corporate identity is common to both, advocacy advertising is usually conducted in response to the public's negative perception of corporate actions or in response to government actions.

In ProActive communications, you take a *pre-emptive* position, not a reactive one. You anticipate, predict and assume a leadership posture. You build support for your viewpoint *before* public opinion swings in the opposite direction. Before emotions heat-up. Before you have a crisis on your hands.

This is a lot easier said than done. It requires a lot of contingency planning, sensitivity, creative thinking and hard work. What happens when the unpredictable occurs? Or, a fuzzy issue suddenly escalates into a heated debate? Yes, you react, but you go immediately on the offensive. You think ProActive and act decisively.

One of the major advantages of issue advertising is that it allows your corporation editorial control over the message. Although this applies more to print media than TV, there are new options in TV that overcome current obstacles and offer greater sponsor control and flexibility. These new TV options will be discussed.

A second advantage affords your corporation the opportunity to go over the heads of government leaders and the media and speak directly to the people and shape public opinion on critical issues that affect them.

A third advantage is the capability to target with a narrow focus on special interest groups. This can be achieved by tailoring your creative message to the self-interests of specific audiences and by selective media placement in print and on TV.

You may want to build friendly alliances and coalitions with private power centers that support your issue. This could include trade associations, labor unions, think tanks, citizen activist and political action groups. You may also want to support a citizen group that will be organized to act as a single-issue surrogate, independent from your corporate structure but under your indirect influence.

A fourth advantage is that issue advertising can stimulate interaction with the public, generating immediate response by telecommunication polling devices and write-in campaigns. This provides a vehicle to forward in-depth literature to support groups and interested individuals. It also allows you to define the demographic and psychographic characteristics of the target audiences sympathetic to your cause.

If you want to increase your rate of reader response by 25 percent or better, consider using coupon inserts with your print ads as the food and drug companies do in consumer advertising. If you want to build public pressure on government legislators, run a double tear-out coupon; one addressed to your corporation, the other to the legislator in the reader's district. Computer programming can target specific legislators by name and address, using subscriber zip codes and publications that offer market-by-market copy splits and editions. The simpler you make it for the reader, the greater the response. Just imagine hundreds and hundreds of big mailbags dropped on your congressman's doorstep . . . to every legislator and senator on your target hit list!

Other benefits of issue advertising include an increased awareness of corporate identity, increased understanding of corporate philosophy and performance, enhanced pride in the company and recognition of corporate leadership.

These benefits have a positive effect on the quality image of your corporation's products and services.

On the negative side, there are some disadvantages that should be reviewed.

The first and most important is that you may not be reaching the right decision-makers who affect change on public issues. This group includes senators, congressmen, congressional staffers, government officials . . . the Washington elite; state and local officials and the bureaucrats they oversee. It includes media influentials, publishers, senior editors and broadcast executives. Plus all the lobbyists and old boy networks.

These target groups are what ProActive people call the center of gravity or *critical mass*. It is the innermost circle that influences action on public issues. While these groups dominate our society, their mind-set can be sensitized by public opinion, their positions softened or reversed.

The second disadvantage of issue advertising is that you may be talking to people of like-mind. Mass media can be used to reach large numbers of people. Unfortunately, you may only attract those groups already favorable to your issue. What you may not get are the undecided and the dissenters, the apathetic people who are too busy to care. Thus, the need to find the ProActive emotional leverage point in your communications to penetrate public indifference. Once you achieve this breakthrough, you can exert public pressure on the innermost circle of decision-makers.

A third disadvantage is that most people consider issue advertising to be self-serving. Target groups may look at issue advertising as one-sided, transferring negative attitudes and distrust to other advertised products and services. This skepticism may spill over to other corporate issue ads; ads that may be better balanced, but suffer the sins of the credibility gap.

A fourth disadvantage could be an investor backlash when some shareholders may not agree with your corporate issue's viewpoint. They could differ on the basis of politics, Republican or Democrat, conservative or liberal; or be strongly opposed because of other reasons. This could result in shareholder alienation, dissent and reaction that could make negative headlines in the news media. A similar backlash could occur with your trade relations, resulting in some loss of business. The degree of acceptable risk should be estimated prior to starting a campaign.

A fifth disadvantage is that it is difficult to evaluate the effectiveness of an advocacy campaign in quantifiable results that affect your bottom line. Most companies evaluate their issue campaigns by keeping track of letters mailed-in by the public and requests for reprints of ads, which are reported to be sizable.

Also, on the negative side, issue advertising appears to have made little impact on legislators and their aides. Their perception of its value as a communication vehicle was ranked low by congressional staffers in a recent survey. While this might seem like a legislator's blind spot, they are not immune to public pressure that can be generated by letters, phone calls, personal visits from constituents and lobbying. Media coverage can be stimulated by letters to the editor and editorial replies on TV and radio, which unfortunately are constrained by limited availability of time and space.

A more definitive way to measure the effectiveness of an advocacy campaign is to conduct a tracking study to measure shifts in public opinion among target audiences. This study should be tailored for your specific issue, analyzing how effectively your campaign has communicated its basic message and persuaded the audience to accept your point of view. This should be accomplished on a time phased basis, giving your creative people the opportunity to fine-tune the campaign.

While every advocacy issue is distinctive, there are four stages in the life cycle of a public issue. They include the development stage when issues emerge from persistent friction and dissatisfaction. The politicization stage evolves when friction increases and advocates start to debate pros and cons. This leads to the legislative stage when attempts are made to resolve the differences by voluntary agreements and enactment of laws. The final litigation stage starts after legislation has been passed. The opportunity to influence public issues is greatest during the early development stage and decreases as the issue progresses. That's why companies like W.R. Grace, Mobil Oil and United Technology take ProActive planning seriously. They try to spot trends *before* they become public issues and formulate ProActive strategy and tactics that respond to emerging public expectations.

Let's look at technique and how to improve the quality of issue advertising.

The first step is to determine your current status. If you are planning to start a new campaign, it helps to do a competitive review to determine what other corporations have done and are currently doing.

One technique that works is to plaster your conference room wall with issue ads, clustering them by issue category. You should dissect each ad clinically, diagnosing each campaign's strategy, positioning and copy platform. You will discover a sameness . . . a dull, boring, stuffy look that creates a doom and gloom impression.

The graphics should be reviewed as a separate entity to help your campaign stand out from the crowd. Most art directors try to achieve a contemporary look. They compete among themselves in design, typeface, layout and illustration, trying to be innovative, but in most cases, doing what everyone else is doing. If formal balance is in, the herd instinct takes over and every campaign uses it. When montages were big, everyone climbed on the bandwagon. The challenge is to be creative and not follow the herd.

Most corporate image and issue ads look alike. If you

don't agree, conduct a recognition test on yourself. Cover up the logo and corporate signature of all the ads on the wall and see how many companies you can identify. Start switching signatures and see how confusing it gets. Try this test on your business associates. You'll be amazed at the lack of recognition, underscoring the need to establish a distinct corporate identity with a bold, innovative approach in copy and graphics.

The second step is to formulate new advertising objectives that are measurable. Develop a strategy that selects the right issue for your campaign. Public opinion polls can be of assistance to select a current issue compatible with your corporation's needs. Be careful you don't pick an issue overworked by other companies or an issue that nobody cares about.

The third step is to position the issue correctly and to sell it as a product. You should use an outside agency with a strong creative capability in consumer products to develop this positioning. They have years of experience in knowing how to talk to the public and business community. They have the disciplines, insights and objectivity to define your campaign's positioning. Because they are outsiders, they can ask the perceptive questions your top management needs to answer; questions operating management may find too sensitive or embarrassing to ask. They can enter into a healthy dialogue that will put teeth into your corporate positioning and create a cohesive advocacy campaign that works.

The fourth step is to develop a balanced copy approach to avoid a self-serving image. Your headline should have an emotional charge, one that hits a responsive cord; one that triggers instant interest in your issue and point of view. Don't be afraid to present both sides of the issue, presenting your facts logically. If there have been mistakes, admit them candidly, and discuss what actions have been taken to correct the situation. Show your human face honestly.

People will gain respect for your company and your issue. The task is to get them to think: "Gee, they're human, just like us. We all make mistakes. They're not so bad after all. The point they're making might be right!"

Try to keep your message simple. Boil down the complexity into everyday conversational language. Listen to your favorite newscasters on TV. They use conversational language that speaks directly to you. There is always a sense of importance when they editorialize. It is easy to grasp, understand and recall. Try to speak in the same informal tone of voice.

Don't overwhelm your reader with too many facts in each ad, trying to prove your points. Moderation pays off. Remember, you're planning a campaign. This requires a single-minded focus, never losing sight of your company's objectives. Keep it loose and flexible. Don't shoot all your bullets at once. If you do, you'll have no ammunition left for your next ad.

Don't talk down. Or lecture. Or distort the facts where they insult people's intelligence. Too much of Mr. Good Guy doesn't work.

The fifth step is to keep a sharp focus on your target audience. Do the necessary homework to have a clear picture of who they really are. When you talk about the public, what specific segments? How do you describe each segment? How do they think about your specific issue? Speak directly to them in terms of their self-interest and how your proposed solution will *benefit* them. As individuals, as corporations, as a nation and as a better world to live in.

The sixth step is to pre-test your prototype ads with your target audience. Their perception and final impression of the ads, what we call "take-away," can provide the insights for final modification to the campaign.

You should take a fresh look at your media strategy to assure effectiveness. Try to look beyond the traditional criteria — publications that everyone uses; reach and frequency. You need more impact and dominance to achieve a greater sense of importance. If your ad is surrounded by other issue ads, it can get lost in the clutter.

Research has proven that combined media is more effective than single media. Three tests were conducted for major companies, comparing TV alone versus print alone versus TV and print combined. In these tests, the level of awareness and preference were significantly higher for combined TV and media.

Although most publishers stress the importance of continuity scheduling, it may be in your best interest to flight your print advertising. This will free-up available dollars to run larger space and multiple space units to help you dominate the magazine. Use spreads instead of pages. Design a hybrid spread to gain impact; yet, save money buying a four-color page that faces one in black and white. Experiment with different space units, using one-quarter page ads at the top of a column in sequence as a teaser or square-thirds facing a four-color page.

One of the biggest problems with TV is that until recently the big three TV networks have not accepted corporate advertising that presented views on controversial issues of public importance. The TV networks have used the Fairness Doctrine of the Federal Communications Commission as the primary reason to deny access for issue advertising. The networks have found it difficult to develop new guidelines. They say that they would like to permit corporations to broadcast issue advertising in a responsible way. If for no other reason than to generate additional income. However, their problem is not knowing how to draw the line and prohibit all the cranks, radicals and crazies, who demand equal air time to espouse their views. The Supreme Court has upheld the network's right to reject controversial advertising.

W.R. Grace contested this policy and won the battle as

this book goes to press. The Senate is currently considering a bill to repèal the FCC Fairness Doctrine. Since there is more to this battle than a formulation of new guidelines, this subject will be discussed in the next chapter.

There are currently other ProActive over-the-air TV options to consider. The Independent TV Network, MIZLOU TV Network, Fox Network and other ad hoc TV networks do not agree with the TV network policy and do accept issue advertising. Local TV stations have not reported any fairness complaints. A new vista of TV programming opportunities have now become available.

Make sure media planners work closely with their creative people during the start-up phase of your campaign to seek new ways to gain greater impact. Copywriters and art directors do not have a franchise on creativity. You want just as much innovation in your media plan.

Let's look at three examples of how different corporations conduct issue advertising. The first question one must ask is how combative do you want to be?

You can advocate *advocacy* advertising where you become the adversary. Or, you can communicate your corporate message, advocating a particular issue.

By championing the cause of advocacy advertising with the TV networks, several corporations achieved a high degree of corporate visibility. This perception enhanced their corporate image and leadership position among their target audiences.

During the energy crisis in the early 1970s, Mobil Oil pioneered a very pugnacious adversarial approach when it decided to challenge its opponents and critics in the marketplace of ideas. It started with the long gas lines and rapidly escalating gas prices. Everyone pointed an accusing finger at the major oil companies, including Mobil. There was a major need to overcome thc sensationalism, misinformation and distortion of the facts that the media was feeding to the public. Mobil confronted the media with a head-on assault, using imagination and flair. It ran a series of high impact ads, positioned opposite the editorial pages in leading newspapers in major cities around the country. It told its side of the energy story, using a factual copy approach, now known as the op-ed advertising campaign. Although public opinion shifted slowly, Mobil got its message across. Consumer requests for reprints of the ads were reported to be large.

Mobil tried to counter the TV networks access policy on the Fairness Doctrine, but to no avail. At one point, it offered to pay the networks for the media cost of a two minute TV commercial and the cost for equal rebuttal time for the opponents. They even gave the TV networks carte blanche in selecting the opponents. The networks remained unyielding and enforced its no-access policy.

In order to set the record straight, Mobil ran one commercial on MetroMedia TV in New York and Los Angeles and a maverick ABC affiliate in Washington, D.C., backing it up with full-page newspaper ads. This led to Mobil's decision to create its own television show, the "Mobil Showcase Theater," which ran on PBS, Public Broadcast Stations, and on an ad hoc TV network. It was a quality culture show that achieved acclaim from corporate supporters and critics alike. Mobil ran its TV advocacy commercial prior to the show and immediately after it, never interrupting the program itself.

Mobil continues to challenge the media and activist groups, expressing its views forcefully, clearly and promptly. It uses its op-ed ad campaign to speak out on a broad spectrum of issues that directly affect the company — from energy, taxes, foreign trade, arms sales to apartheid. This combative adversary role does not mean that Mobil is abusive or unpleasant. It is very aggressive, recognizing that its silence in the past has been counter-productive.

The W.R. Grace & Company, under the leadership of chairman J. Peter Grace, picked up the sword and continued the fight with the TV networks. While maintaining a high visibility adversary role with the media, Grace's ProActive tactics were less pugnacious, more gentlemanly; yet, equally effective. The conglomerate used print and TV to present its side of the issues to the public.

Comparing the adversary tactics of Mobil and Grace, you find Mobil being more reactive than Grace. Mobil's public relations policy is to respond immediately to any adverse opinions. Its advocacy ads speak out on far reaching issues, but tend to be self-serving. Grace, on the other hand, appears to be more ProActive and has a finer, deft touch that seems less self-serving.

The W.R. Grace & Company has been presenting issue advertising since 1978. The roots of its current campaign were linked to the findings of the Grace Presidential Commission, in which Peter Grace served as chairman. The commission report in 1985 recommended new ways to cutback federal spending and stop waste and inefficiency in the federal government. When the report was largely ignored by President Reagan, Peter Grace directed his company to focus on the growing U.S. deficit. Grace believes the national deficit inhibits real economic growth. The company manages many diverse operating divisions in chemicals, natural resources and consumer services. Grace is concerned about the economic limits of growth and corporate requirements to make more than paper profits. To overcome economic stagnation and create new profit opportunities, Grace went public with its ProActive deficit campaign to change the environment and economic factors that inhibit the corporation's future growth.

The company used print and TV to urge congressional action on the U.S. deficit and to seek public support. Its first sixty-second TV commercial featured a beautiful newborn baby who cries when he is presented with a $50,000 deficit bill from the government. The commercial was aired on the NBC and ABC TV networks in 1985.

The following year, much to its chagrin, Grace's newest commercial, "The Deficit Trials: 2017 A.D.," was rejected by the TV networks because it was too controversial. The TV commercial had cost $300,000 to produce. It called public attention to the tragic consequences of unchecked federal deficit spending. The commercial portrays a futuristic courtroom scene in the year 2017. The children of tomorrow are clad in rags and look decrepit. They have brought to trial a remorseful old man from a previous generation, ours. They charge him with bankrupting the future through unchecked federal deficit spending. The commercial does not advocate a solution. This is left to the viewer.

"Why is 'The Deficit Trials' called controversial?" asked Anthony Navarro, Grace senior vice president in charge of communications. "We haven't found anyone yet who is in favor of a growing deficit. Yet, one year the networks think the issue is not controversial; the next year they think it is. The only thing controversial about the ad is the networks' refusal to run it."

Grace garnered a windfall of publicity in its campaign to gain access to the networks for issue advertisers, probably achieving far greater reach than if it had run the paid commercial on the networks. In recognizing the First Amendment rights of the network, the corporation asked the networks to recognize the private sector's First Amendment rights, too. Primarily, to keep the American public informed and exposed to a variety of views.

Pretty heady stuff . . . for a ProActive advocacy campaign. Real assertive leadership.

According to Stephen Elliott, the former corporate advertising director of W.R. Grace, "The visibility opened up all types of doors at all levels, worldwide."

The company hired Joseph A. Califano, Jr., former Secretary of Health, Education and Welfare in the federal government, to press the networks for accountability on their standards for acceptance and rejection of ads dealing with important issues of public concern.

The controversial TV commercial appeared as a feature on many TV newscasts. When a major corporation of W.R. Grace's size takes on the media and cries foul-ball, everyone pays attention. Finding another medium, Grace presented the commercial in 35 movie theaters in Washington, D.C. It was also presented on the Independent TV Network on August 21, 1986 on 152 local TV stations. It was billed as: "The W.R. Grace 60-second ad that the networks refused to run." Pre-publicity and tune-in advertising delivered sizable audiences.

Unfortunately, W.R. Grace won the battle and lost the war. In a cost-cutting decision, Peter Grace cancelled his $3 million corporate advertising budget and disbanded his corporate advertising department. CBS has now acquiesced and will accept corporate issue advertising, along with ABC; the latter only during post-midnight periods. NBC is still a hold-out.

The third example of advocacy advertising is United Technology, a Hartford, Connecticut based conglomerate, which runs a continuing op-ed ad campaign in newspapers in major markets and in national magazines to enhance its corporate image and to participate in the "Great Debate of Current Affairs." The ads encompass a broad range of issues — "Social Security in the Red," "Technology and Jobs," "The Protectionist Illusion," and others. Like W.R. Grace, the ads appear to be thoughtful, perceptive insights into critical issues that affect our country; and not as aggressively self-serving as Mobil.

If you believe in the art of friendly confrontation, the level of combat intensity is yours to choose. You can be creative and innovative . . . without fixing bayonettes.

Or . . . you go for the jugular!

EIGHT

The Media
Is Not the Enemy

Are the news media out of control?

Yes, no, maybe. It depends upon your perspective.

Many business executives are convinced there is an anti-business bias among reporters in the news media, especially on TV. Some of the reporting is deliberate, some reporting may be based on ineptitude.

Ever since the Watergate scandal, many young journalists have wanted to become investigative reporters like Bob Woodward and Carl Bernstein. Not only to investigate, but to become feature writers and get the big story. This is what sells newspapers. The newspaper business is like any other business. The publishers need to make a profit. Look at today's headlines and see how much space is given to war, terrorism, murder, arson, rape and corruption. That's what people want to read. That's what moves newspapers off the newsstands.

Young journalists try to please their bosses. That's how you get ahead. They have been weaned on the pursuit of the big scoop. How they single-handedly uncovered the greatest wrong-doing and exposed the villains to the punishment they so richly deserved. That's the obsession — to become an overnight sensation, from obscurity to fame. Like show business, a star is born!

First comes the recognition, the by-line, the feature column, a best-selling book, an Oscar award-winning film; maybe even a Pulitzer prize for outstanding journalism. Fame and fortune have arrived.

Is this a fantasy? Perhaps, but there is an element of truth in it.

There is also a strong feeling among business executives that newspaper reporters are economic illiterates who do not understand what they are writing about. They take poor notes, don't do their homework, ask stupid questions, take up unnecessary time and can't even spell your name correctly. There is a certain contempt, recognizing that reporters aren't paid well. They are probably a bunch of hacks who couldn't make it as creative people in the real business world. There is also the perception that newswriters take a perverse pleasure in attacking business and should be avoided at all costs.

The perception of TV journalists is even worse. They are deceptive, untrustworthy, irresponsible, yellow journalists who are out to destroy your company. There is never a chance to get an uncensored fair hearing or enough time to state your case completely. When you do speak out, you can be sure of swift retaliation, trying to embarrass you, trying to make you appear stupid and incompetent.

Most business executives are not trained to appear before the unforgiving eye of the TV camera. Nor are they trained to answer difficult questions with one-liners. Their inability to cope with a TV interview has fostered a new industry to train and rehearse executives for this kind of encounter. The thought of a TV interview can send shock waves through an executive suite.

Business executives believe there is a double-standard stacked against them. The press is quick to unite behind the protection of the First Amendment and free speech at the first threat of attack or libel suits, when biased reporting and inaccurate use of information have occurred. Yet, the press does not recognize a corporation's right to have the same protection.

The Supreme Court decided in 1978 in the Beliotti case that corporate speech was entitled to First Amendment protection, eliminating most of the previous restrictions against such speech. With this landmark decision, corporations ventured into the marketplace of ideas, demanding that they now have the mandate to respond to TV *on* TV and should be allowed to do so.

The media is quick to defend itself against all of these charges. Print and broadcast executives conceded that the news industry is not perfect, but they want to do their own house-cleaning and correct whatever is wrong from within. They also reject criticisms of anti-business vendettas and cries of yellow journalism.

They point out that most reporters are trained as generalists, not specialists. They don't expect their people to become experts in economics, law, health, education, politics, international affairs and sports, since they may be covering any one of these activities on a given day. While there are some specialists, most reporters do not have a narrow expertise. However, they should have the professionalism, talking knowledge and journalistic disciplines to cover the story properly. Their job is to search for the facts, seek expert opinion, collect and evaluate information and present the story coherently, honestly and objectively.

But do they?

If business coverage appears to be biased, incomplete or poor, perhaps business should take part of the blame. Reporters complain constantly that senior business executives do not make themselves accessible for interviews or for confirmation of news. They don't want to be quoted.

They don't want to discuss sensitive information about their industry, their competition or their own companies. They constantly try to hide all the blemishes and cover up what is really going on. It's almost like a smoke screen that fogs your vision so reporters can't see the facts for what they are.

Reporters like to characterize their antagonists . . . or victims, whichever term you prefer. There is the CEO who thinks he is *Stonewall Jackson*, an institution unto himself. The media be damned! They are not going to get to him. He stands tall and strong in the wind, above the din of battle . . . wondering why he isn't getting good press.

Then there is the CEO who acts like an *Ostrich*, hiding his head in the sand, waiting for the storm to pass over; confirming nothing, denying everything; with his rear-end exposed, waiting to get kicked in the behind . . . which usually happens.

There is the *Razzle Dazzler*, the gladhander who really digs public relations and tries to snowball tiny bits of minutia into glowing feature stories, never playing square, always over-selling and getting little publicity in return.

There is the *Wimp* who is nervous, insecure and disorganized. He is afraid that anything he gives out will be held against him. He is so terribly self-conscious of his precarious status that he only gives out incomplete information and chews up precious time.

There is the *Chronic Complainer* who knows only two words: "Gimme more!" No matter how good the story, he keeps looking for the next one. Pressing and pressing, making himself so unpopular that he creates a huge void between himself and the press.

There is the *Knight in Shining Armor*, the good guy who sees no evil, hears no evil and knows no evil. He is all things to all people, the unselfish corporate citizen. He is so good that nobody cares. His approach is as extinct as a dinosaur.

There is also the *Iron Maiden*, the female version of Attila the Hun, who guards the castle and won't let a reporter through the gate, protecting everyone from intruders. No matter what tricks reporters play to interview the key people, she is always there to thwart them. And keep her company in the dark.

Then there are *Honest John* and *Reliable Barbara*, two sweethearts whom every reporter loves. They have got their act together, know what reporters want, give it to them quickly and completely and are always available to take their phone calls. When they don't have the answers, they'll get them fast. They have lots of ideas that they discuss openly. They consider reporters to be their peers and friends. No wonder they get all the action.

Now that a love-hate relationship has been established between media and business, let's try to bridge the gap and try to find a middle ground. Are journalists really that treacherous? Are they really out to get us?

The media, for all of their idiosyncrasies, are not really a bad sort. I have had the privilege of being part of their fraternity and have carried three press cards for many years. One from *Broadcasting* magazine, the second from the *North County News*, a weekly newspaper in Westchester, and the third from MIZLOU TV News. I must admit that I was grossly insulted when I was practically thrown out of the CES Press Room in Chicago, when they found out I was a public relations executive. If they had known I was also an adman, I probably would have received bodily injury. Although I was guilty of infiltrating their domain by using my press card, I was curious (a sign of a good reporter) and wanted to know what went on behind the scenes.

We all need to look behind the scenes to get a better appreciation about how the media works, so we can become allies, not enemies. We should enter into a healthy working relationship, where professionals respect one another. There may be times when you need to agree *not* to agree, but this can be accomplished without getting emotional or starting a vendetta. A corporation should be able to advocate a point of view on any issue of public interest without becoming an adversary.

Okay, then what is really behind the battle between the TV networks and companies like W.R. Grace, Mobil Oil, and anyone else who wants to use the airwaves to address an issue of public concern?

Part of the underlying problem is the FCC Fairness Doctrine. How can the TV networks develop guidelines to prohibit the broadcast of inflammatory commercials from the Klu Klux Klan, American Neo-Nazi Party, Communist Party, anti-church and hate-monger groups? How do you provide equal time for the right-to-lifers and pro-abortion groups who can generate strong emotions, which may have a negative impact on commercial advertisers who are trying to sell their products and services on TV? While radical commercials may serve the interests of the First Amendment, they do little to promote goodwill toward local TV stations and their advertisers.

You can not be aware of the intensity or power of activist groups until you see a local TV station's telephone switchboard light up and get overwhelmed. It is a question of economics, where owners of local TV stations ask: "Why put our current business at risk?"

Where do you start? Who do you let in? Where do you stop? It is like crawling through a minefield, where your next move can be a disaster! That's one of the reasons why the networks would like to keep the status quo on issue advertising.

Is there a better way?

Joseph Califano of W.R. Grace said publicly that the TV networks need to develop new policies that will promote rather than stifle debate; policies that are fair, consistent and understandable.

Two-thirds of the American people get their news from television. During the prime time evening hours, three out of four TV sets are tuned to network programs.

Califano stated that the big three networks have near monopoly power in determining the extent to which television contributes to a well-informed citizenry and the free marketplace of ideas. "Inconsistent, arbitrary and capricious action to allow some ideas on network TV and keep others off is unfair to advertisers and viewers alike. Serious issue advertisers like W.R. Grace are entitled to know what the rules are."

A more productive dialogue between the TV networks and advertisers should lead to a better balance of viewpoints over a reasonable period of time. What was left unsaid in the request for new guidelines is the battle for control.

Do the TV networks want to relinquish the control and implied censorship that they hold over advertisers? This control runs counter to the First Amendment, but it is a fact of life. Will the TV networks relinquish this control without government intervention and regulation?

The TV networks not only can deny access to issue advertising, but they also can deny access to product and service advertising. An agency must submit every TV commercial to the TV networks for acceptance and continuity clearance. This means that an advertiser and its agency must submit documentary evidence to prove every point in its commercial. This leads to hours upon hours of extra work, documentation and legal bickering, which clients find aggravating and counter-productive. The TV networks become judge and jury, questioning an advertiser's honesty . . . almost as if you are found guilty before-the-fact and need to prove your innocence.

Copywriters bemoan the fact that lawyers have gotten too involved in the creative process. An advertiser ends up with lawyers talking to lawyers, instead of copywriters talking to consumers. This is how the system currently works. How bureaucracy feeds upon itself. How one battery of lawyers confront another battery; FTC and FCC lawyers switch sides to advise the private sector and TV networks how to deal more effectively with the same regulatory government agencies the lawyers once represented. Perhaps, it is time for somebody to blow the whistle and say enough is enough! How long should advertisers have to contribute to the *Lawyers' Benevolent Association*? It is not a healthy situation.

The TV networks prefer to work within the grey, obscure area where guidelines are not definitive. This puts them squarely in the driver's seat and places advertisers at their mercy. There is no recourse or court of appeal when they say no. Your only option, and I have used it more than once, is to *bypass* the TV networks and their owned-and-operated stations, and negotiate directly with the local network affiliates and independent stations, who will accept your commercial . . . the way you want it. Uncensored!

The majority of the time, the local TV stations will accept your commercials if you conduct yourself in a responsible manner.

The media appears to have learned a lot from these creative confrontations and now tries to apply a greater degree of understanding when covering a story. Publishers, editors and broadcasters are aware of their power to shape public attitudes about business. If you, as a business executive, approach them honestly and openly, you can achieve more balanced coverage.

How do you do it?

You should develop a ProActive policy of "full disclosure" . . . even when it hurts. You need to enforce this policy rigidly and let the press know you are doing it.

We are not suggesting that you hang out all of your dirty linen for everyone to see. It means you are going to do your ProActive planning well in advance, so you are prepared and have nothing to hide. Unexpected problems may occur. Some may be sensitive, proprietary, or could cause damage if the competition learns about them. This type of information is confidential and cannot be released. However, if there are problems that a reporter can dig out for himself, interviewing middle management and lower level employees, especially someone who has been recently dismissed, you better be prepared to address the problem candidly. You need to define the situation, state the facts for what they are, good and bad, and outline what corrective action is planned and when it will take place. If you don't come out in the open promptly and accurately, the problem can blow up in your face.

You do not have to trumpet unfavorable news the minute it occurs, but when media inquiries are made, don't dodge them. Be courteous and cooperative. Try to understand the reporter's goal, to get a good story. His focus is the public interest — suspicious, inquiring and somewhat distrustful. Yours is a private interest — protective, growth oriented and also somewhat distrustful. There must be a neutral ground, where media and business can participate in more balanced coverage.

When meeting with the press, there are different levels of disclosure that can be used. The first and most important priority is to establish the ground rules with the reporter at the beginning of the interview. If he or she agrees to your qualifications, then proceed. If agreement is not reached, then assume that everything you say will be quoted "for the record" and attributed to you.

One qualification is to talk "off the record." Everything you say during the interview cannot be used by the reporter. Be careful that you establish this ground rule at the beginning. If you wait until the interview is over and then say it is "off the record," it is too late.

Another qualification is "not for attribution." Here the reporter can quote everything you say during the interview, but cannot attribute the quotes directly to you. However, the reporter can refer to a "company source." If you don't want the information you are granting to get back to you in print, better think twice about giving the interview. It is better to determine in advance how the reporter plans to source the information you plan to give out, rather than see "leaks" traced back to you afterwards.

A final qualification is a "backgrounder." Everything you say during the interview cannot be quoted, but it can be used as general information for story development.

While we believe in the principle of "full disclosure," it should be structured from a *marketing-driven* point of view. If a reporter asks for confidential sales and profit statistics, you do not have to provide them if you are representing a private company. The simple answer is: "We are a privately-held corporation and company policy prohibits the release of this information." The reporter cannot get too angry with you, because it is a company policy that says no, not you. However, you should show some form of cooperation by providing percentage changes for sales or share of market or tracking studies; something tangible that the reporter can write about. A stonewall will get you nothing but journalistic anguish . . . and possible retaliation.

If you are representing a public corporation, there is a different set of ground rules. A good inquiring reporter can dig out some of the information from your corporate annual report, Form 10K and quarterly reports. It seems better to lead them by the hand so they get the facts straight, rather than leave them to their own devices and possible misinterpretations.

That is why it is preferable to have a "talking paper" in front of you during the interview, outlining what you want to say. Check off your points one by one or go back at the end to be sure you didn't miss something important. Remember, it is your interview. Stay in control. If possible, provide the reporter with a packet of information, including your "talking paper" and "backgrounders" with general information that you think may interest the reader. Don't overwhelm the reporter. Keep it short and simple. Everything you provide will be appreciated, since it makes the reporter's job easier.

How do you cope with sensitive interviews and unfriendly situations?

If that sensitive telephone call from an inquiring reporter hits you cold and unprepared in the middle of a meeting, you can get into serious trouble quickly. It never pays to shoot from the hip, because you may say the wrong thing and regret it. If you tell them to call back, it may be considered a putdown and you are now on the defensive. Therefore, your first requirement is to have a game plan, a standard operating procedure for this kind of contingency. Don't hesitate to ask for your agency's help. It should be written in outline form for quick reading, flagging different types of contingencies. What to do when Ted Koppel calls to invite you to participate on *Nightline*? Or, Mike Wallace wants to interview you on *60 Minutes*? Or, a senior editor from *The New York Times* calls?

You need to establish the ground rules at the beginning and recognize the importance of a clear and balanced exchange. You need to determine the substance and thrust of the interview, what questions will be asked, what type of information is desired, the length of your participation and the time for rebuttal. Find out what preliminary fact finding has been accomplished, the sources used and any gaps that need to be filled in. Let the interviewer know that you will record the TV interview on videotape or on a tape recorder so you can have a record of the interview that can be checked for accuracy.

Try to stay ahead of the reporter, providing fact sheets that can benefit the interview. Mention other responsible sources that should be checked. While you can't control the entire interview, you can take precautions to see that the press gets complete and accurate information.

Make every effort to structure the interview so you will be treated fairly. Discuss how the interview will be edited, so your comments will not be taken out of perspective. On TV, different editing techniques can be used to distort, mislead and portray an impression that is dramatically different from what really transpires. To avoid this danger, insist that your comments be aired without prior editing.

If you sense that you will not be treated fairly or that you will not be given enough time to present your side of the issue completely, you have the prerogative to decline the invitation for the TV interview. Tell them why you do not want to participate and see if they will modify their approach to accommodate you. Be reasonable, flexible and search for the middle ground.

Accepting the TV interview is just the beginning. If you have never been interviewed on a network show before, you should attend a special training course that prepares you for it. Their curriculum usually includes how to dress, the make-up needed, how to sit and position yourself comfortably before the camera, what to do with your hands, how to field surprise questions, how to make your point and be persuasive, how to laugh and win in a TV encounter. Each TV show is different and the do's and don'ts are rehearsed under carefully simulated conditions. When you see your first simulated interview on videotape, you will know that you need all the help you can get.

Newspaper and magazine interviews are easier to cope with. There is less of an encounter and more of an old fashioned, give-and-take, question-and-answer period. Reporters try to be objective. If you have got something to say, you are not limited to twenty seconds as you are on TV. Reporters will take down every word you say, sometimes taping the interview so they can be sure their facts are correct. They will use your background information as long as it adds substance to their story.

If you believe a newspaper or magazine published an unfavorable article that distorted the facts, you can demand a retraction and clarification. Publications will admit an error when they make one and will print a retraction if they agree with you. Unfortunately, the first impression can be a lasting one, and the retraction does not undo the damage caused by the incorrect story.

When a story is written accurately, but still presents your company in an unfavorable light, you can respond by writing a "Letter to the Editor," which most likely will be published. Or, you can go the Mobil route and create an op-ed ad to clarify the record. You can also request a face-to-face meeting with the publication's editorial board or seek an ombudsman to act as an intermediary to help resolve the differences.

Okay, what do you do when the network refuses to accommodate you and insists on its right to control the response content? If you can prove that your company has been damaged because of inaccurate editorial, you can sue the network for libel. However, you must prove "malicious intent" to win, which is difficult to do. A final option is to petition the FCC for reply time under the "personal attack" doctrine.

You can also produce videotape rebuttals and distribute them to independent TV stations, movie theaters, educators, special interest groups, selected target audiences, government and media influentials.

You should start planning ahead for the day when corporate issue advertising will be accepted on all three TV networks. Once the barriers come down, where do you want to place your commercials? *The Today Show* on NBC appears to be a popular choice. Or, would you prefer to appear on *CBS News with Dan Rather*, or *NBC News with Tom Brokaw*, or *ABC News with Peter Jennings*; or, budget permitting, schedule a road-block on all three? What about the magazine-type formats? Do you want to appear on *60 Minutes, 20/20, Nightline, This Week With David Brinkley* or a special news documentary? Better start polling for the popularity of TV shows among your target audiences.

You should also look for low intensity, non-controversial opportunities to gain TV visibility for your corporation — on TV and radio talk shows, special events, community relations and sports activities. The editorial environment helps present your company in a more compatible perspective, enhancing your corporate image and credibility.

Try to build friendly relations with the media, where they see you in a pleasant, non-adversarial role. Get to know them better as individuals on a first-name basis. Plan an open house and invite them to visit your company to look around. Create a special event or new product happening, so there will be a reason for their attendance. Give them carte blanche to talk to your staff and employees. Let them see the human side of your organization and how everyone performs. If your company is doing well and the morale is high, they will walk away with a favorable impression. This will prove helpful when they write their next story. Keep your communication channels wide open at all times. Talk to your friends at the press when times are good . . . as well as during times of stress. You never know when you will need a favor.

Regardless of the size of your company, you can make the press a part of your team. Embrace them and get as close as possible. All you have to do is try. You will never control them, but it will certainly be worth the effort.

Remember: Make love, not war! More can be achieved. And everybody wins!

NINE

How to Beat
the TV Networks

The TV networks appear to be losing their influence on mass America because of three factors: an arrogance of power, technological change and fragmentation of the television industry.

These three factors, when clearly understood, can be harnessed to your corporate advantage. New ProActive tactics can be used to beat the networks.

The battle for control between the TV networks and corporate America will continue to be fought at different levels of intensity. Until the networks clean up their act, they will continue to be attacked for their lack of responsibility, contrived news stories, libel suits, docu-dramas and news programs that have become entertainment vehicles. All three networks are guilty of structuring their programs to sensationalize the news, losing a great sense of objectivity.

Television will always be an intrusive, emotional, close-up medium with tremendous power to influence its viewing audiences. How many times have TV news cameramen scripted and rehearsed a scene before filming it as a hard news, candid story? How many times have TV news cameramen shot a scene with less than a dozen angry people and portrayed them to look like a wild mob scene? The close-up nature of the camera tends to dramatize and exaggerate.

How many times have newscasters injected themselves into their news stories to establish their own sense of importance, tinged with a sense of humor, rather than reporting the news objectively, which is their mandate? Watch how newscasters use all of the dramatic techniques usually found in entertainment programming. When they report a crisis where deaths are involved, watch their facial expressions and listen to their shocked tone of voice, sensationalizing their stories. For business problems, they present a face of gloom with a deep tone of voice, serious and sad. For celebrations, a face of joy coupled with an enthusiastic voice of cheer. Newscasters are human and they do reflect the emotions and happenings around them. But isn't their conduct just good theater?

Why?

So they can build bigger and more loyal viewing audiences. And get better ratings.

How many times have TV commentators appointed themselves to be your news interpreter . . . to tell you what the politicians and corporate leaders really mean, what they omitted, what they fuzzed over and what they should have said? How many times have their comments intruded into your thoughts after a major news event or political debate . . . before you had a chance to think for yourself?

Who appointed the TV networks to be the self-annointed guardians of the truth? Their thought-provoking analyses confuse the issues. Their "Big Brother is looking over you" mentality has created a backlash of public resistance. Our new ProActive tactics can take advantage of this backlash.

Technological change and fragmentation have made a

negative impact on the three major networks. There are over 850 TV stations in the U.S. today. CBS, NBC and ABC, having dominated the industry since its inception, have encountered competition from many new sources. Network affiliate stations are demanding more independence and local control over their programming. Cable TV should increase its current reach of 45 percent of total TV households in the U.S. to 65 percent by 1990, offering a wide choice of programming. Local independent TV stations have combined into station groups and the Independent TV Network to make their voices heard. The superstations have grown in importance, offering additional programming choices. Rupert Murdock's fourth major TV network, the Fox Network, presents new challenges.

Another prime threat to available TV network viewing time comes from the home video industry, where VCR coverage should grow from its current base of 18 percent of total TV households in the U.S. to 40 percent by 1990, possibly higher. The use of VCR has changed America's viewing habits. Many network shows and special events can be videotaped off the air onto VCRs for later viewing. Videotape rentals have become big business, increasing in popularity as club prices reduce the cost per use, providing viewers with an affordable option of watching over-the-air programming or renting a good movie.

High technology will fragment the industry further. One community after another is being wired for cable TV. If Cable TV can get wired into Forest Glen, Pennsylvania, hidden in the out-of-the-way mountainside near Lake Wallenpaupak in the northern Poconos, it can go anyplace. Satellite TV and direct broadcast TV systems are changing the landscape of small town and rural America, providing consumers with a greater programming selection.

The pre-eminence of network programming and its share of total viewing will decline. People have become more selective in their viewing habits. Their tastes have changed and will continue to change. They have learned to zap back and forth between programs, getting quick glimpses and information bursts, looking for instant gratification. TV remote controls and VCR fast-forward speeds up the process, helping viewers search for something new and more exciting.

The public's demand for better quality programming will increase. Yet, how do you define *quality*? How do you equate it to the anachronistic rating system that the three networks rely upon, which seems to be dictated by the *lowest* common denominator? The consumer desire for better programming will be fueled by increased competition, new trends in programming and heavy promotion.

New quality programming will be created for entertainment shows. It should also be created for public information to serve a social responsibility.

We have created a new ProActive concept to fill the gap in public affairs programming. Our new TV property provides a corporation with an *uncensored*, sponsor-controlled, flexible format . . . where corporations can now respond to TV *on* TV! The opportunity also applies to a Third World country or private enterprise.

The concept overcomes the TV network access rule, where corporate issue advertising and special docudramas have not been acceptable. The concept also overcomes the TV network obsession with total control over programming. The concept offers an opportunity that *bypasses* the TV networks completely; yet, reaches 75 percent of total TV homes in the U.S. and more.

The concept also solves the problem of network domination of the news, overcoming TV magazine formats that slant and distort the news. Since Congress requires broadcasters to encourage discussion of all sides of an issue, major advertisers can now have this opportunity.

Our concept: we plan to produce an open forum where corporations can set the record straight! There will be no news media represented on the show, either as hosts, moderators or debaters. We want to encourage a spirit of *uncensored* open debate on major *controversial* issues that have a strong emotional impact on a mass TV viewing audience. Two or more sides will be invited to present their case honestly, fairly and in good taste. It will be a "no holds barred" kind of contest.

There will be total flexibility. Each side will have the same amount of time to present their views and give a rebuttal. Each side has the option to use videotape footage, 35mm color highlight slides, pre-recorded sound tracks, multi-media effects. Whatever it takes to tell its story effectively. Let the best man win!

Our producers will make every effort to avoid the editorializing that the TV network news commentators do. I personally resent the *thought-control* that TV network commentators *inflict* on the American people . . . on me, immediately after a Presidential telecast.

To avoid this possiblity, our producers have established strict criteria for the selection of our central character, who will serve as host and moderator for the show. He will be a non-newscaster, selected from the ranks of TV announcers, actors, sportsworld, academia or government. He must have good TV stage presence and the dynamic, intellectual caliber to serve as an impartial interlocutor. His job will be to monitor the debate — to ensure a smooth, orderly flow of each side of the issue. He will not care which side is right. His task will be to guide both sides of the issue, asking questions to keep the debate moving. He will remain aloof, objective and unemotional. At no time will he try to influence the viewing audience. This includes his facial expressions, tone of voice and body language. None of the little tricks newscasters use to slant the news.

As soon as the first sponsor is lined-up, our producers

will conduct a national star search to find the right personality. If high visibility is a corporate objective, the star search should be supported by a heavy advertising, promotion and publicity campaign.

The name of CFI's new TV program is: "The Court of Public Opinion. You Be The Judge." It is planned as a sixty-minute show. It can be scheduled quarterly or monthly.

What a masterful way to beat the TV networks at their own game! Every American wants to root for the underdog. Whether you agree with the proponents or not, they will at least have their day in court.

To stimulate audience interaction, we plan to use AT&T's 900 telephonic system as an affordable, instant polling device. Viewers can call in their "Yes, no" decisions on an issue and see them tallied electronically on-camera. Although the 900 system is a straw poll and not a projectable national sample, it will provide insights into the public's perception of a controversial issue. The national tally will be dissemminated to newspaper editors and TV news desks at over 550 TV stations across the U.S. via a satellite link-up for the same night and next day newscasts.

If promoted properly as a special news event, the follow-up publicity can reinforce your corporation's stand on a controversial issue, recapping the audience response and its demand for results. Post-publicity can be sent to government and community leaders, media influentials, shareholders, employees; anyone your corporation wants to influence. Behind-the-scenes photo coverage can be featured in corporate newspaper ads, newsletters, sales literature, stockholder reports; press releases to national, trade and special interest magazines. Videotape documentaries can be edited to different time lengths for shareholder and employee meetings, community affairs and trade pre-sentations. The possibilities are unlimited.

The TV production, networking and station clearance will be planned, coordinated and executed through the

MIZLOU TV Network, the nation's leading independent TV network. Its president is Vincent C. Piano, a dynamic and decisive leader, who has run the company for 25 years. Vic, as everyone calls him, is determined to make this new program a *quality showcase* production. There are two options for networking and station clearance. Option One is to use the MIZLOU TV Network exclusively for over-the-air broadcasting, offering a quality station line-up in the top 50-100 markets. This reaches approximately 85 percent of total TV households in the U.S. Option Two is to double-dip and combine the MIZLOU TV Network in the top ten markets with one or two national cable TV networks — the Financial News Network (FNN) and the USA Network, delivering a combined reach of 75 percent of total TV homes.

The first option provides ultimate flexibility. The program can be produced and videotaped live, but can be rebroadcast at any future date of the sponsor's choice. Although we can assume that immediacy is important, the sponsor can elect to adapt the broadcast scheduling to the needs of the different markets by both date and day-part, scheduling your program against weaker rated shows.

The second option allows you to focus on your target audience more effectively. As Vic says: "You're counting heads, not hands." The cost of the second option is significantly lower.

The greatest cost variance will depend upon how local TV stations respond to the controversial programming. Will they demand a complete buy-out, the current prognosis? Or, can MIZLOU negotiate an arrangement similar to its sports and entertainment programming? The difference could double the price of the show.

If the local TV stations can not sell the local time to local advertisers, MIZLOU will need to negotiate a complete buy-out to offset the station's lost revenue. The question is, will the stations try to sell the time locally?

Local advertisers should welcome the opportunity to participate in a quality showcase that provides a "Court of Public Opinion" on controversial issues. If the stations promote it properly at the local level, sizable viewing audiences can be anticipated, which should encourage local advertisers to participate.

Any company that perceives itself as a pillar of the community and desires an image of social responsibility is a good prospect. Local companies should be willing to stand-up and be counted . . . as the underdog's champion, a defender of free speech for everyone. Banks, insurance companies, department stores and public utilities should be encouraged to support this open forum. They can disassociate themselves from the specific issue, but stand behind the right to speak out. To give the underdog his day in court. And to let the public be the judge.

The problem of obtaining local clearance may be overcome in two stages: negotiating a buy-out initially to get the first show on the air; and upping the ante for local participation once the show is successful.

Corporate objectives and available budget will dictate which TV network option will be used. The format of the show has been structured to provide flexibility for sponsorship. "The Court of Public Opinion" can be brought to the American public each quarter by the same sponsor or by a different sponsor per show.

The corporations that get in line first will call the shots! They can probably write their own contracts, protected by multi-year zero-based increases. MIZLOU's TV standards and practices are flexible and can be adapted to corporate needs. It makes it a lot easier to do business this way.

Let's look at the high visibility a sponsor will get during the program. The sponsor's corporate name will be linked dramatically with the show, featured in the opening and closing credits and visually on a banner, stage center. The sponsor gets an opening and closing billboard, plus the option to run three sixty-second advocacy commercials during the show or six thirty-second commercials. There will also be tune-in publicity and advertising to generate public interest in print and on TV.

You can't buy this kind of TV exposure on a major TV network for any price! It is high visibility at its peak.

Depending upon the production requirements and station clearance problems, our concept is a bargain when compared to network pricing. Our best guesstimate for Option Two, using the MIZLOU TV Network in combination with a national cable network is $350,000 net per show. For Option One, using the MIZLOU TV Network alone, the price could double. This latter price could be reduced by selecting the top 30 markets, reaching 54 percent of total U.S. households.

Compare these estimates to the cost of one TV prime time thirty-second spot, which costs approximately $150,000. Six thirty-second spots would cost $900,000! More than double the cost of MIZLOU Option Two.

MIZLOU can clear a quality station line-up for any type of show. It is a question of timing, money and sponsor requirements. The benefits: ultra *flexibility* and maximum *sponsor control*. Plus a TV format that can drive home your message and enhance your corporate image.

The costs for using AT&T's 900 polling service to generate public interaction is inexpensive. The equipment requirements are minimal. The system screens-out people who are marginally interested. Each telephone caller is charged 50 cents on their telephone bill per 900 call. The system is easy to use and administer.

What issues are acceptable? How controversial?

Any advocacy issue is open game as long as a corporation is willing to sponsor it. If you are willing to pay the price, we are ready, willing and able to put it on the air. We will *not* play censor!

Anything and everything goes! We want to encourage free speech, not inhibit it. We want companies to focus on controversial issues that will arouse emotions and generate maximum public interest.

Our producers are not overly concerned about the possibility of a corporation trying to shock the viewing audience. They do not anticipate a deluge of obscenity, bad taste and vulgarism, since a corporation will have to live with the verdict of "The Court of Public Opinion." Corporations will apply their own constraints, looking out for the profit motive and their own self-interests.

There are many issues. Energy, environment, chemical, toxic waste, government spending, liability insurance, civil rights, aerospace and defense, trade tariffs, terrorism, low intensity wars, drugs, crime, apartheid and more.

Who will select the opponent to debate the other side of the issue?

The guy who picks up the tab gets to choose his opponent. It's like being the heavyweight champion of the world. He picks the contenders. If he wants to fight a bum-of-the-month, he will end up with few people watching TV. If he picks a top contender, he might be in for the fight of his life . . . a large TV audience . . . and a big, fat purse. As executive producer, we plan to work closely with our sponsors in selecting opponents who will provide a balanced view. To give the sponsor exactly what he seeks . . . an honest-to-goodness battle and debate.

Our concept should be supported by a ProActive public relations program, stressing that it is in the public's self-interest to support a corporation's right to respond to TV *on* TV . . . on "The Court of Public Opinion."

"You be the judge!"

TEN

Deep Penetration

During my 30 years on Madison Avenue, I have sat through countless client meetings, listening to CEOs and their marketing directors complain about how they only skim the surface of their markets. If they could only penetrate deeper into the guts of their market, they could really expand their business.

One ProActive tactic that can accomplish this goal is called the "CFI-MIZLOU ProActive Option." It offers your company the opportunity to sponsor an exciting televised special event, which has a wrap-around promotion that can be tailored to get into the guts of your market.

Our tactics require careful planning and execution, using the national televised special event as your focal point. The wrap-around promotion starts at the grass roots level and can involve your consumer, distributor, dealer; anyone you want. It builds methodically on a statewide or regional basis, adapting to your marketing requirements. It culminates with a national TV show that reaches 85 percent of total TV households in the U.S. on a quality station line-up. The entire marketing promotion and field work can be a *turnkey* operation, where the producer plans and executes all of the marketing support packages and the operation itself. Or, your marketing and sales staffs can be involved as much or as little as you prefer.

Our challenge is to get the attention of the CEO who will recognize instantly what can be gained from this type of integrated marketing promotion. Short of his involvement, the screening process takes over. The staff gets in the way, finding different reasons why the TV promotion will not work or why they can't justify it with numbers.

What they are really saying is that they don't want to get involved in grass roots marketing. It requires a lot of hard work, tedious hours, follow through and coordination to get all of the people on the firing line to do what you want them to do. It is difficult to work with imprecise data or to accept the fact that research cannot track this type of promotion accurately. So your staff schedules meetings and talks about the need for grass roots marketing, while they wring their hands in utter despair. "If we could only find a way!"

Well, there is a way! But it is not for the faint-hearted, the lazy loafer or the nervous Nellie.

It is for the hard-charging CEO. The dynamo who knows what he wants and won't accept anything less. A CEO who is willing to listen to new ideas. A CEO who knows how to make it happen.

This is the CEO we'd like to meet. This is the CEO who should be banging on our doors to let him in.

Tell us who you want to reach. How do you define your target market? Are you looking for a promotion vehicle that provides an elegant, quality image to reach adults, male and female, aged 24 to 54 . . . for a company in the beauty, fashion, automotive or wine field?

We've got it.

Are you looking for a promotion that will capture the fancy of high school teenagers?

We've got it.

Are you looking for the sports-minded market, males 18 to 44, with spendable discretionary income?

We've got it.

Are you restricted by government regulation not to advertise your products on TV, but still would like some corporate visibility on TV?

We've got it.

Do you have special-interest products for gardening or hunting and do you want to reach a narrowly defined audience?

We've got it.

Are you looking for something that's never been done on TV that can capture the imagination of the American people from coast to coast?

We've got it.

Are you thinking of creating a special event that nobody has thought of, including us, and would like to do it?

We'll do it!

Let's look at a variety of different packages as an example of how the "CFI-MIZLOU PlayAction Option" can work for you.

The first opportunity is a special event that can provide a quality premier showcase for your company and product line. It has all the glamour, glitter, elegance and style that you can hope for.

It provides a corporation with a unique opportunity to dominate an emerging growth trend that is sweeping across the country. Ballroom dancing is back! Everyone is dancing together again, just as we did in the '40s and '50s. It has captured the attention of editors and broadcasters, who have publicized the trend for several years.

The professional dance people are anxious to put ballroom dancing onto network TV. They organized a company called the American Ballroom Company, which includes management from the Fred Astaire and Arthur

Murray national dance franchises, and independent dance schools. John Monte, the younger brother of orchestra leader Victor Montenegro, is president of this group. John is one of the most well-known, personable dance masters in the professional dance industry. Anything that he does has the master's touch.

The American Ballroom Company conducts a national dance competition called the "U.S. National Ballroom Dance Championships" or U.S.B.C.s as it is known in the trade. It is an exciting, beautiful event, where over 1,000 professional and amateur dancers from all over the U.S. come to compete. The U.S.B.C.s also have open dance events for worldwide competitors. This competition is like the Olympics of ballroom dancing.

The dance competition is magnificent to watch. The big band sound and the Latin American beat are back in full youthful swing . . . from formal black tie 'n' tails and elegant, evening gowns . . . to sparkling, seductive Latin American and disco costumes. The dancers vie for championship crowns in professional and amateur events, competing in the tango, rumba, cha-cha, foxtrot and jive (formerly called the lindy.) There is the quickstep, which Fred Astaire made famous in the movies, where dancers are so light on their feet that they practically glide across the ballroom floor. There is the Viennese waltz, which brings back the grace of centuries ago. There is the proud bolero, paso doble, mambo and disco hustle. There is also collegiate competition called formation dancing, which is as good as Broadway's best chorus lines.

The costume ensembles for the men and women range from sophisticated blacks and whites to the outrageous, sequined, vibrant look. There are feathers and frills. Color on color. Traditional and avante garde. A virtual showcase for fashion and beauty.

We had a 22 year-old male macho chauvinist working

for us during the U.S.B.C.s. When he saw the first film clips and the beautiful women, Marty Holmes exclaimed: "I've got to learn how to do that. I want to be able to glide and slide across the floor like the pros." He had been to several ballrooms and wanted to be part of the action. Young people like Marty are clamoring to learn. Ballroom dancing is coming back fast — in the cities, suburbs and on the college campus.

Our agency handled the publicity for the U.S.B.C.s for two years when they were conducted at the Waldorf-Astoria in New York City . . . before relocating to their home turf in Miami. We also handle the advertising for the Fred Astaire Dance Schools in New York. From a publicity point of view, we had tremendous success. Excellent coverage was obtained prior to the event, during the four days and nights of the competition and immediately afterwards. CBS, NBC, ABC and the leading TV independents gave us over 35 minutes of *free* airtime, which was worth over $3 million. Major photo stories appeared in *The New York Times, Daily News, Post, Newsday, USA Today, Gannet Group, Bergen Record, New Jersey Star-Ledger, Independent Press, Village Voice*; plus follow-up feature stories of the U.S.B.C. champions in their home town metro newspapers. Stories also appeared in *Newsweek, Dance, Backstage* and *Dancing USA* magazines.

Here is an opportunity to get in on a crest-of-the-wave, tie-in with over 15,000 dance studios around the country; and tie-in with your local dealers at the grass roots level. The U.S.B.C.s are willing to rename the competition with the sponsor's corporate name, promoting it prominently. For example, it could be called "The Clairol U.S. Ballroom Dance Championships" or "The Gallo U.S. Ballroom Dance Championships" . . . or, recognizing the growing importance of Japanese world-class dancers, "The Nissan U.S.B.C.s" or "The Panasonic U.S.B.C.s" or "The Seiko U.S.B.C.s" . . . it's time to dance!

The organizers have agreed to create a national network of dance contests, starting at the state level and advancing to the regionals and finally the nationally televised event. Approximately 80 ballroom dance competitions are conducted on a regional basis. John Monte can link these regionals to the national U.S.B.C.s, similar to the way the Miss America Pageant is conducted at the grass roots level. The program can be launched slowly, starting with six regional events in the first year, or, it can be expanded quicker on a broader scale.

Here are some promotion ideas to demonstrate the strong marketing clout that you can obtain locally.

Every drug store, department store, specialty store and mass merchandiser can become the sponsor's headquarters for the event. Every dealer showroom, jeweler or beauty salon can participate. A complete promotion package with banners, posters, handouts, point-of-purchase displays and co-op ads can hype the event under your corporate name. Contestants can pick up their applications at your local retail outlets to enter the competition. Scoring sheets and a procedure brochure to "Score Along with the Judges" can be distributed to coincide with the national TV show.

Finally, you can speak in earnest when you tell your retailers and dealers that you are giving them real promotional support to build their local store traffic and volume. There are also opportunities for field marketing at the 80 regional competitions, where the sponsor can demonstrate products, give out samples and literature, and integrate a sweepstakes contest into the promotion.

The national U.S.B.C.s TV show can become the sponsor's "Social Happening," where tables can be reserved at ringside for your executives and guests. A full hour prior to the Grand Finale will be reserved for your guests to "Dance with the Professionals." Editors will be invited to attend and dance with the stars. Is there a better way to capture their enthusiasm and support?

The sixty-minute TV special will be produced and broadcast on the MIZLOU TV Network, reaching 85 percent of total TV households. A celebrity hostess will be selected, based upon sponsor requirements. Rita Moreno and Juliet Prowse have performed in the past. The sponsor gets six thirty-second commercials during the program, avoiding the clutter of spot scatter plans, plus the opening and closing billboards and credits. The sponsor's top management can participate in the on-camera awards ceremony, which also gets good photo coverage for post-publicity in the consumer and trade press.

The TV show will be videotaped, edited and broadcast at a scheduled date coordinated with the sponsor. Highlights of each day's championships can be edited down to two-minute news clips and fed by satellite for the same night, next day news coverage to 550 TV stations in the U.S.

The sponsor will get strong corporate and product visibility within the program in a manner that cannot be obtained on network TV for any price. Huge banners with the corporate name will be seen in many dance sequences. The corporate name will appear on the presenter's podium, commentator's TV booth and as a centerpiece on the awards table. It will all be executed in good taste. When the final telecast is completed, the sponsor may look at his one-hour TV special as a *sixty-minute commercial*, rather than the six thirty-second spots that he gets.

The U.S.B.C.s and MIZLOU are flexible, providing sponsor control and a *turnkey* operation. The costs vary, based upon sponsor requirements. The estimated cost of this prime time one-hour TV special is $350,000 net — a real value when you consider all of the local marketing support you will get. It is also a bargain: the entire cost is 50 percent *less* than what you would pay for six thirty-second spots, which can easily get lost in commercial clutter.

Another marketing opportunity targets on the teenage market. Is your company in the soft drink, cosmetic, fashion or another business that caters to teenagers? Are you looking for a promotion to generate high interest levels? Are you looking for a traffic builder that will get you into the guts of the market?

This unique *turnkey* promotion combines a special event in the top 25 markets with a national TV special. The promotion will focus on a regional high school dance contest, conducted in regional shopping malls across the U.S. The winners will travel to the final competition, which will be televised on the **MIZLOU TV** Network, reaching 85 percent of total TV households.

The sponsor's name will be integrated into the promotion's name, called: "The National High School Dance Championship." Strong community involvement is anticipated, since we will be working closely with the promotion director of each shopping mall. Parents, friends, teachers, neighbors and families will show-up in strength. If promoted properly, we can draw teenagers from all of the high schools in the regional area, pitting contestants from one school against the other. School spirit gets involved, adding to the excitement of a major media event.

The prime motivating factor to get teenagers to participate is the *promise* of competing on national TV. Every teenager wants to become a star. This promotion will fulfill that dream. Fifty high school dancers will be finalists and compete on national TV.

This concept was tested successfully in Arizona and California without the benefit of a national TV show. Local support and press coverage were excellent.

A one-hour TV special will highlight the regional differences in teenage dancing. The lindy, disco, Texas two-step, Georgia Rock and Latin American beat . . . whatever the kids consider fun. Their costumes will be a bright and colorful sight to behold.

The field marketing opportunities are unlimited. Contestants will have to go to their local retail outlets established as headquarters for the promotion. Retailers can tie-in with banners, posters, point of sale material and dance programs. Another good opportunity for sampling, premiums, sales literature.

This is an effective way to penetrate the school market, since the mall promotion director has established contacts. Pre-publicity and word-of-mouth at the school level will bring out the crowds. Local TV stations will do remote telecasts, along with local newspaper coverage.

The sponsor gets high visibility on the MIZLOU TV Network, including six thirty-second spots during the show, opening and closing billboards and participation during the awards ceremony. Since the TV show is planned for a weekend, the cost is lower, estimated at $275,000 net.

The promotion is planned over nine months. Talk about getting into the guts of your market. This promotion should be a natural!

Another marketing opportunity is the sports market. The MIZLOU TV Network is in its 18th year of televising post-season collegiate football bowl classics. Vic Piano, who is frequently called "Mr. Football," has pioneered this concept. For the first time, Vic has decided to offer these bowl packages for total sponsorship, rather than selling spots to individual advertisers. Some of the bowls have greater magic than others. For example, the Independence Bowl in Shreveport, Louisiana and the Freedom Bowl in Anaheim, California, which are played on December 20th and 30th respectively, can capture some of the same kind of excitement and patriotism seen on the Miss Liberty Centennial festivities in New York on July 4th, 1986.

If your corporation is trying to build a strong corporate image that ties-in with our country's heritage, this type of special event should be considered. There is a limited inventory of football bowl games available; six, possibly eight games. Vic's game plan is to negotiate three to five year contracts with rate protection for each sponsor.

A corporation can achieve high visibility, enhancing its quality image. Being identified with a prestigious sports event will enhance employee morale and provide a unique platform for consumer and trade promotions.

Your corporate name and logo will be identified on all signs, posters, graphics and news coverage. There will be strong corporate visibility during the game and at half-time when corporate executives participate in the on-camera awards ceremony. You will have the right to use the bowl name and logo in advertising and promotion.

Your company can create a travel incentive package for your salesforce and leading dealers, using the football bowl tie-in to promote MVP sales contests. The sponsor will get 250 bowl tickets to give away as prizes, bringing your best customers to the game.

There are other fringe benefits, too. The sponsor's name will appear on the scoreboard and cover of the football bowl program. There will also be four scoreboard and two public address announcements during the game.

The sponsor gets three minutes of commercial TV time, plus opening and closing billboards on the MIZLOU TV Network, reaching 85 percent of total TV households. As an additional bonus, the sponsor will get two minutes of commercial time on a national TV cable network.

Needless to say: "The early bird gets the worm."

There are other MIZLOU TV sports promotions, targeted to an upscale market, focusing on tennis, golf, ocean speedboat racing, triathalon and sportscar racing packages. Your sponsorship of any of these events can be tailored to your requirements, similar to the TV marketing promotion packages described previously.

If your company is in the cigarette or liquor industry, MIZLOU TV can provide good corporate institutional visibility, focusing on signs and banners that feature your corporate name and logo as the sponsor of the event. You have the option to run three minutes of TV commercial spots for non-restricted products or you can sell off the time to another advertiser.

There is another special event moving out of the starting gate, which has lots of excitement and potential to achieve deep market penetration. It is called the "Great American Horse Race and Pony Express Classic" and is planned to run coast-to-coast with all the possible tie-ins imaginable at the local level.

The "Great American Horse Race" was run successfully, coast to coast, in 1975. The concept of combining it with the "Pony Express Classic" was test marketed successfully in six regional races. With the focus on endurance, self-reliance and independence, the "Pony Express Classic" should capture all the excitement of Buffalo Bill Cody and the Wild West. The organizers plan to sell "Ponygrams," which will be carried by Pony Express pouch to a bank in San Francisco. It will be deposited in a time capsule for safekeeping and will not be reopened for 50 or 100 years. Just think of the claim that a sponsor can make: "We'll still be around when your grandchildren come to collect it!"

What a natural sponsorship for Wells Fargo, Bank of America, American Express, MasterCard or one of the air freight couriers.

Advance publicity people along the route will assure local TV and press coverage. The race will be conducted over a 30 to 60 day period, providing the sponsor with many opportunities for local field marketing.

The MIZLOU TV package is flexible and will be planned in a similar manner to the ones described previously. Costs are contingent upon the size of the winner's purse and the combination of the MIZLOU TV Network and a cable TV network.

There are other TV marketing promotions available for national sponsorship. The "All-American High School Jazz Festival" is presented annually in Mobile, Alabama. The MIZLOU TV show will spotlight the six best bands in the U.S., consisting of 25 to 30 members per band. Their big band sound is targeted to a mass market — from 15 to 75 years old. Pre-publicity will provide a sponsor with access to the high school market — displaying posters and banners and distributing premiums at the grass roots level. The sponsor's cost is estimated at $275,000 net.

If you want to feature some of the most beautiful, vivacious women in the U.S., there is the "National Professional Football Cheerleader's Contest." Preliminary plans call for shooting sequences in selected NFL cities with the big event shot at the Fontainbleau in Miami. There are many national and local campaigns that can be wrapped-around this promotion. Visualize three beautiful cheerleaders leaping with joy while presenting your products, exclaiming: "Three cheers for . . . !" The sponsor can run national ads and adapt them locally, featuring the local NFL cheerleaders promoting your products in each NFL market.

The "CFI-MIZLOU PlayAction Option" can create almost any type of TV marketing promotion, limited only by our imagination . . . and yours. We certainly can achieve the market penetration you require. We can also put a lot of big points on your scoreboard!

ELEVEN

Grass Roots

There are a lot of ways to get into the guts of the market
. . . . with or without TV. It takes vision, flexibility, and
determination, coupled to ProActive marketing and
promotion. This applies to companies that distribute
products through retail outlets in all channels of trade —as
well as retail chains, service establishments and franchises
that sell goods and services directly to the consumer. When
you recognize how rapidly the mass market is fragmenting,
you need to redefine your marketing objectives to capitalize
on new ProActive opportunities.

One only has to look at new demographic and life-style
trends: the maturing of the baby boomers, the yuppies, the
suburbanites, the new breed of cliff dwellers, the greying of
America; the growing importance of the career woman, the
single parent, new two-on-the-aisle shopping trends and the
growing viability of the ethnic and minority markets; rising
expectations and local differences of geographic regions.
The mass market buckshot approach is becoming more
costly and less efficient. It is being replaced by a targeted
rifle approach, repositioning a brand by target audience
and regional and local marketing opportunities.

As retailers consolidate their strength, using sophisticated computer read-outs of cash register sales, they will make greater demands on manufacturers. The battle for shelf space will become more competitive. The promise of national advertising support will no longer suffice. Retailers now demand more local advertising and promotion allowances to stock your product and "push" it through to the consumer, monitoring its rate of movement, dollar sales and profit margins through computer analysis. This becomes especially challenging for companies fighting to launch new products, where buying committees have the decision-making power to determine if a new brand will replace an old brand on the shelf.

When I was a client, serving as advertising manager for Savarin and Medaglia d'Oro coffee brands and later for Simplicity, management would ask: "How can business be expanded at the grass roots level?"

This same question was asked when I worked with the national merchandising managers at Sears, supervising the national advertising campaigns for major home appliances, home entertainment products, personal appliances, housewares and fashion.

The same question was asked when my wife, Charlotte Haller, managed a family retail business called The Fashion Scene, a full service fabric sewing center and dealer for Singer, Viking and White sewing machines.

The same question comes up everytime we meet with our clients and prospective clients. "How do we get into the grass roots of your market?"

We had the answers then, we have the answers now.

The same fundamental ProActive marketing principles apply . . . whether you are selling a tangible or intangible product to different market segments; or selling the services of a regional franchise, retail chain or single retail establishment; or selling a travel destination, hotel, airline or economic development for a Third World country.

In every instance, the product concept and how you position or reposition your company to attract local market segments are of paramount importance. Once you focus on the BIG IDEA and create a personality and image for your company, product or service, you need to develop the ProActive merchandising and marketing promotions that get into the guts of your market.

There are many success stories in retailing that demonstrate the conceptual planning that goes into a grand opening of a new store or a service establishment. Unfortunately, a lot of the excitement and fanfare are lost after the initial opening, because there is little creative follow-through on a sustaining basis. After the first shot, most companies settle down into traditional price point advertising and promotion. Their companies grow and reach a sales plateau, varying 10 percent up and down, never achieving their full sales potential. While price point promotion will always be an integral part of retailing, you need to develop new ProActive marketing promotions that build a bigger market, attract new customers, increase repeat business among current customers, and reinforce the image, expertise and service of your company. These promotions can forge new sales peaks, improve slow periods, broaden your customer base and create better interaction with your consumer.

If you are a specialty store retailer or a franchisor with a unique concept, you may have about six months' lead time before a competitor knocks you off. The major chains can move with lightning speed as they analyze the market to take advantage of new product trends. They can create a new department and merchandise mix that competes with your rapidly growing business. They might be located next door, down the road or in the vicinity of your trading area. Once that happens, you can anticipate increased competition from mass merchandisers and other specialty chains, who will cut into your share of market. This has occurred with book stores, auto repairs, video rental and computer center franchises. Even the successful retail chain, The Banana Republic, faces strong competition from department stores, touting the hot selling African safari look. Getting knocked-off is a fact of life that manufacturers, retailers and service companies cannot avoid. Your challenge is to plan ahead . . . and stay ahead.

Let's look at several case histories. Of all the companies that I have worked for, Simplicity had the greatest understanding of what ProActive planning and grass roots marketing was all about. My stint at Simplicity was during the days of the home sewing boom.

From 1965 to 1979, many companies enjoyed one of the greatest resurgences of business in an industry that had refused to die. It didn't just happen. Simplicity helped make it happen. Although the ProActive marketing concept hadn't been formularized at that time, Simplicity helped pioneer many of its principles. Without Simplicity, the home sewing revolution would not have happened.

Women began to sew again. They sewed to fulfill a creative need as a form of self-expression. It became the "in" thing to do; part of the do-it-yourself craze. Women began to admire each other's handicraft. This, in itself, was a major breakthrough, overcoming the stigma that home sewing was only for people who could not afford to buy ready-to-wear clothes.

The new product concept came first. Simplicity focused on fashion and created easy-to-sew Jiffy patterns. There is a skill level involved in sewing, and the quick and easy patterns overcame the consumer fear of failure. Simplicity ran a TV and print celebrity campaign: "If I can sew, you can sew." Sales began to skyrocket.

Simplicity used a grass roots strategy that achieved a leadership position in the industry, accounting for more than 50 percent of all fashion patterns sold. Simplicity had a simple corporate philosophy that went along with its name. The company would build a bigger market, maintaining its share. Their business would increase as the market grew. And grow it did.

Simplicity developed an education program that penetrated every high school and middle school in the country. They provided sewing books and literature for home economic classes. They put the focus on fashion and fun. Almost every teenager learned their sewing skills from Simplicity; and, to a lesser degree from Singer, which also had a school program. Simplicity ran a major advertising and publicity campaign in *Seventeen* and *Teen* magazines, teaching an entire generation to sew and be creative.

Sewing became one of the few hobbies that mothers and daughters could do together. Management recognized this fact early and fed feature stories with photos to the leading women's service and fashion magazines. The TV networks captured the glamour of home sewing in their newscasts of fashion happenings. Newspaper columnists devoted entire columns to the subject.

A national retail promotion program was offered to major department stores. Fashion stylists travelled to each city and presented a traditional fashion show, which featured Simplicity patterns that were made into model garments. The department store promoted the special event, featuring the stylist as a celebrity in local newspapers, radio and TV. Sewing clinics were held after each show to answer questions and give advice.

The company published three magazines to promote home sewing. They also published the *Simplicity Fashion News*, a slick, smartly designed monthly fashion digest that was sold to all of Simplicity's retail accounts for free distribution to the consumer. The back cover had extra space for the local store imprint, address and telephone number. These free "take-ones" kept women interested in what was new in home sewing.

The management at Simplicity had great vision and

created ProActive marketing programs that provided their retail accounts with the selling tools needed to sell the consumer at the grass roots level. It was this vision that led the Haller family into one of the most exciting ten-year periods of our lives.

As advertising manager, one of my duties was to supervise the selling of advertising space in the Simplicity magazines, managing the activities of the salesforce. I had prepared a presentation for one of our new salesmen to use. On one of these presentations, I listened to myself selling the virtues of the booming home sewing market. I asked myself: "If it is such a booming market, how can my family take advantage of it?"

That's how it started. I always had an entrepreneur spirit. Looking for the BIG IDEA, I created a unique marketing concept in fabric retailing, introducing a new kind of shopping environment. The new store had a look and attitude that was totally different from a traditional store. The primary difference was the approach to selling fabrics . . . the focus was placed where it belonged . . . on fashion and service. On the promise of helping a woman look great by helping her create her own style. We didn't want our customer to think of our store as just another fabric shop. We positioned it as something "special" . . . as a full-service home sewing center, where customers could shop and compare various brands, all under one roof, before making a buying decision.

The merchandise mix included a complete line of fashion fabrics for clothing and home furnishings; seven pattern lines; Singer, Viking and White sewing machines; and a sewing school to teach the newest sewing techniques to adults and teenagers.

Our company was named: The Fashion Scene.

We opened our store in a quiet hamlet in northern Westchester called Shrub Oak, New York. It was a large store, 4,000 square feet, located in a neighborhood shopping center across the street from Lakeland High School.

The store was designed to look like a theater with small fashion boutiques, merchandising sportswear, evening-wear, childrenswear and lingerie fabrics in special departments. A large stage was constructed inside the store. It had a large screen, 8 feet tall by 24 feet wide, coupled to a multi-media projection system that included eight slide projectors and a stereo sound system. The multi-media system was used for fashion shows and daily activities.

We used ProActive tactics to create interest in our new store, generating news and then promoting it. I met with the publishers of the local newspapers and with radio station managers. Television was not used because the store was located in the northern tier of the New York TV market. TV's high cost and wasted coverage were prohibitive. If cable TV had been available, we would have used it.

Our ProActive publicity focused on our grand opening. The town supervisor and local politicians were invited to attend a tape-cutting ceremony, covered by local news photographers and reporters. We planned our first fashion show . . . to get people to come to The Fashion Scene. About a month before opening, we decided we wanted a band to play an opening song, our song. A high school band competition was held, a battle of the bands that had good press coverage. A young rock group from Lakeland High School won and played during our first two fashion shows. A friend wrote a song: "Come to the Fashion Scene!"

On opening night, we had a packed house and standing room only. Everyone came dressed-up as if they were going to the theater in New York City.

I came to the mike, saying: "Welcome to The Fashion Scene. Here we are. Off-Broadway, 45 miles north!"

That opening line got a great round of applause. We used it at all of our fashion shows, which became the most talked about and best attended special events in Westchester and Putnam counties.

The Fashion Scene was an instant promotional success, positioning itself quickly as the fashion and sewing expert in our marketing area. Like Simplicity, it didn't just happen. We made it happen! We got into the guts of the market in a way that will make everyone a ProActive believer.

The marketing tactics were consistent. Multi-media fashion shows were used to draw people to the store, customers and prospects, women who sewed and non-sewers, adults and teens, men and women. Themes were created for each show, promoting specific merchandise. They were selling shows . . . to get people to buy while they visited the store and to get them to think about sewing. The fashion shows were used to build a quality image, and, to motivate the consumer, to involve her in the latest sewing techniques and to entice her to shop frequently.

The store advertised consistently in newspapers and the *Pennysaver* and on radio. Two campaigns served different purposes. Large space ads and radio commercials promoted the fashion shows. Traditional smaller space ads featured seasonal themes, using comparative price promotions. In retailing, if the newspaper ad doesn't pull in the first three days, the ad is a failure. Promotional goods were purchased and advertised at attractive prices to build store traffic and sales.

ProActive publicity was *marketing-driven* and made the difference. The fashion shows became the community's major special event of each season. Pre-publicity was generated for each show, focusing on people, fashions and community involvement. During the first year, there were four major shows — the grand opening in June, back-to-school in August, the holiday show in October and the spring show in March.

Each fashion show was presented as a major news event . . . with the focus always on "Look what's new!" We worked closely with all of the newspaper editors to get maximum post-show coverage. We received the best support from John Chase, the publisher of the *Yorktowner*. I developed a special relationship with the *Yorktowner*, where I created a full fashion page for each of our fashion shows. I took the photos, wrote the headlines and copy and laid-out the page. It ran as editorial, featuring the glamour, excitement and fashion news. Reprints were made of the full-page editorials and distributed at the store, adding to our credibility. The editorials were also used to penetrate the local school market and community groups.

When I was at Simplicity, I was told that the school market was a tough market to crack. It had layers of bureaucracy, where you started at the state level and worked down to county before approaching a home economics teacher. If you approach local schools with tactics that benefit the student's best interests, you can avoid the bureaucracy and make great inroads at the grass roots level.

My wife Charlotte, who supervised the store, wanted to organize a Fashion Scene Teen Board, which would represent the seven high schools in our marketing area. Char had created and organized teen boards before at Gimbels and Gertz department stores, so she had the experience. We prepared a professional presentation, which outlined our school program. We went directly to the high school principals and got permission to meet with their home economic teachers. From that point on, it was pure chemistry . . . our ability to persuade and the initiative of the teacher. They all recognized the benefits their students would get from our program and endorsed it.

We had over 150 girls tryout and compete for The Fashion Scene Teen Board. This became an annual, high visibility event, generating pre-publicity coverage to announce the tryouts and post-publicity to announce the 20 winners. Being selected for The Fashion Scene Teen Board became the most coveted high school "club" in the community. The girls were used for fashion photography and as runway models. To be eligible, a girl had to know how to sew, because she would model a garment that she made herself. It would promote a pattern and fabric that Char selected to tell a fashion story. A girl had to be personable and in good standing at school. She had to be photogenic and have good stage presence. Being a good dancer helped, because we danced the girls through many of their numbers. Some of the girls on the Teen Board, who were experienced home sewers, worked at the store after school and on Saturdays. They became the fashion and sewing experts in the eyes of the teenage community.

I named our teenage show: "Lollapallooza." When the girls first heard it, all I heard was: "Mr. Haller, Lollapa-what?" But once they got into it, it became a real lollapalooza! A big hit. I took photos of the 20 girls over three weekends with Char serving as stylist. I bet I photographed our models against every barn, stonewall fence, waterfall, cliff, bridge, wagon wheel, meadow, country club, motor lodge and restaurant in our area.

When you get teenagers involved, you get the entire community . . . families, friends, schoolmates and teachers. If you make celebrities out of them as we did, you have a winner. After each fashion show, we ran one slide projector on automatic, selecting the best photos that featured the patterns, fabrics and trims we promoted.These photos were projected on our large screen continuously during regular business hours for everyone to see.

The fashion shows became so successful, we had to sell tickets after the first year to maintain crowd control. At one show, I counted 425 people. It looked like wall-to-wall faces peering back. If someone had shouted: "Fire!" there would have been a panic. When we limited tickets to 300 per show for the three evening performances, we had crossed the professional threshold. People hurried to get their tickets when they went on sale, so they wouldn't miss-out.

Adult models were also used in the holiday and spring fashion shows. These women were former models, who liked to sew and lived in the suburbs raising children. This group was named: "The Suburbanites." Little children were used, who danced to "lollipop" music, stealing the show. Grandmothers and male models were used, too.

There were other grass roots programs. Mini-fashion presentations and sewing machine demonstrations were made to community groups — home extension and 4-H Clubs; churches, synagogues and temples; women's business and luncheon clubs. This lower level activity generated press coverage and strong consumer interaction, resulting in new customers and increased sales.

Always on the lookout for new markets, Char noticed a lot of women who attended our shows couldn't sew or didn't have the patience or time to learn; yet, they liked our fashions and fabrics. Targeting this market segment, Char started a customized dressmaking service, hiring 14 dressmakers to sew custom-made clothes for these new customers, using our patterns and fabrics. This led to creating our own fashion labels: "Fashion Scene Originals" and "Lollapalooza." Both were promoted actively at our fashion shows and in print ads. Char also promoted bridal fabrics, naming the boutique, The Fashion Scene Bridal Salon.

Our staff paid great attention to the home furnishings market, an integral part of our business. Far more fabric yardage was sold to this kind of customer than fabric for clothing. Char and I had always liked the Scandinavian look. We watched the Marimeko look grow in popularity, but couldn't buy the line because there was a franchise store in our market. Recognizing that there was an emerging new market for wall graphics, we scoured the industry until we found two suppliers from Sweden and Finland with their own distinct looks. We provided our regular customers with this new look and also targeted a new customer — people who couldn't sew, but wanted wall graphics framed for their home and apartment. We promoted this concept in advertising and publicity and watched it grow to account for 11 percent of our total sales. When needlecraft became popular, we promoted it, too.

Our tactics never wavered. Look for new concepts to interest our customers and prospects. Keep our finger on the pulse of the local market. Create new promotions that can be advertised and publicized. Introduce new concepts at the fashion shows. Use pre-publicity to draw the traffic and post-publicity to promote the concept; and then merchandise it. Use a continuity program of small space display ads to sell the merchandise. Offer mini-fashion and sewing presentations to community groups. Listen to their needs and create new concepts to benefit them. They will visit your store and become loyal repeat customers.

As The Fashion Scene approached its fifth anniversary, we learned that a regional shopping center called the Westchester Mall was going to open two miles away. Making the tough decision that merchants are forced to make, we closed the Shrub Oak store and moved to the Westchester Mall. Because of the high rental costs, we reduced our space to 2,400 square feet, which did not permit a multi-media theater operation. Although the new store had a lot of character, it began to look more like a traditional fabric sewing center.

After opening, Char and I conducted one more fashion show, this time for the entire mall, coordinating merchandise from many of the stores. It became too much of a hassle. We discontinued the fashion shows and the teen board.

By moving from a neighborhood shopping center to a regional mall, major changes occurred. Our staff now worked a 12-hour day split shift, seven days a week. They experienced walk-in traffic that we never had before. Sales *doubled* in the first year and showed increases each following year. We continued to advertise and promote at the grass roots level, emphasizing the sewing school and mini-fashion presentations. Supervised by Char and our managers, Fran Schiel and Bonnie Milano, the staff continued to build a loyal following. Constant attention was paid to fashion and sewing skills, never forgetting that *service* was the most important product.

At year ten, ominous warning signs appeared on the horizon. Many women customers had rejoined the workforce, which left limited time for home sewing. If I ever timed a decision well, it was the decision to close The Fashion Scene. We conducted a successful going-out-of-business sale, paid-off our creditors and retired from retailing. The next year, the home sewing industry went "belly-up," and has never fully recovered.

If you want to achieve deep market penetration, you should develop ProActive grass roots marketing programs that can be tailored to the needs of your local markets. While you may not require the glamour we created at The Fashion Scene, there are many ways to *personalize* your services to set you apart from competition.

Another good example in the retail field is home grown. After we closed The Fashion Scene, our manager, Bonnie Milano, moved with her family to Tom's River, New Jersey. She used some of the same ProActive marketing principles when she joined Kassenoff Cabinets, a retailer specializing in custom-made kitchen and bath cabinets. Recognizing new opportunities in what had traditionally been a male dominated industry, Bonnie took to the airwaves on radio, appealing to a woman's point of view. Since women spend far more time in the kitchen than men, Bonnie talks to women conversationally: "Are you tired of the same old drab kitchen? Hi! I'm Bonnie from Kassenoff Cabinets. Come on in and let me help you design the kitchen of your dreams." Bonnie's commercials, like those of Mariette Hartley, are warm, friendly and inviting.

Bonnie has become a local celebrity, where prospects come to the store and ask for her by name. Since designing a new kitchen has a low incidence of purchase, Kassenoff uses a two-color ad in the yellow pages. When people are in the market shopping, they'll look for Bonnie's store in the yellow pages. Kassenoff also promotes its cabinets at the Home Improvement Show, held at the county mall. Bonnie is planning a cable TV test to attract new customers and build sales to a higher level; they have been increasing at an annual rate of 30 percent over previous years.

In the auto repair and service franchise fields, there are many opportunities to *revitalize* your sales. If you are in the service business, why is there so much discount and price-point advertising? Without a clear, unique positioning, every service establishment starts to look alike, blending into the neighborhood like the corner gas station. Different ProActive tactics can build a distinct *personality* for your business . . . propelling sales upwards!

If your company distributes products through retail outlets, a new sense of urgency should be given to creating ProActive marketing promotions that "sell in" and "sell through." If you do not develop programs for the grass roots level, you may find yourself held captive to retailer demands for increased promotion allowances, which you cannot control, influence or accept.

If you really want to get into the guts of your market, you need to listen . . . and then listen some more.

TWELVE

The Retailer Is King

The retailer and dealer still reign as king.

When *your* consumer, the customer, enters *their* store, despite all the millions of dollars you may have invested in national advertising, the retailer can still influence the sale, switch your customer to another brand or lose the sale completely and let your customer walk.

Your ProActive marketing campaign needs to win the support of retailers: to stimulate their brand loyalty and to urge them on to greater sales heights. To get them to "push" your product, rather than relying on advertising to "pull" it through. A "push, pull" strategy will always prove more effective.

You need to motivate your retailers to use all of the ProActive marketing tactics and sales promotion material that you provide to help build a bigger market. To generate more store traffic. To help them close the sale. To get more of their customers, the consumer, to buy your product. And to infuse them with the same "Can do" spirit that you use to get results.

How do you motivate the retailer?

What ProActive marketing tactics can you use?

Any dealer will tell you that the answer is a five letter word: "Money!"

Bigger profit margins, advertising case allowances, co-op advertising programs, free goods, bonus-goods, dealer loaders, spiffs . . . anything and everything, except kickbacks, which can cost the buyers their jobs and get them thrown into jail.

Once an industry or company gets involved in this type of merry-go-round, it is hard to get off. Yes, it is essential to provide good profit margins to the trade. But do all of the giveaways produce greater sales volume and velocity for your brand . . . or are you trading off promotion dollars for the pseudo-security of protecting your brand's position on the shelf?

When you think ProActive, you plan a marketing program that gives the dealer an *incentive* to sell your product on both a short and long-term basis.

We have developed a composite of 14 marketing concepts that have worked effectively for many of our clients in different classes of trade.

1. *Sales training:* Seminars, video cassettes, leave-behind workbooks and training literature, including product information, features and benefits, selling tips and demonstrations, can be of great value, especially for chain store and franchise operations. The results are better trained retail sales people who now have a better understanding about how to sell and demonstrate your product; plus a grateful management who will see the payout at the cash register. Enough emphasis can't be placed on providing this type of service on a continuing basis. With more PCs and word processors being used, consider formatting your training programs onto IBM compatible disks for distribution and reference.

2. *Caravan Promotions:* Visiting celebrities, who are skilled demonstrators, fashion stylists, sports figures, home

economists or experts in their respective fields, can draw
sizable audiences, build store traffic and increase sales.
This can include celebrity photo and autograph signing
sessions; how-to clinics, seminars and demonstrations;
fashion shows and video presentations. These promotions
should focus on an exciting theme that has broad appeal.
They should be supported by local advertising, publicity,
in-store displays announcing the coming event. Caravan
trunk promotions can be packaged to travel to different
cities simultaneously on a scheduled basis. While the "show
and tell" segment of the presentation should be structured
to tell your story effectively, there should be an informal
segment to encourage audience participation — to keep
consumers involved so they will buy now — before they
leave the store.

3. *Travel Incentive Contests:* One exciting way to get
sales personnel to "push" your brand is to promote a free
dream vacation to a romantic resort for two, based on
realistic and attainable sales goals that can be achieved.
Distributors, sales reps and dealers should be included in the
marketing program. The promotion should be based on
achieving incremental sales goals. They should be monitored
and promoted on a monthly basis. Sales interest can be
sustained over a six to nine month period. These incentive
contests can be subsidized or self-funded by building the
cost into your cost of goods. The "breakage" factor, which
includes budgeted funds that are not spent when
participants do not achieve the sales goals, will reduce some
of the cost.

When planned with an exciting theme and hosted
properly, the travel promotion will build enthusiasm,
goodwill and brand loyalty . . . plus the desire to win
again; to qualify for next year's dream vacation. Your
targets will be last year's peak performers who should
achieve even greater sales heights; the near-winner who can
be encouraged to make an even greater sales effort to win

this time; new dealers and even some of your marginal accounts who may now go all-out to win.

For companies with overseas manufacturing facilities, the promotion could include a VIP factory tour plus a first-class royal grand tour of the area. There is no substitute for a factory tour, where the trade can see firsthand the size, scope, substance and quality control of your resources.

The trade promotion can be extended to the consumer level, offering special discounts as a sales closing device to motivate consumers to buy now . . . to help the salesperson win a dream vacation. Corny, but it works! It all gets down to the pizzaz of the marketing promotion and how effectively you promote it. CFI has an affiliation with a company called Travel Group Concepts that specializes in this field with numerous success stories in all business categories. A glamorous *turnkey* promotion can be tailored to your company's objectives and budget, delivering on the other end, so everyone returns from their free vacation elated about the marvelous time they had.

4. *Merchandise Sales Contests:* A continuity marketing program can be developed over an extended period of time, awarding gift prizes of valuable merchandise based on incremental sales performance. A well planned program and selling theme should stimulate eligible participants to reach higher sales performance levels. A flexible multi-level program can be designed, providing a total package that includes the announcement theme letter, merchandise catalog, score sheet, monthly newsletter and point awards, program conditions and other graphic devices.To gain maximum value, the sales goals should be attainable, so everyone can win.

Step-ups should be planned to motivate participants to accelerate their sales efforts to reach higher levels that offer higher priced merchandise they desire. The marketing program can be tailored to your needs, creating a special catalog with selected items to avoid offering competitive products as awards; or using available catalogs. Fulfillment requirements should be analyzed, since it takes about three months to create, organize and distribute the promotion plus six to nine months for the campaign. It may be preferable to drop-ship the merchandise awards, rather than distribute them from warehouse inventory, to ensure that the winners will receive the most current merchandise, not last year's close-outs.

While not as dramatic as travel incentive programs, merchandise promotions tend to get more people involved at both the high and low levels of sales performance. They are generally less expensive to execute.

5. *National TV Advertising With Dealer Tags:* The problem with most national TV advertising is that it promotes a brand, but does not *direct* the consumer to a specific store in a local market. Some ProActive companies involve their dealers and retailers in their national advertising by creating 25-second TV commercials of network quality, allowing 5-seconds for one or more dealer tags that are integrated into the end of the commercial, listing dealer name, address and telephone number. The media programs can be funded by the manufacturer or subsidized on a participating basis, where the retailer may contribute 25 percent to 50 percent of the local media cost. The manufacturer usually picks up the cost of producing the commercial, which most dealers cannot afford.

The media schedule is purchased by the manufacturer for each market on a volume basis, buying a package of many quality spots during the three to four week advertising flight. The goal is to get as many of your dealers in a market to participate, scheduling them for different flights. For radio, dealer tags are usually allotted 15-seconds on a 60-second commercial.

The results: increased store traffic and sales; plus a participating dealer who "pushes" your product. While logistical requirements are significant, this type of promotion is superior to using a national toll-free 800 telephone number. Dealers usually think of dealer-tagged commercials as *their* commercial. They will always be skeptical about an 800 number, wondering whether they are getting all of their inquiries or if they are being directed to another dealer.

6. *Regional & Market-By-Market Dealer Listings:* One established technique that still works is to sell a marketing program with a strong selling theme, where participating dealers get listed in your ads in regional and local editions of national magazines. These promotions are based upon minimum inventory purchases. Counter-card and "take-one" displays for the consumer should be included in the promotion package. If your selling theme is provocative, the directional thrust of the dealer listings will increase brand sales. There are new media opportunities to consider, targeting your consumer in some of the new service, life-style, city and suburban magazines.

7. *Product Sampling:* If you plan to launch a new product or boost market share for a food, confection or beverage product, in-store taste testing can achieve excellent results. If your product has strong appetite appeal, you should plan a special themed merchandising event, combining in-store sampling with an introductory price-off coupon to generate immediate trial and purchase. A bounceback, price-off coupon should be integrated into your product's label or package to stimulate repurchase, or to cross-sell another product.

In-store sampling is a highly specialized technique. Remember: Murphy's Law will prevail. "If something can go wrong, it will." A professional company should be retained to plan and coordinate your program with the supermarket chain headquarters and the individual stores, assuring that adequate retail stock and samples are on-hand at each participating store; and setting-up and supervising the cooking demonstrations or food servings on the store premises. Your objective should be to get your brand on the shelf with multiple facings and to generate a high rate of turnover. A fail-safe sampling promotion can be the best insurance to maintain good trade relations.

8. *Dating Goods:* While you may not want to be the retailer's banker, another effective tactic to expand distribution is to offer six months "dating" on merchandise at a trade show. For example, a manufacturer can sell a dealer merchandise at a June trade show, offering to ship the goods immediately; up to their credit line. The dealer would not be required to pay for those goods until January 15th. This sounds like an offer the dealer can't refuse.

When the dealer sells-out all of the merchandise and wants to reorder, which usually happens well before the Christmas season, he will have to pay the manufacturer for the sold merchandise, since his credit line is used up. At that point, the new orders are purchased on normal credit terms, net 30 days.

Another incentive is to offer "anticipation" to dealers, where they get a two percent cash discount if they pay their bills within ten days of invoice.

9. *Balanced Merchandise Exchange:* Another way to expand distribution for new dealers is to offer a "guaranteed sale," and to sell the merchandise initially on consignment. The dealer pays for the goods sold in accordance with your credit terms and can return the unsold merchandise for credit. This can be a risky policy, since you may see a lot of merchandise coming back. However, if this is what it takes to "force" distribution with a key account, then it should be worth the gamble . . . just as long as there is an understanding that future purchases will be made according to standard credit policies.

Another tactic is to offer a balanced exchange of merchandise, where the dealer can exhange slow moving goods for faster moving goods or new merchandise on a dollar for dollar basis. Some companies that offer exclusive products with strong consumer demand require a two for one dollar ratio of new orders in exchange for returned goods. Whatever the ratio, it behooves the manufacturer to distribute goods that "sell-through"; and to make some accommodation to get the dusty, slow moving goods off of the shelf. This policy can pre-empt dealer complaints and maintain a healthy trade relationship, where the dealer will "push" your brand.

10. *Promotional Goods:* Every dealer needs to buy products at special promotional prices, which can be put on sale at a full mark-up. Manufacturers should design products that can be merchandised to the trade at higher mark-ups, so retailers can sell them at regular prices, before marking them down for a seasonal sale, retaining their normal profits.

Unfortunately, dealers are only offered slow sellers and close-out models at reduced costs for promotional sales. What they need and don't get are special promotion models with basic features that can be sold profitably in limited quantities to draw new customers to their stores. These promotional goods can be used as a step-up to sell the higher priced, full-featured regular merchandise. The buyers at Sears are masters of this merchandising policy, attesting to the company's long term retailing success.

While this may not be considered a dealer incentive program, it is smart merchandising and will help the dealer increase his storewide sales. It will also reinforce your company's position as an integral part of the dealer's team; and vice versa.

11. *Key Market Accounts:* Some companies allocate sums of money to expand distribution in major markets that are selected on the basis of sales potential. Advertising funds can be offered to dealers for their use in newspapers, store flyers, TV and radio, based upon their volume of dollar purchases and the market's index of sales potential. One FTC precaution: any deal you offer to one retailer must be

offered to all retailers in the same fair manner. While it is important to develop new markets, a manufacturer can lose control of his advertising. When you give carte blanche to chains and dealers, you may be buying new distribution, but your advertising dollars may not be building consumer awareness and preference for your brand. If you get into an arm-twisting situation where you must give in, try to build the extra cost of the advertising into the cost of goods that you sell to the retailer. That way he gets his advertising, and you don't dilute the effectiveness of your national advertising budget.

12. *Couponing and Rebates:* Coupon promotions are one of the most effective marketing tactics to build store traffic, increase sales and build strong trade relations. Research surveys indicate that four out of every five families in the US. save and redeem coupons. A new five-year growth record was set in 1985 with a total of 6.49 billion coupons redeemed. While 1986 data has not been reported yet, the growth trend is expected to continue.

Coupon price-off promotions can achieve many objectives. Primarily, they are used to stimulate trial and convert new triers into repeat purchasers; and to increase sales to consumers and the trade by sustaining sales with present users, winning back former users, encouraging larger quantity, repeat purchases; and to counter competition and gain a competitive edge. Couponing provides an effective sales tool to stimulate greater retail trade support, to build or reduce inventories, and to get better shelf position and store displays.

Distribution can be targeted to specific audience profiles on a geographic basis through direct mail, group mailings, newspapers, magazines, Sunday supplements; or combined with sampling and demonstrator programs — in-store, near-store, in high traffic locations and shopping malls, and at special events. The A.C. Nielsen Company, an expert in the field, can provide guidelines and check lists on how to conduct a successful promotion and fulfillment and how to merchandise it effectively to the trade.

Rebate promotions have grown in popularity in recent years, especially in the marketing of housewares, small and major appliances, home entertainment products and automobiles. Rebates have become an integral part of the consumer promotion mix. When some companies have tried to drop their rebate programs, they found themselves quickly reinstating them, because of competitive pressures, declining shelf space and decreasing market share. Smartly honed rebate programs, supported by advertising and publicity, will continue to generate sales in large volume, especially during slow selling seasons.

Some manufacturers try to rebuild brand loyalty through *added-value* promotions in order to reduce their dependency on price sensitive rebates. Most retailers predict that rebates will be here for a long time. It gives the consumer a reason to *buy now*.

Everyone seems to benefit from couponing and rebates. Consumers can purchase items at reduced prices and stretch their budget further. The dealer can turnover his inventory much quicker, increasing store sales and profits. The manufacturer can open new markets, introduce new products, expand distribution . . . and keep his dealers happy, giving them what they want.

13. *Sweepstakes & Contests:* A successful sweepstakes promotion can stimulate impulse sales among new users and present users for most product categories, providing a sense of immediacy to get consumers to act now before the offer expires. If your promotion theme is exciting, the dealer will get behind your promotion and support it. One of your primary goals is to dominate the participating stores during your promotion, using window banners, streamers and in-store signs; coupled to stand-alone island displays for your merchandise. The concept should be simple in design and execution. The promotion should be supported by high

visibility advertising and publicity, consumer and trade.

The contest awards can range from a large cash prize to a fabulous trip around the world to a guaranteed lifetime income, backed-up by a broad variety of smaller cash and merchandise prizes. The larger and more valuable the prizes and the more winners available, the greater the response rate.

Keep in mind that you can also have a trade promotion, offering prizes to the salesperson or dealer who distributes the application to a winning consumer. A double hit can generate good trade relations.

Federal, state and local lottery laws can affect your sweepstakes and vary from state to state. Hire a sweepstakes specialist, who can guide you through the maze of details to produce the desired results.

14. *Big Brother Programs:* The more you can do to assist the dealer, the greater the rewards. While we have touched on it piecemeal throughout the book, there is no franchise on a good idea. Dealers are very aware of this fact. A good promotion can provide *added-value* to your products. They are welcomed by the dealer if they satisfy specific needs. Their needs, not yours.

When you think ProActive, you should plan a comprehensive dealer marketing communications kit, tailored to the dealer's local marketing needs. This kit should include an overview of your company's brand strategy, your promotion calendar and dealer support you plan to provide. Samples of national print ads and TV storyboards or photoscripts, along with the local media schedule, should be included. If you alert your dealers well in advance about your national advertising plans, they can tie-in at the local level.

Your broadcast program should offer dealers the option to tie-in with dealer-tags for TV and radio, sending sample cassettes to them.

Newspaper mat sheets for local advertising should be

provided in different sizes, providing the graphic elements in the event the dealer wants to create his own ads.

Your display program should include samples of themed displays for store windows, counter cards, shelf talkers, streamers and freestanding merchandise displays with header cards. When sales literature is available, "take-one" counter displays can prove their worth. There is a mixed belief in our industry that a great amount of display material never gets taken out of the box and is thrown away, so why bother with this expense. This situation does occur at major chains and specialty stores, even when quality display material is provided. However, it is not smart to generalize. There are some chains, franchises and dealers who will use your displays if you make them available. Thus, the need to talk, listen and understand their individual merchandising policies.

If your dealers need promotional support, try to provide it. If they don't want a specific program, find out what they need. If they don't know what they need, then keep trying until you hit the right magic button.

Keep the dialogue flowing. Try your very best to get onto their wave length and communicate. Show them that you care. Give them something extra to talk about, something that will help them "push" your product and close the sale, so they will never let *your* customer walk.

THIRTEEN

The ProActive Crystal Ball

If we really had a ProActive crystal ball, we would become instant billionaires and retire to a life of leisure. However, since this is not the case, let's look at research and see how it can be used to help your company predict and influence the future.

Research for the sake of research can be a costly and unnecessary expense. For research to have a payout, it must be *actionable*. To be actionable, it must be brought into the planning process at an early stage. It can help test and validate different concepts and executions. It can reduce risk and help avoid failure. It can also get in the way, if not used correctly, and keep you from making a big score.

When research is actionable, it is an investment. When it is "nice to know, but what do I do with it?" it quickly becomes an expense. When it is conducted at cut-rate costs on a "crash" time schedule, it has limited value and should be avoided. Poor research is worse than no research. If the budget is not available to conduct research properly, it is better to skip it altogether and rely on good creative and marketing judgment.

As creative marketing people, we have learned to live

with researchers and their evaluations. We trust the good ones and rely on their analytical judgment. Their interpretative skills are often interlaced with intuitive judgment, based on years of related research and product experience. The difficulty is being able to see through the numbers. To look at research findings as indicative, not absolute. ProActive research can spot new trends and innovations, shifting social behavior and values, changing demographics and life-styles. The trick is to make it work for you. To forecast. To predict.

But don't let the "tail wag the dog."

I have seen good strategic campaigns killed before they saw the light of day, because of flawed research procedures and sampling techniques. Once a company buys into a research resource and methodology, it becomes the gospel. It takes on a life of its own, frequently leading you in the wrong direction. Yet, you must play the game and accept the results, bad consequences and all, never questioning the procedures. It takes months to overcome and dislodge a flawed study or technique. ProActive timing and advantage may be lost.

ProActive research, if introduced early enough, can be an adjunct to the creative process. However, when research is brought in too late, it becomes a critic and a "finger pointer," a Cassandra that comes in at the eleventh hour and forecasts doom. In many cases, marketing managers look at research in an adversary role. Market research was conducted as an afterthought, because no one thought about it in time or someone wanted to prove a point or someone wanted an escape hatch or disaster check. What they are doing is using research as a security blanket to fall back on if something goes wrong.

Whatever the reason for conducting it, the research now presents a challenge to somebody's decision. Someone has given his stamp of approval to the product concept and to the advertising campaign. If time constraints were not a problem, the research findings, suggesting product modifications, might have been welcome. However, since they now threaten somebody's position and stature within the company and could cause an embarrassing and costly delay to the start of a new marketing program, the research findings and future use of research will be questioned and probably resisted.

There is a simple solution to this perplexing problem. A ProActive research procedure needs to be formalized so that it becomes a mandated, integral part of the strategic planning process. If research is designed into the planning flow at specific stages, early enough to be used and accepted, the people and ego problems will disappear. This does not suggest that you issue a mandate to conduct unnecessary research. Stages can be eliminated if they are not considered essential after "due consideration." What is important, however, is that you mandate "consideration." Now, your research, marketing and public relations staffs become allies and plan the research requirement as partners in the ProActive communications process. Your planning schedule for product development and test marketing should allow sufficient time to conduct the research, so satisfactory time will still be available to adjust, improve and fine-tune the product before national expansion and distribution.

The starting point is to look at your strategic objectives and to design the research program to fulfill the needs unique to your company. This encompasses public opinion polls, market segmentation studies, perceptual mapping, motivation studies, concept testing, product testing, package testing, advertising pre-testing, tracking studies for awareness and persuasion, qualitative and quantifiable attitudinal studies, retail audits and more. Or, you can do less, tailoring your research program to fit specific marketing needs and budget constraints.

In developing the product concept and unique positioning for your product, we have found focus group interviews to be helpful and economical when used properly. You can obtain in-depth consumer attitudes, which result from group interaction, where one respondent reacts to stimuli introduced by the group moderator and to the comments generated by other group members. A chain reaction occurs as different members react to statements from different members, uncovering hidden motivations and anxieties. The total group output is greater than that of any one person. Since the individual member can be influenced by other group members as they reach a consensus, the technique should be kept within its perspective as an indicator that needs to be validated in a quantified full-scale study.

The primary use for focus groups is to generate or validate pre-developed hypotheses after screening the new product concepts, package designs and prototypes of advertising concepts. In many instances, untapped product appeals, consumer benefits and consumer terminology are discovered. Consumers do not talk about a new product in the same terms that you will find in a company's brand management review. One individual comment can be worth the cost of the entire endeavor.

At the beginning of each session, the tone is set. Anything goes. There are no right and wrong responses. All participants are kept at ease. The moderator's role is to keep a natural flow of conversation going and to involve everyone in the discussion. Respondents are told that if they get into areas not relevant to the topic, the moderator will get them back on track. All areas are probed carefully, eliciting as many attitudes as possible, based upon a topic guide established beforehand by brand management and the research staff. The moderator is constantly alert to follow-up on areas raised by respondents, which appear to be important, but may not have been included in the topic guide. The moderator is trained to prevent a dominant personality in the group from assuming a leadership role, which could limit conflicting attitudes. Virtually no subject is taboo or too sensitive to discuss in group sessions . . . if handled in good taste. As long as respondents are convinced that you are not trying to peek through their private keyhole, they will talk freely. In fact, the lack of normal conversation surrounding certain topics frequently makes the discussion more stimulating.

Ideally, eight to ten respondents are needed for each group session. Participants should be selected according to defined audience criteria. As a minimum, they should not have participated in a group session during the past year — to avoid using professionals or experts.

The rule of thumb is to use three different groups for any one variable (e.g. users of specific brands, different sexes, different socioeconomic groups, etc.) Any one group can be an oddball. Two groups may still be atypical, but which one? With three groups, you have a tie-breaker. In selecting the markets, you should achieve geographic dispersion, selecting representative markets where you plan to market your product.

The key to a good group session is the report. Any individual with a nice personality and intelligence can be trained to conduct a good group interview. But the payoff is the analysis. A report that merely restates what was said in the group's transcript leaves much to be desired. The end product should be a keen marketing interpretation of what the research told us about the consumer's perception of your product concept and what implications this has for subsequent marketing actions.

One advantage of group sessions is that it allows creative people to observe the interview from behind a hidden one-way mirror. This allows us to see people's expressions and their body language as they state an opinion or react to one. The little nuances that occur can give you a totally different impression ·than if you were just reading a transcript. Usually, the creative people who attend these sessions are copywriters, art directors, brand managers, new product managers, account executives — all of the key people responsible for developing new products and creating brand positioning and repositioning.

Melvin H. Ross, an N.Y.U. colleague and president of Ross Research Center, which is CFI's research arm, has pioneered a new methodology called *SYNO-GROUPS*. The technique combines elements from focus group sessions and synectics, involving double group sessions with the same group of respondents. The first segment runs the normal two hours, while the second segment takes three to four hours. If the group consists of housewives, the first segment is conducted in the morning, breaking for lunch and reconvening in the afternoon. If working women or men are required, the first segment is conducted in the evening during one week and followed-up with the second segment the next week. Attendance is excellent since a substantial participation fee is only paid after the second segment of the group interview.

The first segment concentrates on a specific topic — product usage, likes and dislikes, unfulfilled needs, desired features and benefits, why product usage was stopped, new applications and any gaps in the marketplace. During the time between the first and second segment, the creative people who were observing the session, put together new product concepts and alternative positionings, based on the input elicited from the group; plus any new hot ideas that may come to them.

During the second segment, the creative people join the same group as co-moderators. They present the product concepts and alternative positionings to the group.

Respondents are told to think creative and not to worry about technology, assuming that whatever great ideas they develop can actually be designed and manufactured.

The concepts are shown in one of two forms . . . a rough drawing and a headline, which are illustrated on a large layout pad; or if graphics are not appropriate, in written paragraph form. After the respondents are exposed to a new concept, everyone is encouraged to say something positive about it. Then there is a general reaction, positive and negative, with group interplay taking over. The moderator asks the group to describe what modifications are required to really fit their needs.

The art director than makes changes to the illustration or draws the changes on a clean layout sheet. The copywriter may ask for changes in the headline. When paragraph descriptions are used, the copywriter will revise the sentences. The changes may be modified two, three or more times until a group consensus is reached. Then the creative team presents the next product concept and the same cycle occurs again.

The enthusiasm of the group is contagious. The respondents actually see their ideas come to life. The new technique has been extremely effective in developing many new products now on the market and others currently in various stages of research and development; and in repositioning established products in mature markets that needed to be revitalized.

Focus group interviews provide the input for full scale motivation studies that are statistically sound and projectable. They also provide creative people with a general direction for the next research stage to formulate a unique positioning.

There are a number of ways to create a unique positioning or repositioning for your product or brand. You can conduct a complete analysis and review of competitive advertising claims for the industry and category in which your brand is competing. The brand management staff, working in tandem with your advertising agency, or each group working separately, will write positioning statements on a judgment basis for your competitors. While you may not have the precise wording that your competitors have tucked away in their files, you can come pretty close to the basic thrust of their positioning strategy. You may also discover that some competitors do not have a distinct positioning at all and are treading on thin ice, staking their future on name and claim and pretty graphics.

To avoid the pitfall of conducting a competitive analysis on a subjective basis, you can plan a sophisticated market segmentation study, combining attitudinal research with perceptual mapping of competition among present purchasers and prospects for your product. Although you may have a clear understanding about the nature of your business, there have been many case histories of dramatic corporate turnarounds when management learned that they were targeting their advertising to the wrong market segment, and compounding the problem by communicating the wrong message. These ProActive studies can reveal new opportunities to improve existing products and uncover new ideas for product innovation. The studies are expensive, but worthwhile.

Once you define your market segments and target audience correctly, understanding your brand's juxtaposition with competition, you are ready to design a Persuasion Test to determine how to position your product and what to say to the consumer. The findings of your focus group interviews and other qualitative research should be reviewed for input. The features and benefits of your new product should be identified. Then, a list of your product's primary features and attributes are written, combining them with a series of individual consumer benefits. These statements are written in simple prose, listing a benefit for each product attribute. You want to explore as many directions as possible. The end result could be as many as 50 different claims, straddling the entire spectrum of possibilities. Each product claim is written in consumer language. It is a simple declarative sentence and is not to be confused with the writing of headlines, which comes later. A great amount of coordination and review will occur between the client and agency to assure that the list is complete, since it will become an integral part of the Persuasion Test.

Criteria should be clearly established for the selection and screening of your sample, which must be statistically valid and projectable. Your target audience must be defined in precise terms. Their attitudes toward your product claims can be totally different when they are in the market to buy, as compared to when they are just looking or not interested at all. This is especially true for high priced, considered purchases like refrigerators, ranges and air conditioners, which differ significantly from high turnover impulse products. Your criteria can discriminate by age, sex, income, education, home ownership, geographic considerations, light and heavy users, product purchased within the last six months, intent to buy within the next three months, who makes the buying decision, who is the influencer and other specifics that apply to your product.

The cost of screening will increase in direct proportion to the criteria you establish and the difficulty encountered in finding qualified respondents on a random basis. However, you should place sufficient emphasis on screening for the right prospects, since the results of your study will rise and fall on their response.

The Persuasion Test is conducted among the screened sample by trained interviewers, who will conduct personal interviews in high traffic central locations. The survey is structured to determine a preference ranking of product claims, attributes and consumer benefits. A research technique called a factor analysis is used, compiling the data statistically by cluster and individual rankings for importance and uniqueness; and finally for persuasion. The results are like a road map, revealing the direction and routes that you should follow. On the basis of this study, a good creative team can develop a sharp positioning for your product and create an advertising campaign that can pinpoint the consumer's needs. We have used this ProActive research technique for many clients, and it has not let us down.

I should also add that we have worked for clients who could not afford to conduct the research to develop a unique positioning. When this happens, we do a competitive analysis and create the positioning the old-fashioned way. We think. We start writing. We poke at it until we hit paydirt. There are times we skip ahead. We use intuition and go straight for the jugular. We write the headline and it is right on-target. Smack in the middle of the bull's-eye! Then we go back and write the positioning statement.

This fast-forward, switch-to-reverse thinking is something most copywriters don't talk about. It is not supposed to happen this way. We are supposed to create by the numbers, sequentially. If I could get a dollar for every time a positioning statement was written this way, I'd be a rich man.

There is another ProActive research technique in the conceptual stage to consider that is still a closely guarded secret. It is a proprietary computer model that Ross Research uses to predict the "rate of trial" for new product introductions. It is called the Ross "Trial Rate Predictor Model" and it has been validated at high levels of accuracy for many packaged goods, products and services. Recognizing that the correlation between a consumer's "intent to buy" and actual purchase can vary significantly, Ross achieved a major breakthrough.

The computer model can predict what actual consumer "trial" will be within 1.8 to 2.4 percentage points of the actual sales data. Consumers are presented with a concept statement or a prototype ad and asked for their reactions, including their buying inclinations, which are recorded on a purchase intent scale. A prototype of the product and package are then offered to the consumer in a product test. In the call-back, consumers are asked for their final reactions to determine if the product held up to its promise. This information is then input into the computer model for a final score, which will predict a "trial rate" that may or may not correlate with your marketing goals. Thus, predicting success or failure.

The sample consists of a minimum of 400 targeted respondents, who are selected at random according to pre-planned marketing criteria. The final data is quantifiable and projectable.

With your positioning and creative concepts completed, what ProActive research techniques are there to assure that your advertising executions are effective?

I prefer not to engage in the debate regarding the effectiveness of copy testing under simulated conditions . . . other than to say we do not believe in it. People do not watch television in shopping malls or in theaters. They do not read magazines when someone is waltzing them through its contents. Research respondents are not advertising experts, and we shouldn't ask them to fulfill that role. We know repetition of advertising is what sells products. While it is great to have "norms" or an average ranking to compete against in your product category, what does the "norm" really say? It tells what other ads and commercials achieved statistically in relation to each other, using samples which may not relate to your prospects.

Many companies try to save money by testing TV commercials in a preliminary storyboard form called animatics, rather than testing in final executed form. Animatics are videotaped illustrations and a rough sound track of the key frames in the 30-second commercial, which look more like a kid's Saturday morning TV cartoon than a quality commercial. The animatic technique is not appropriate for all types of commercials;. If the commercial uses a stand-up announcer or there is a simple product statement or demonstration, the commercial may score relatively well. However, if the commercial uses a celebrity or tries to establish a mood or involves the viewer with quick cuts and dissolves to create excitement and desire, the animatic format gets in the way and the commercial does not score well. Second, the animatics are usually shown under forced simulated conditions in shopping malls or theaters with only one exposure, which is not the way TV viewing occurs in real life.

TV is an intrusive medium. With all the TV commercials screaming for attention and the TV clutter getting worse, new commercials should be pre-tested on-system at home under actual conditions, using finished commercials and repetition within actual programs. Cable TV now presents a low cost target approach.

Major marketers like Procter and Gamble, Phillip Morris, Anheuser-Busch, General Mills, Campbell Soup, IBM and others are using cable TV to test variables such as copy content, commercial effectiveness, media mix, seasonality and frequency against different target audiences in different geographic regions of the U.S.

The ASI Research Company in New York runs two services on cable TV to measure TV effectiveness: Recall Plus, which is day-after recall of the TV commercial, providing in-depth evaluation of the commercial's performance; and Apex, measuring motivation and persuasion. The TV commercials are inserted into prime time family oriented programs. Random samples of 100 each are used in two different geographic areas.

The A.C. Nielsen Company is experimenting with their new ERIM Testsight Service, which combines cable and over-the-air testing in selected markets, measuring consumer response and household purchases with scanners at participating supermarkets. The ERIM program can test several marketing plans . . . heavy TV frequency with couponing versus a regular TV schedule and heavy newspaper advertising and couponing.

Cost efficiencies are attractive on cable TV and can reduce an advertiser's budget 20 percent to 50 percent, compared to other over-the-air testing methods. In addition, some cable operators have established low cost production capabilities and can produce quality commercials at a fraction of the going rate. If special effects and high paid talent are required, the cost goes up. It pays to seek out these cost saving opportunities.

Let's look at your advertising and public relations program from a campaign point of view, where frequency and continuity have been employed. If sales and market share goals are your criteria, then shipment data and retail store audits by companies like A.C. Nielsen, Audits & Surveys and others are probably your best barometer. However, how does the sales data correlate with your communications? What trend information is available to evaluate the effectiveness of the communication elements in your overall campaign?

Tracking studies can provide the diagnostic insights to evaluate your campaign over a period of time. Each tracking study should be designed to fit the needs of the company. It should be conducted on a long term basis, spanning the life cycle of your advertising program. Each study has a pre- and post-evaluation, starting prior to the commencement of advertising and ending immediately after the final advertising flight. Benchmarks should be established to evaluate changes in brand awareness, advertising awareness, attitudes toward company and product attributes, specific issues and purchase preferences. Major markets should be selected for testing and control. They should not be changed during the course of the study to avoid unnecessary distortion. A target audience is selected at random, according to pre-planned criteria for each wave of the research. Screening for respondents and personal interviews are conducted in high traffic, central locations. Trend data is evaluated at the end of the advertising year, which can be scheduled on a calendar, fiscal or seasonal basis. If the campaign is effective, it should show increases in both the rate of change and the relative levels of the various benchmarks. If the post-measurements are flat or decline, diagnostic evaluation can usually pinpoint the problem. Corrective actions can then be taken.

Some of the principles used in tracking studies are used effectively in the world of politics, where public opinion polls are used extensively. Computerized techniques have been developed to identify key market segments and sub-segments and report changing attitudes quickly. Trend reports spot the effect that specific issues have on the shifting attitudes of these targeted segments. The reports can be correlated by different demographic criteria. Telemarketing and direct response techniques can be used to pinpoint the target segment, using zip code directories. This provides an excellent opportunity to create narrow focus campaigns that talk to the specific interests of the people you most want to influence.

Is there a message here for product marketers?

Yes, if you believe in ProActive planning, you can design your own crystal ball. If you design your research to be *actionable*, the results should be crystal clear.

FOURTEEN

On the Side of the Angels

The consumer is everything.

Setting your ProActive crystal ball aside for a moment, there is no substitute for being on the firing line with day to day contact with the consumer. It is almost like being an infantry commander. You need to have live combat experience before you can be truly effective. Until you get this experience or hire someone who has, you will always be one step behind.

How do you train advertising and public relations practitioners to function as skilled ProActive marketing professionals?

The first step is to cross-train them in each other's craft, so they can have a full appreciation and understanding of each other's disciplines.

The second step is to send them into the trenches, where they can experience the sights and sounds and smells; and develop a sixth sense about what actually happens and what is needed on the firing line. They need to overcome their ivory tower mentality and get hands-on marketing experience.

Select your rising stars and send them into the field,

assigning them to work as sales people for your most aggressive customers. Not just for a one or two day visit, but for a two-week tour . . . twice a year. Make them understand that they are being sent into the field as players, not observers; they should roll up their sleeves and learn-by-doing; and upon their return, they should be able to say: "I've been there. I know what is needed."

Put them on the selling floor during the slow winter season, when no amount of advertising and pump priming will get consumers to leave the comfort of their homes to start shopping. Encourage them to talk to the consumers who do venture out and learn firsthand how difficult it is to overcome consumer apathy, especially when consumers are not in a buying mood. Let them watch the pros in action and see how they overcome consumer resistance and close the sale. Let them learn what sales support is needed, what works, what doesn't work, why it doesn't work and what support can be used by other retailers across the country.

Send them back into the field for a second two-week tour during your customer's busy season, when consumers are out in strength on a buying spree . . . not necessarily looking for your brand or product, but shopping and buying; turning loose of their hard earned dollars that can buy your product or someone else's. Let your people learn the retailer's axiom: "The consumer is always right" . . . even when they are wrong. Let your people experience some of the pressures of retail selling — the consumer questions, complaints and haggling; even share the frustration that comes when defective goods or unwanted purchases are returned for credit. Let them suffer the fatigue of standing long hours on their feet without a break, while maintaining a friendly, courteous composure. Let them see how easy it is to lose one's concentration when faced with numerous interruptions and menial tasks of packing and unpacking, pricing and marking of goods and all the chores that never seem to be accomplished.

Let them learn the art of selling . . . not just how to build interest and demonstrate your product, but the art of closing a sale. If they can learn from the masters . . . and they can only learn-by-doing . . . they will develop ProActive selling skills that will be a windfall for the balance of their business careers.

There are many sales people in the business world who have been selling for years and think they are experts at it. Unfortunately, they can be found guilty of committing two sins. Both relate to skills and experience.

In the first sin, they may have learned everything during their first year on the job and never learned another thing after that. When they say they have 10 or 15 years experience, what they should say is that they only have one year's experience and never progressed any further.

Selling is one of the most competitive professions. The good sales people never stop learning. They are always on the lookout for new sales techniques to overcome difficult selling situations. They are hungry for new information about your company and products, and why your products are superior to the competition. The more they know, the more they sell. And the more they sell, the bigger their pay checks. These are the people whom your rising stars should seek out; the pros, not the amateurs.

The second sin is unpardonable, but relatively common. How many times have you seen sales people talk themselves into and out of a sale? It is a vexing problem that can be overcome by a better understanding of the psychology of selling. Once a sale is made, sales people should stop talking, write up the order and ring it up. Or, they should thank the buyer for the order, pack-up their satchel and get going . . . before they unsell what they have just sold. Too many sales are lost this way!

These are some of the lessons your people can learn by being on the firing line. Let them share the anxieties and fears retailers live with from day to day. Encourage them to mingle with both high and average sales performers, and discover how some of these people can let small personal problems inhibit their sales performance, which may have a negative impact on the sale of your products. Your people need to learn what makes these people tick; how to motivate them . . . to find out what promotion support material they need and what incentives will turn them on to sell your product more effectively.

Your people should also tour your factory to see how your products are actually made, the research and development and quality control that goes on behind the scenes. The more knowledge and information your people have, the greater their contributions to the growth of your company. Let them talk with the engineers and foremen and assembly line personnel. Let them visit your warehouse and loading dock facilities and look at all of the goods moving out. Once there, if they could just imagine, for a moment, what would happen if sales suddenly stopped and shipments came to an abrupt halt. Goods would back-up on the loading dock, forcing a shut-down on the assembly line. Workers would be laid-off and a tremendous backlash could occur, depressing the economy of the entire community . . . and your company's bottom line.

A factory tour can have a lasting impression, especially if one shares this fantasy; a fantasy that underscores the responsibility and importance of marketing. ProActive marketing can keep your factories open and your goods flowing. Factory tours should be scheduled on an annual basis to sharpen the marketing skills of your people. The more they talk and listen, the more they learn. The more they learn, the better they communicate.

While I have focused on products sold in retail outlets, the same principles apply in business-to-business, high tech industrial, travel, insurance, investment and service industries. Your people need to learn as much as they can about your customer and your customer's customer. This can be accomplished by formalized training programs, assigning your rising stars to the most appropriate real world environments, where they learn-by-doing.

The third step in ProActive training is attitudinal. When you think ProActive, you go for the jugular. You need to zero-in on the bull's-eye and hit it repeatedly. The implementation plan is just as critical to success as your strategic and tactical plans. They should be detailed to the nth degree so they are *actionable*, including milestones and accountability to monitor progress.

When you think ProActive, you must be able to deliver as promised. No excuses. No alibis. No rationalizations. No walking away.

In ProActive marketing, the only thing constant is change itself. Hopefully, some of the new ProActive tactics and marketing principles discussed in this book will stimulate you and start you thinking in new directions.

If you accept the ProActive challenge, you need to plan ahead. To *act decisively*, instead of reacting. To forge a new *pre-emptive*, leadership position for your company. To innovate and control your marketing communications . . . and your company's destiny. To build new and bigger markets. To leapfrog ahead of competition . . . and stay ahead! To make your company grow faster.

In the final analysis, people and attitude will make the difference. If you want to be on the side of the angels and enjoy good fortune, fire-up your people with our brand of ProActive creative firepower. Success should be within easy reach.

RUBEN DARIO CENTENNIAL STUDIES

RUBEN DARIO

CENTENNIAL STUDIES

Edited by MIGUEL GONZALEZ-GERTH *and* GEORGE D. SCHADE

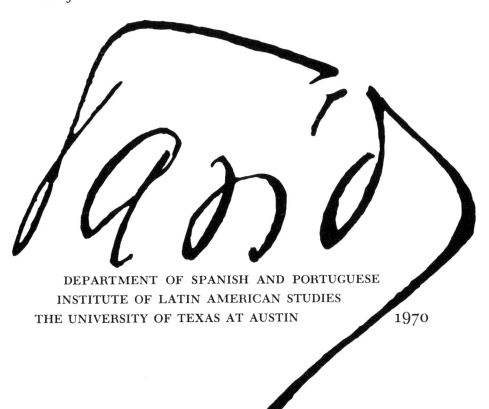

DEPARTMENT OF SPANISH AND PORTUGUESE
INSTITUTE OF LATIN AMERICAN STUDIES
THE UNIVERSITY OF TEXAS AT AUSTIN   1970

FOREWORD

IN FEBRUARY OF 1967 the University of Texas at Austin celebrated the Rubén Darío Centennial by presenting a series of lectures and other cultural events organized by the Department of Romance Languages. The present volume contains the five lectures given on five consecutive afternoons.

The scholars who took part in the symposium represent countries that played a geographical, intellectual, and sentimental part in the life of Rubén Darío: Argentina (Anderson-Imbert), Chile (Torres-Rioseco), Cuba (Florit), Spain (Enguídanos), and the United States (Phillips). One might say that only France and his native Nicaragua are missing, unfortunately. Professor Miguel Enguídanos examines the inner tensions which made Rubén Darío aware of his being one with the world and comes to the conclusion that, contrary to the postulates of recent times, a lush poem like "Era un aire suave" is not only characteristic of Darío's sensibility but also as much a work of art as the broody "Lo fatal"; while at the same time the poet somehow foresaw the wave of dehumanization which now threatens us. Professor Eugenio Florit points out a number of details in Darío's coming to grips with the problem of form and shows how the young man who was to become a lyric star of the first magnitude occasionally foreshadowed himself in unsure yet interesting compositions. Professor Allen W. Phillips presents a thoughtful and well-documented study of the friendly relations and mutual regard that existed between Darío and Ramón del Valle-Inclán, the great Spanish modernist and expressionist who cultivated the peculiar kind of literary satire called *esperpento*. Professor Arturo Torres-Rioseco comments on Darío as a "classic poet" and contends that what was once regarded as obscurity in his work actually stemmed from a general lack of culture among many of his readers, especially since after 1888 (when he published *Azul*) Darío moved confidently toward an integration of language and emotion which responded to his preference for classical forms. Lastly, Professor Enrique Anderson-Imbert analyzes what is perhaps the Nicaraguan's most significant literary production next to his poetry, namely, his short stories, among which are many that develop on the plane of the fantastic. Anderson-Imbert concludes that, although frequently Darío marred his fiction by relating it to his occultist obsessions, he sometimes shows himself to have been a master of the prose narrative as well as of the poet's instrument.

It is important to note that the symposium was planned in such a way that the lecturers had complete freedom to choose their own topics and did so independently. Yet the reader will discover, as did we who were there at the time of oral presentation, a surprising unity among the essays. There is a line of vision and feeling that runs from the first to the last, highlighting recurrent themes of great significance, such as the permanent value of poetic art, the relations between the works of a given writer (in this case Darío) and those of his contemporaries, as well as the inner relations among his own works, and the element of foresight in literature or the ancient identification of the poet and the prophet (*vates*).

We wish to thank Professor Ricardo Gullón, who first conceived this centennial celebration and did much to get it under way. For their assistance we should like to express our gratitude to Professor Theodore Andersson, former Chairman of the Department of Romance Languages, to Professor Ramón Martínez-López, Vice-Chairman of the Department of Spanish and Portuguese, and to the members of the organization committee for the celebration: Professors Luis A. Arocena, Michel Dassonville, Beverly J. Gibbs, K. Carter Wheelock, George G. Wing, and particularly to Dr. Nettie Lee Benson, Latin American Collections Librarian, for making accessible many key items from those collections, and Professor Pablo Beltrán de Heredia for planning and executing a splendid book exhibit in the lobby of the Academic Center as well as a very handsome program-brochure. We also wish to convey our special thanks to Mrs. Esther W. Phillips and to four young scholars here at the University, Miss Anne Bonner, Mr. David Flory, Mr. John Wilcox, and Mrs. Cecile Wiseman, for giving so generously of their time to translate the essays included here, and to Dr. Stanley R. Ross, Director of the Institute of Latin American Studies, and his Publications Committee for their assistance in financing the printing of this book. Finally, with the name of Mrs. Julia Reeves, who typed the manuscript, we wish to close these lines of appreciation.

MIGUEL GONZÁLEZ-GERTH

Table of Contents

INTRODUCTION
by George D. Schade

STRADDLING THE NINETEENTH AND
twentieth centuries, Rubén Darío (1867–1916) triumphantly ushers
in the literary movement known in Spanish America and Spain as
Modernism with *Azul* (1888) ('Azure'), a collection of poems and
stories, and *Prosas profanas* (1896) ('Worldly Songs'), a volume of
verse. His pivotal work, however, and the masterpiece of Modernism,
which had such a tremendous impact on Hispanic literature, was
published in 1905, *Cantos de vida y esperanza* ('Songs of Life and
Hope'), a book of poems of such vitality that one feels one has lived
there and shared in its experiences: its gnawing doubts, deep anguish,
and at the same time, quenchless appetite for life. Several other outstanding collections of verse followed: *El canto errante* (1907) ('The
Errant Song'), and *Poema del Otoño* (1910) ('Autumn Poem'), which
contain individual pieces that haunt the memory and fire the imagination. In addition to his poetry, Darío produced a large corpus of prose
work: some fine short stories ranging from the jeweled anecdotes of
Azul to splendid Gothic tales of suspense and horror; critical notes on
and often flamboyant appreciations of contemporary writers, *Los raros*
(1893) ('The Odd Ones'); a rather slap-dash but charming autobiography; travel impressions, *España contemporánea* (1901), etc.

Confronted by his work on this centennial anniversary of Darío's
birth, the critics have been busy trying to assess once again his place in
Hispanic letters. During his lifetime Darío enjoyed enormous re-
nown, but in the half-century since his death, the poet's star has
plummeted in the minds of some: a writer garlanded and anointed
during his brief years on earth, then duly interred in the Histories of
Literature and Anthologies of Hispanic Poetry, jettisoned in favor of
more modern voices often of harsher, bleaker tones. Undeniably, some
of these poets, like Pablo Neruda and Octavio Paz, who follow Darío
in Spanish America, are towering geniuses, but to prefer their poetry
should not automatically make one scorn Darío's.

Rubén Darío was born in a humble hamlet in Nicaragua. At the
age of fifteen he began his nomadic wanderings, visiting neighboring
El Salvador; at nineteen he embarked for Chile where he spent several
crucial years in his literary development and published his first sig-

nificant book of poetry. Later he lived for fairly extended periods in
Argentina, Spain and France, and in these three countries produced
the bulk of his best creative work: compelling poems of enduring
beauty, style and dignity. During his short and active life Darío undoubtedly suffered a great deal, but he also drew in deep, hearty
breaths of life. At times he plumbed abysses of alcoholic dissipation,
but his poetry soared heaven-ward in a constant endeavor to attain
spiritual beauty. Now his home and haunts (in Nicaragua, in Spain,
etc.) have become places of pilgrimages, and his lasting fame seems
assured.

All attempts to gloss over Darío's genius by churlish critics are
doomed to failure. If we select from the best of his work, not only
Cantos de vida y esperanza, but also *Prosas profanas, El canto errante*
and *Poema del otoño,* the truth of this genius emerges clearly. His
poetry has substance and surface, a supporting wall as well as the
brilliant stucco façade. *Prosas profanas* delight our senses with their
rich tapestry of recurring exotic and mythological patterns. They are
like pictures with finish and glaze. This richness and refinement of
phrase is combined seductively with an unerring sense of rhythm and
music to enchant our ears as well as feast our eyes.

The perfection of form continues in *Cantos de vida y esperanza.*
Darío, the master craftsman, the distiller of exotic essences and per-
fumes extracted from many lands and arts, does not falter. But his
earlier tendency toward rhetoric and ornamentation often gives way
here to melancholy poems full of shadows and blendings, self-probings
and doubts, the hermetic seclusion of the inner world, the anguish
which characterizes so much of twentieth century literature. Death
becomes more apparent thematically; it is a part of life and until it is
accepted, life is perhaps but a subterfuge.

In several poems of *El canto errante* a very modern note is struck
where Darío startles us by employing deliberately common, conversational phrases, which are so conventional in present-day poetry, but
atypical of Darío. His hedonistic "Autumn Poem" again represents
Darío at his best—magnificent verses pulsing with the heartbeat of
life.

Unprecedented and unmatched in the annals of Spanish American
literature, Darío's poetry fertilized a whole generation, and his influence continues to be felt. On re-reading his poems, we find that they
give pleasure and stimulate reflection; we discover more beauty, more
meaning in them.

The Department of Romance Languages of the University of Texas celebrated his centenary in February, 1967, with a week of symposia, exhibitions of his books, and lectures by distinguished scholars on various aspects of Dario's work. These lectures are published here in English translation in the hopes that the English-reading public in this country and Great Britain, in recent years more aware of Hispanic letters, will find them provocative and interesting, and perhaps be stimulated to read Darío himself.

A work may be many things at the same time, but it is important to know what the essential things are in it. The quarries our authors seek in the following pages are some of these essential things in Darío's poetry and prose. We offer them as a tribute to his memory.

2

Cuando el áureo Pegaso
En la victoria matinal se lanza
Con el mágico ritmo de su paso
Hacia la vida y hacia la esperanza,
Si alza la crin y las narices hincha
Y sobre las montañas pone el casco sonoro
Y ... hacia la mar relincha,
Y el espacio se llena
De un gran temblor de oro,
Es que ha visto desnuda a Anadiomena.

Gloria, ¡oh Potente! a quien las sombras temen!
Que las más blancas tórtolas te inmolen...!
Pues por ti la floresta está en el polen
Y el pensamiento en el ... vencen!

Gloria, oh Sublime que creas la existencia,
... en quien siempre hay futuro en el útero eterno,
... tu boca sabe al fruto del árbol de la Ciencia
Y al torcer tus cabellos apagaste el infierno.

MIGUEL ENGUÍDANOS

INNER TENSIONS IN THE WORK OF RUBÉN DARÍO

translated by Cecile Wiseman

So MUCH HAS BEEN WRITTEN about the work of Rubén Darío that I have to be cautious. Anyone who wants to say something new about his work is immediately confronted by a formidable obstacle: not only is his critical bibliography already very extensive, since he is considered the Spanish-American poet par excellence, but also some of these studies are of very high quality. Pedro Salinas' book, *La poesía de Rubén Darío,* stands out among the very best. I will confess at once that for me this book has been as much guide and inspiration as obsession and nightmare. To say something more, something that will penetrate deeper into Rubén's work than what Salinas has already said, is, frankly, very difficult.

Salinas combined his great critical talent and his exceptional humanity and personality, with an even rarer gift—he was himself a true poet. Thus he could penetrate the subtleties of the poetry of Jorge Manrique and Rubén Darío from multiple personal perspectives: that of the poet, that of the critic and professor, that of the emigrated Spanish liberal—never free from his Spain, but in love too with this new world—and that of the whole man, the well-bred man of good taste.

Salinas' book about Darío is the child of an epoch. Its essential concern is with themes: to find the true themes of the poetry. It is concerned as well with style: how and why the themes are expressed as they are. But although Salinas' work is a difficult mark to surpass, and even though read with the respect that such an admirable effort deserves, it presents still only one point of view. Subtle and penetrating, but not final. No one human point of view is absolute. At the end of his book Salinas, with his usual integrity, recognizes and points out this limitation. He covered a great deal of territory, but nevertheless he himself, in his conclusion, points us toward the areas still unexplored in Darío's vast work. His methodology not only admitted other possible approximations, but also suggested the direction that other kinds of studies could follow. I could not have written these pages if

I had not read this challenging message in the last lines of Salinas' book. He says:

Thus I see the themes of Darío's poetry—the central and the minor ones— not as drawn by my judgment or prejudice, but as evident and completely objective facts in his poetic reality. Three active principles, *anguished eroticism* (the inevitable intertwining of the acts of creation and death), *social concern,* and the idea of *art and the poet,* function in his poetry, perfectly distinct, each one seemingly enclosed in its own orbit. In the realm of objective reality they are undoubtedly completely independent. But fate brought them to live together in the poetic creation of Rubén. Is it possible for these three great themes to have coincided in his spirit, merely dwelling in the same shelter, keeping themselves apart and sepa- rate without any form of fecund contact or enriching communication? It is unquestionable that the themes do not touch at any point, if they are considered one by one, *abstractly.* But they have one thing in common: independent among themselves, the three are still dependent upon the same master, the spirit of the poet. . . . The themes don't touch each other, but do all three touch the same soul?

Clearly Salinas understood that considering Darío's work as a jig- saw puzzle—and the image is his, not mine—into which all the funda- mental pieces had to be fitted before the ultimate and final image was revealed, left one task still undone. In his own words, it was still necessary "to discover the latent capacity for coherence among them," among the fundamental pieces. Salinas, then, did not over- look the need for carrying the search for understanding to what I have proposed as one of the chapters of my work: to determine how the poet lived his visions in anguished inner conflict.

Proclaiming anguished eroticism as one of Darío's themes, Salinas saw the necessity for going even further:

Anguished eroticism kept Darío in a *state of constant war with himself.* The two antagonists into which his nature was split hardly gave him an instant of rest—moments of exalted and jubilant unconsciousness, truces that divided the acts of his drawn-out tragedy. The poet felt his spirit possessed by the terrible truth that *struggle* is the inescapable fate of any erotic desire that wants to endure. This gave birth to a *growing longing for peace.* . . . This *tragedy of the poet* began, as we know, the first day of battle between the erotic and the temporal, between Eros and Chronos.

The "constant state of war," or the "tragedy," in which the poet lived, a supremely erotic-melancholic consciousness, is something that goes beyond what Salinas looked for in Darío's poetry. It is neither the root of his work, nor as abstract and basic as "theme," but it has to do with what Ortega called the true nature of man: his drama, his history; it is something still to be done in this sea of contradictory forces that is life. Salinas saw, when he finished his rare and wonderful book, that the poetry that he had just explicated as had no one until then, slipped away from him again through this aspect of its nature, the vital and existential aspect. It doesn't matter. Faithful to his methodological postulates, he had carefully avoided this problem from the beginning. The results of his effort were not empty. In its time and place Salinas' book is unique. In our time and place, it is the beginning of understanding and point of departure for new explorations. We could not have done without it.

I shall try to explore, in my own way, the path toward the "something more" in Rubén Darío's poetry that Salinas left open for us. I have a certain advantage over him—neither personal nor intellectual —in that I live in another time, one more favorable to such an exploration. Today these questions interest us more. The anxieties of the present have better prepared us to understand the vital transformation of the poet's inner tensions into the perennial formulas of a higher language, that is, into poetry. Rarely in the history of man has anyone lived—morning, noon and night—with the tense awareness that existence is a menacing and "permanent war."

To set off on this difficult path I have to establish some working hypotheses:

FIRST: Poetic creation is the most intimate, deeply-felt function of the poet's life. The acts that we call poems aren't merely accessorial; even less are they means of escape from the reality of life. Perhaps they are very unique forms of life—unique in their intensity and transcendence. They could be called "specialized" acts. It is indisputable that the poems, once they are created, are objects independent of their creator. They are living things. But, for this very reason, mightn't we think that they will keep forever alive the image and semblance of that part of their creator which was immortal?

SECOND: It is necessary to try to understand the constant labor of the poet in the flow of time. In what follows I must trace the "chain of events-poems," emphasizing among them the ones that seem most significant, but without losing sight of where they have come from and where they are going in the totality of the work. Books like that of Salinas have been, above all, magnificent photograph albums. Is it not time now to attempt a cinematic vision of all that has to do with the creation of a body of poetry?

THIRD: Neither the life nor the work of the poet must be fragmented, as they have been so often, until we come to believe that there is more than one Rubén Darío. In the unfolding of the poet's life, each season is child and consequence of the one that came before. The spring, summer, autumn, and winter of his poetry will have to be understood as the dynamic integrants of a unity existing in a spatial and temporal continuum.

FOURTH: I have eliminated, at least in this part of my work, any consideration of the influences of other writers on Darío. Not because I find this problem uninteresting or unimportant for the complete understanding of the poet's work; on the contrary, I hope to tackle it at the proper time. But here I am more concerned with showing what the poet contributed to his epoch, what he gave of himself to his contemporaries, than what he received from them. In the moment of fulfillment of the creative inner tension, external influences—personal or literary—had already been assimilated and become integrated parts of the poet. I shall leave aside, then, the problems of Modernism. I don't want to move from the level of flesh-and-blood life. I consciously and purposely will avoid abstractions that I believe to be devitalizing.

FIFTH: Every poem is charged—as if it were an electric battery or a very complicated clock—with inner tensions. Here, stating my most important hypothesis, I should explain what I mean by *tension*. It goes beyond the always inadequate dictionary definition: "The state of a body subjected to an action of forces that stretch it," since I am speaking of the consciousness of a man and his creative spirit, not of a body. Applied to the poet, then, tension will be the action of a force, or vital urge, upon his spirit. There will be more than one: the process of existence, in relation with his personality, will keep on subjecting him to "tensions." But in the poet's case, inner tensions will not only determine his conduct, but will also approach what the Stoics called "tension" (τόνος), a fundamental concept of their philosophy and attitude toward life, that could be defined as "a principle of unification of the disperse." In other words, the poet's inner tensions, the results of his way of experiencing life, will not only torment him with their pressures—as they do every man—but will also make him aware of his unity with the world. I believe that these tensions cause his constant desire to merge himself with the universe, to express it, to make it live in his words, to squeeze out its quintessence and give it to his readers. These tensions are, in short, the energy that maintains the particles of his being in cohesion. To use another technological metaphor, they are his electric charge; true poetry, then, will be charged with a kind of radioactivity. Which explains the burns it inflicts upon those of us who come genuinely close to it. What I have said about my last working hypothesis is true for all great poets, especially for the modern ones, and in especially great measure for Rubén Darío. In the fine inner tensions of his poetry lies the ultimate secret of his work.

My methodology in this task obliges me to examine the poet's work at length. (I intend to make all the necessary explorations gradually. These observations are part of a book on the work of Darío which I am currently writing. However, the working hypotheses outlined above apply to the entire book and not merely to the present chapter.) At this point it is better for me to be very selective and reserve until later my faithfulness to the order of the poet's vital experiences. I too must be careful and watch out for pitfalls, and, at best, establish some poetic-existential coordinates in Darío's work that will let me test the validity of my hypotheses.

Darío's biographers have established the important facts of his everyday life. They aren't hard to enumerate or understand; I will mention a few that are related to his precocious infancy and adolescence.

Rubén was born in a remote and insignificant corner of the Hispanic world. His town was poor, his family was poor—not only in material things but even more in spiritual means. His childhood was dominated by the stigma of abandonment, separation from his parents, sadness and insecurity. Some claim that the child Rubén found himself surrounded by gossip that cast doubt upon his paternity. He was brought up by a great-aunt and uncle, good people but eccentric. His uncle and godfather was a colonel in a small country, a fervent liberal who held degrees in law and philosophy, a disorderly reader. He treated him like a true father, but, to add misfortune to misfortune, he died when Rubén was still a child. The lack of a real home was compensated for by the boy's precocious development. Among his various precocities— political, erotic, alcoholic—his gift for verse was apparent very early. It is said that when he was eight years old he was already known as the "child-poet." Early in his adolescence he became famous as a local poet. His international consecration, we must remember, came with the publication of *Azul* . . ., when he was twenty-one. In other words, he found rapid recognition in the craft for which he seemed pre-

destined. To balance accounts in everything else his life was an un-
broken chain of failures and personal misfortunes. He was never free
from insecurity, or even from extreme hardship in facing the vicissi-
tudes of everyday life.

But all this is important only because the constants of loneliness,
bitterness, and misfortune are present in Rubén's poetry, from his
first stumbling efforts to his greatest and most enduring poems. It
can be said, obviously, that there have been other lives as unhappy as
Darío's, and unfortunately there will be many more, and that—as
Salinas said—the relation between the innumerable events that the
poet lives as a simple human being and the exceptional acts that are
his poems has still to be proven. Although I realize the difficulty of the
problem that Salinas poses, I refuse to separate those exceptional facts
of life, the poems, from the existential context in which they are produced. This affirmation, which I find myself repeating over and over,
is at the point of becoming a downright platitude; but I believe my
insistence is necessary, because what I ask of my readers is a simple
act of vital commitment to poetry. An act so simple, and so obvious,
that its necessity can be overlooked. What I ask is nothing more than
to insert the poems into the chain of insignificant events, and consider
them higher events, that is, to see them and feel them like events of
life that are culminating and revelatory of the whole chain. Neither
biography nor psychology is to be feared, if the scholar's perspective,
like that of the reader, is directed from the poem toward life, and not
from life toward the poem. In the poems, I insist once more, we find
the true life of the poet.

This poem, one of Rubén's earliest—written when he was fourteen
—and of little literary value, is worth considering:

> Lector: si oyes los rumores
> de la ignorada arpa mía,
> oirás ecos de dolores;
> mas sabe que tengo flores
> también, de dulce alegría.

> (Reader: if you hear the faint sounds
> of my unknown harp,
> you will hear echoes of pain;
> but know that I have flowers
> too, of sweet joy.)

The little poem (intended to appear on the title-page of a proposed first book) is composed mimetically of obvious resonances and literary allusions—the harp, the echoes of pains, the flowers of sweet joy. It is not at all noteworthy or exceptional. The lines would have been forgotten and never recovered if they had not been Rubén's. The poet himself dismissed them, not wanting them to be published. Alberto Ghiraldo, Darío's heirs, and the scholars have salvaged them. And they do in fact serve a purpose.

The purpose they serve for me is to point up the fact that at this early stage the boy-poet, even though derivatively, was already speaking of some "faint sounds," some songs, charged with inner tension. The conflict is very simple, but conflict nevertheless: "If you hear the faint sounds . . . you will hear echoes of pain; *but* . . . I have flowers *too*, of sweet joy." The vertices of tension are clearly established, the charge and irradiation of that anguish is not very effective, but its direction couldn't be clearer: to make us hear the faint sounds of the harp, the inner, unknown music that speaks to us of the contradiction between pain and joy. Perhaps the literary model for this early exercise was Bécquer or one of the other Romantic poets, but the intention, the desire, to tell us that life is made up of pains and joys, is it only a literary cliché, not really felt, or is it already a true intuition of what awaited the poet?

All this would be gratuitous or irrelevant if there weren't a line of continuity that could be traced from that little poem of 1881 to the great poems, like the autobiographical one that opens *Cantos de vida y esperanza*: the constant presence of that first tension. And even more: Rubén tells us in that poem, as he looks back on his first years:

> Yo supe de dolor desde mi infancia;
> mi juventud. . . ¿fue juventud la mía?
> sus rosas aún me dejan su fragancia,
> una fragancia de melancolía. . .

> (I have known pain since childhood;
> my youth . . . was it really youth?
> its roses still lend me their fragrance,
> a fragrance of melancholy. . .)

The examples are very numerous and should be studied in detail, their chronology established, and the variations and modifications, as well as the outcome, of the pain-pleasure vertices traced.

I am going to proceed selectively in order to test the viability of some of my hypotheses. I will consider two examples that not only seem to me highly significant, but are without doubt two of Darío's best poems. They are "Era un aire suave . . . ," written about 1893, the first poem of *Prosas profanas,* and "Lo fatal," the last poem of the book *Cantos de vida y esperanza,* written before 1905.

I begin with "Lo fatal" for a particular reason. Today, as yesterday, the reader makes his own anthology of Darío's works. He excludes poems and prose that he considers to be of transitory merit, fashionable in their time but no longer saying anything today. This is natural. In his recreative task the reader searches for that part of the poet's work that has not only resisted the attacks of time, but that he feels to be closest to his own sensibility. It is necessary to consider how much the fashion of the selector's era will influence his choice. It is possible that many times synchronization with the contemporary weighs more than the desire to find permanent poetic merit.

"Lo fatal," without question, is a great poem; but, at the same time, it has become the classic example of composition by Darío that we cite unblinkingly, saying that "this is the part of Rubén's work that deserves to be saved." I wonder if the fact that today many of Darío's readers would consider "Lo fatal" worth saving, but might relegate to oblivion "Era un aire suave . . . ," does not have more to do with the "fashion," or preferences of today's reader, than with the true value of the poem.

Consider "Lo fatal":

> Dichoso el árbol que es apenas sensitivo,
> y más la piedra dura, porque ésta ya no siente,
> pues no hay dolor más grande que el dolor de ser vivo,
> ni mayor pesadumbre que la vida consciente.
>
> Ser, y no saber nada, y ser sin rumbo cierto,
> y el temor de haber sido y un futuro terror. . .
> Y el espanto seguro de estar mañana muerto,
> y sufrir por la vida y por la sombra y por
>
> lo que no conocemos y apenas sospechamos,
> y la carne que tienta con sus frescos racimos,
> y la tumba que aguarda con sus fúnebres ramos,
> ¡y no saber adónde vamos,
> ni de dónde venimos. . . !
>
> (How fortunate the tree, almost without feeling,
> and even more the hard rock, because it feels nothing now,
> for there is no greater pain than the pain of being alive,
> nor heavier burden than conscious life.

To be, and to know nothing, and to be without a sure direction,
and the fear of having been and a future terror...
and the certain dread of being dead tomorrow,
and to suffer from life and from shadow and from
what we don't know and scarcely suspect,

and the flesh that tempts with its fresh clustered fruits
and the grave that awaits with its funeral wreaths,
and not to know where we are going,
nor from where we have come...!)

Read today, this seems to us one of Rubén's most profound poems. What it communicates—its feeling that pain and absurdity are the dominant notes of human existence—has disquieting resonances for us.

How many times, as we leaf through the paper in the morning and read articles that tell us of social, economic, political, and now cosmic absurdities, and others that detail the ins and outs of the latest atrocity, how many times don't we feel exactly the same mood expressed by the poet? Today it is a group of respectable citizens that questions very seriously the human dignity of people who have a higher proportion of melanin in their skin. One morning we hear that someone is defoliating an entire jungle, with great efficiency, of course, burning out the trees, the animals, and the people who lived there. We can suppose, like the poet, that the rocks at least felt nothing. Another day we read that the dangers of cigarette smoking have been proven, to find, on the next line, a statistic showing that in view of this fact, the number of smokers has increased. Another morning we're told of prodigious machines that go to the moon and to Mars, take pictures of these mysterious heavenly bodies, send the pictures to Earth, and publish them: we look at them and see—that there is nothing there. We hear too, every day, about the politics of brinkmanship.

The poet had anticipated our sensibility back in 1905: "... to suffer from life and from shadow ... and not to know where we are going, nor from where we have come ... !" "Lo fatal" is unquestionably a good poem. But it is also true that we read it today, and prefer it to others, because it expresses so exactly what we feel inside of us, giving voice to the anguish of our time.

At the beginning of the century Rubén had already felt and expressed modern man's existential anguish and sense of loss. He was seeing the advance—in fact he had already expressed it bitterly in the stories of Azul ... in 1888!—of the frightening dehumanization that followed from the subordination of the spiritual to the material;

the subordination of man to the thing, the artefact. "Lo fatal" is the naked expression of pure existential tension. The polar vertices of the tensions are perfectly clear in the poem:

Mineral and vegetable existences—rock and tree, in order of vitality —opposed to human existence—conscious life, feeling.

Being—with a consciousness or inclination for knowledge—opposed to "knowing nothing."

To feel the passing of time, opposed to a refusal to accept condemnation to temporality.

The fear of having lived before and forgotten—it is known that Rubén was a spiritualist—opposed to the terror of returning to live another earthly existence.

The tempting flesh, demanding the erotic act of creation, opposed to the grave, of funereal flowers.

The unknown origin of man, opposed to his uncertain final destiny.

These are the constant vertices of tension, successive or alternating, of human existence. Rubén feels them and lives them in the poem, stripping his soul naked before us with an almost absolute candor and intensity. He bares for us the very heart and bowels of his poetry. He hasn't dressed up this poem with the irritating, glittering, or ultra-sonorous draperies that we have come to expect. Almost all that remain are the rhythm of the lines, unmistakeable and always masterly, and two sensual metaphors: "frescos racimos" ("fresh-clustered fruits") and "fúnebres ramos" ("funeral wreaths"). The poem's stylistic charge is in the verbs: *to be* (several times), *to know* (also various times), *feel, be dead, suffer, suspect, tempt, wait, go, come*; all of them in repetitive play, being conjugated in different tenses. The nouns too: *life* (twice), *pain* (twice), *tree, rock, burden, direction, fear, terror, dread, shadow, flesh, fruits* ("racimos"), *grave, wreaths*. Notice that the simple enumeration of the poem's verbs and nouns almost gives us the experience of the entire composition; although, naturally, we know syntax to be especially important in this poem. One construction in particular stands out, being repeated thirteen times in a poem of thirteen lines: the accumulation of terms joined by the copulative conjunction "and." It is this repetitive construction, accumulating tensions, that communicates to us the pain and fears of the poet, and that produces the great discharge of existential agony.

Rubén Darío himself, in his *Historia de mis libros* (1909), explained his intentions in their vital and historical aspect:

In "Lo fatal," against my deep-rooted religion, and despite myself, a phantasm of desolation and doubt rises like a fearful shadow. Certainly, there has existed in me, from the beginning of my life, a profound pre-occupation with the end of existence. . . . I have been filled with anguish when I examined the basis of my beliefs and discovered my faith to be neither solid nor well-founded enough when conflicting ideas have made me waver, and I have felt myself lacking a constant and firm support. I have known the cruelty and idiocies of men. I have been betrayed, repaid with ingratitude, slandered, misinterpreted in my best intentions by the evil-minded, attacked, vilified. And I have smiled sadly . . .

It would not be difficult to select and study other poems by Rubén like "Lo fatal," where the poet, human and profound, smiles *sadly* at men's idiocies, or tells us of the anxieties that trouble his heart. I mention only "¡Ay, triste del que un día. . . . !," "Augurios," "Melancolía," "Thanatos," from *Cantos de vida y esperanza*, "¡Eheu!" from *El canto errante*, "Poema del otoño," from the book of the same name, and the poems "A Francisca." There are many more of this kind. Consider, for example, "De otoño," also from *Cantos de vida y esperanza*, a key poem for the understanding of the poet's reversion and his concentration on the inner song, where he says:

> Pasó ya el tiempo de la juvenil sonrisa:
> ¡dejad al huracán mover mi corazón!

> (The time of the youthful smile has passed:
> let the hurricane move my heart!)

Or the spine-tingling "Nocturno," poem XXXII of *Cantos de vida y esperanza*, of maximum importance in understanding how the tension of the poet's soul turns the dial of his poetry:

> Y el pesar de no ser lo que yo hubiera sido,
> la pérdida del reino que estaba para mí,
> el pensar que un instante pude no haber nacido,
> ¡y el sueño que es mi vida desde que yo nací!

> (And the regret of not being what I would have been,
> the loss of the kingdom that was meant for me,
> the thought that for an instant I could have not been,
> and the dream that is my life since I came to be!)

What I have said is perhaps not new. The group of poems to which I have referred is, as I pointed out earlier, the part of Rubén's work that the readers of our time would salvage from a shipwreck. The rest, especially the most characteristic poems of *Prosas profanas*, don't awaken much interest; they are considered—when they are paid any attention at all—as exquisite frivolities, or as porcelain museum pieces. Today few readers would jump into the water to save the work of "the other" Rubén Darío.

"Era un aire suave . . . ," from *Prosas profanas*, is a poem that moves hardly anyone today, and that, at best only scholars and specialists in Spanish-American literature read with any interest. Nevertheless, I think that we are committing a great error of historical perspective and aesthetic appreciation. As I said earlier, the judgments fashionable in our age are suppressing real efforts to understand and feel the enduring merits of that poetry.

To begin with, I find highly doubtful—and a grave historiographic error—the dichotomy made between the Rubén of before and the Rubén of after *Cantos de vida y esperanza*. Those who believe in this dichotomy have not asked themselves whether a creative existence is not perhaps a biological and historical continuity. The reality that is a succession of physio-biological moments in the poet's life has a corresponding parallel, even more complex and rich, in the succession of moments in the self-formative process and in the creative process. In order to know the life of a man, what a man really is, we have to know his history. Among the innumerable events that happen during his existence, the ones that make him *him*, the ones that shape him, are his most individual, original, and creative acts. We, the majority of human beings, don't get far along this road, and, at most, our formation culminates in the acquisition of a unique personality and a collection of abilities. But there is a minority, made up of the original thinkers, the inventors, the artists, the poets, who possess the gift of making, of shaping, not only their personal history, but also that of the majority. They bring about great and transcendent events. How can we understand a poet's life, or the guts of his life that is his work, if we mutilate it, or even worse, if we don't make an effort to relive it on its own terms?

Rubén Darío's whole life passed in incessant movement. Always in tension, because, disliking the succession of nights and days that it was his lot to live, he tried to cast off these contingencies and direct his soul, and his work, toward an ideal world; a world more like a utopia, metamorphic and changeable, than an ivory tower. The great adventure that was his life, despite sorrow and misfortune, can be understood and justified only by reading, really reading, *all* his poetry. The study of his anecdotal biography should be subsidiary to that of the flow of his work. The sufferings of one who knew himself to be defenseless, not at all pragmatic, a Chorotega Indian, who went stumbling through life, matter to us because, as he was careful to tell us, he had the hands—creative hands—of a marquis. His aristocratic dreams reflect more the exaltation of the human spirit than an aspiring social vanity. His aristocratic and exquisite ways, acquired with great effort, were part of being a poet. They are a pathetic adventure, ended happily only in his work, and they caused Rubén more pain than joy. He indulged in certain worldly vanities during his term as minister of Nicaragua in the court of Alfonso XIII, or during his trips through the Hispanic world, where he had become an idol; but they were all very precarious. The uniforms and palaces were only lent, backdrop to a farce in which he himself never really believed. His poetry—more than the documents and chronicles of the period—tell us the whole truth.

Tying all the loose ends, I read "Era un aire suave . . ." Yes. The poem seems to be, at first sight, the dream of an ideal, exquisite world. The music comes up and a female character appears: the marquise Eulalia, a literary fiction who embodies literature, dreams, a vision of the eternal feminine—"laughter and fickleness" ("risas y desvíos")—and an illusion of an aristocratic and supercivilized world. Lavish aestheticism. Verses and lines that would irritate other poets—among them Unamuno—because taken out of context, they were acoustic pyrotechnics. Remember the most famous verse, the one that provoked the wrath of the harsh and austere don Miguel:

> ¡Amoroso pájaro que trinos exhala
> bajo el ala a veces ocultando el pico;
> que desdenes rudos lanza bajo el ala,
> bajo el ala aleve del leve abanico!

> (Amorous bird that breathes out trills
> under her wing sometimes hiding her beak;
> that hurls forth coarse disdain under her wing,
> under the treacherous wing of the light fan!)

But if we read the poem ("Era un aire suave . . .") with care and awareness of those inner springs that stretch from the poet toward every horizon, until the creative and unifying tension is produced, we will notice that the gentle airs heard in the gardens and salons of

the palace, the laughter of the marquise, her coquetries, are heard
and contemplated from a distance, from outside the gratings that
separate the garden, and its fortunate inhabitants, from the common-
ers. There, banished, in his condition as the humblest of men, is the
poet. In the poem the marquise Eulalia surrenders herself to the page-
servant-poet; but she does it in the garden, hiding herself from those
of her class in "el boscaje que cubre la amable glorieta" (the foliage
that covers the inviting bower). Afterwards the exquisite Eulalia keeps
on laughing and flirting; the party goes on . . .

When we get to the last five lines, we realize that it has all been a
dream. The poet doesn't know where or when he saw the marquise,
nor when he heard her laughter. The time and space in which it all
took place was only an illusion. The dream's effect is cruel, the poet
is hurt:

> ¿Fue acaso en el Norte o en el Mediodía?
> Yo el tiempo y el día y el país ignoro;
> pero sé que Eulalia ríe todavía,
> ¡y es cruel y eterna su risa de oro!

> (Was it perhaps in the north or in the south?
> I know neither the time nor the day nor the country;
> but I know that Eulalia is laughing still,
> and her golden laughter is cruel and eternal!)

The laughter hurts the dreamer, naturally, because he knows that
he is excluded from the dream. That is the poem's real inner tension,
its secret. The poem is not an exquisite porcelain museum piece, but a
sad song of the longing to possess that porcelain. The frivolous laugh
of the marquise never ends: "Eulalia ríe todavía." Rubén hears it
always there within, in the dream-salon that he can never enter in
prosaic reality.

Obviously there are differences between the Rubén of *Cantos de
vida y esperanza* (1905) and the Rubén of *Prosas profanas* (1896).
The poetic ingredients, the magnitude of the different inner tensions,
can vary from one period to another, and this variation will be evident
in the final product, the individual poems; but the differences are the
logical result of living in time—a process always painful for Rubén,
and the Gordian knot of his poetry. They will be seen with greater or
lesser clarity, but a good reader will always find the poem's extremes
of tension and its emotional trajectory.

A letter written by Rubén in 1904 to his loyal friend Juan Ramón

Jiménez, when he was preparing and selecting the *Cantos*, is quite enlightening in this respect. Rubén says, among other things:

I am going to send you the poems very soon [those intended for the volume *Cantos de vida y esperanza*]. You'll see. There's a little of everything. But for the first time there is what Rodó didn't find in *Prosas profanas*, the man who feels. It must be that when I wrote them, *although I was suffering* [italics mine], I was in my springtime and that consoled me and gave me courage and joy.

Our current injustice to the so-called first Rubén, then, shouldn't surprise us. If writers who were really so close to him, like Rodó and Unamuno, didn't see the underlying suffering and gentle melancholy in his springtime verses, how can we expect it of ourselves, here in another age—atomic and apocalyptic?

Today it is difficult to relive Rubén Darío's imaginary adventure of marquises, Versaillesque gardens, princesses, and swans. We prefer to say that they died away, thank God, his visions ended forever. Eager for the simplistic formula—and wanting to pass quickly over something that no longer charms or intrigues us—we reduce it all to the statement that the poetry of gentle breezes, lyres, gardens, and marquises, was a fashion that fulfilled its function in a given moment—the end of the nineteenth century and the beginning of the twentieth —by battling against the ugliness, prosaism, and vulgarity prevalent then. But by simplifying so drastically, we deny ourselves the understanding of the high tension with which these poetic visions were charged—and still are charged—for the reader. We refuse to feel with Rubén the spiritual tension, the inner shock—beyond all changes of fashion—that drove him to dream his deliriums or chant his hymns, to find an outlet for his tremendous verbal and imaginative exuberance. We don't sympathize with this poetry because in us the organ for feeling it and enjoying it has surely atrophied. It is possible, too, that we have come to the extreme of being incapable of seeing the hunger for higher beauty and humanity that can be felt by a man born in the lowest, darkest, and remotest roots of a village, rich in sensibility but poor in fortune, justice, and happiness.

Rubén Darío was born in Metapa, an insignificant spot; all his life he walked in a dream of lakes and distant palaces. But it would be unjust to call him an escapist for this. He became a cultured man, in his own way, a way that was partly that of the Hispanic world, that is, improvised, autodidactic. He lived concerned with the great and small things that happened around him. He felt himself committed to many causes and ideas of his day. He was a modern man—more than a Modernist—and he knew as few did, in those years at the end of the century, that a flood of dehumanizing dangers was coming upon us. In a curious parallel with Unamuno, Rubén undertook a humanizing mission. He already knew, in those years, that the idea of satisfying only the material needs of the villages was inadequate. He, who had known every kind of privation, knew very well that the hunger of the poor is not "hunger" in the singular, but "hungers," in a resounding and demanding plural. Hunger for human dignity; hunger for mastery over nature, things, time, and distance; hunger and thirst for justice; hunger for beauty, cleanliness and health; and above all, the hunger of hungers, that of the spirit.

Rubén realized that a great historical era, one given direction by successive aristocracies, was coming to an end in his time. He saw on its way a violent flood of Prussian artillerymen, of pragmatic Yankees, of English stockbrokers; he didn't foresee the coming of the super-bureaucrats, especially the Bolsheviks. He thought the flood inevitable, but he feared, with reason, that something worth saving would be lost in it. Something superfluous, without apparent social function, not even edible; something that couldn't be used to build the modern anthills intended for the perfection of mankind. Something that Rubén, timid, always somewhat of a child, progressively deeper in alcoholism, useless for everything but writing, symbolized, saw, sang, questioned, grieved, in a swan.

Rubén's swans weren't —aren't—papier-maché decorations, con-trivances of Wagnerian stage machinery. They were chaste and noble heraldic symbols, pennants of challenge, and much more. Improbable animals that seem artificial to us today, forgotten in lakes and rivers by the poets of other times. Anachronistic, even a little vulgar, if you wish; but they're there still. . . . Bad readers of Rubén that we are, we haven't realized that the poet put more expressive force in his persistent use of the word "still" than in the laughter of the marquise Eulalia or in the whiteness of the swans.

Although in remote times swans had been the dream of minstrels, or the emblem of knights (Cisneros), they had come to be only a part of the closed garden of the few. Rubén, from the critical vantage point of his lifetime, asked them, the few, not to forget the last song, nor why the swan sings it. The many, those who were going to tear down forever the gratings of the world's Versailles, he asked not to strangle the swans, to learn the lesson of art and mystery hidden in their form. Once more the old myth could be life-giving. The swan must not be strangled. He must be saved, fed, left tranquil and majestic in his lakes, to see if the old humanizing gods, taking form once more in him, would come down to earth to impregnate new Ledas: seamstresses, typists, working girls, free now from servitude to the land or to rich masters, but about to fall into the dehumanizing trap of the factory, the office, the union, and the party. The swan could do something to combat the mediocrity of the middle class Ledas that today, a hundred years after Rubén's birth, is already in possession of the world. Bread for everyone! by all means, but why not swans too? thought with hope and pain the good Indian of Chocoyos.

Today, a hundred years after he was born, we think about the poet and are saddened as we contemplate the spectacle of these masses of whites, reds, blacks, yellows, and greens that can conceive of no other bird than the chicken bred on an industrialized farm, and that prefer the racket of parades at Macy's, in New York, or in Moscow's Red Square, to the tranquility of the lakes.

The following words come from a letter sent by Rubén Darío to the Cuban writer Manuel Serafín Pichardo, on August 21, 1907:

One of the things I most appreciate in you, my good friend, is your loyalty to the purity of Art in the midst of life's ugliness. There are so many toads and so few swans!

In this simple lamentation directed to a friend and poet, in the intimate language of a letter, we can see resumed the maximum inner tension that moved Rubén. He knew himself to be physically, socially, and practically closer to the toad than to the swan. The tension between the ugliness of life and the purity of Art mattered to him more as that tension in itself—a striving toward human fulfillment—than as an aesthetic posture. He praised his friend's decision to dedicate himself to lofty humanizing ideals: the toads are so many, but the swans so few! If there is so much toad in each of us, why not dream, why not strive to become a swan?

RUBEN DARÍO

AZUL...

VALPARAISO

IMPRENTA Y LITOGRAFIA EXCELSIOR

14, CALLE SERRANO, 14

—

MDCCCLXXXVIII

EUGENIO FLORIT

THE MODERNIST PREFIGUREMENT IN THE EARLY WORK OF RUBÉN DARÍO

translated by John Wilcox

IN THE FOLLOWING PAGES, I PROPOSE to convey some of the ideas that occurred to me as I read the poetry that Rubén Darío wrote prior to *Azul*. Obviously, for such a task I have had to lean on certain studies that have already been done on the subject, and also on certain opinions expressed, even though in passing, by distinguished colleagues and critics.

In the first place, the poet's precociousness and his truly prolific output have to be borne in mind. His early work begins around 1878, when he was hardly eleven years old, and goes on to 1888, the date of the first edition of *Azul*. If we include in this production all the verse Darío wrote up to that year,[1] we find ourselves dealing with almost half, and perhaps more than half, of the total number of his poetic compositions. In them, as is natural in an exceptional case such as this, we do observe from the outset stutterings, approximations, or prefigurements of what his poetical language was destined to become within a very few years. My dear friend, Enrique Anderson-Imbert, among others, has already indicated in his excellent introduction to Ernesto Mejía Sánchez's edition of the poems, how Rubén Darío, before his journey to Chile and when he was still in his native Central America, had begun to feel the influence of French writers of the time: Coppée, Mendès, Gautier. His initiation into the harmonious groves of Victor Hugo, thanks to his friend Francisco Gavidia, should be included here.[2] It is clear, says Anderson-Imbert, that before his journey to Chile he sympathized with Parnassian ideals of "art for art's sake," "but even after having glimpsed the course he would have to take, he went round and round like a distracted dove that circles the city, delaying the moment at which he must part to deliver his message."[3]

It is some of these wanderings that I would like to mention, even if they do no more than mark a few of the milestones on his trajectory. I hope that the reader will discover with me Rubén Darío's struggle,

as I like to call it, with form; a form in pursuit of which he was end-
lessly engaged. Let us recall the final poem of *Prosas profanas*:

YO PERSIGO UNA FORMA . . .
Yo persigo una forma que no encuentra mi estilo,
botón de pensamiento que busca ser la rosa;
se anuncia con un beso que en mis labios se posa
al abrazo imposible de la Venus de Milo.

Adornan verdes palmas el blanco peristilo;
los astros me han predicho la visión de la Diosa;
y en mi alma reposa la luz, como reposa
el ave de la luna sobre un lago tranquilo.

Y no hallo sino la palabra que huye,
la iniciación melódica que de la flauta fluye
y la barca del sueño que en el espacio boga;

y bajo la ventana de mi Bella-Durmiente,
el sollozo continuo del chorro de la fuente
y el cuello del gran cisne blanco que me interroga.[4]

In addition, there are some curious points to be found by those who
wish to steep themselves in Darío's relations with poets who were
older or younger than he. The admiration and enthusiasm that the
name of Rubén Darío awoke in the young Juan Ramón Jiménez is
known to all. I say 'the name' because Juan Ramón himself has said
and written on different occasions that, when he saw Darío for the
first time in April of 1900, he had read few of his poems. Graciela
Palau de Nemes states that, in spite of Juan Ramón's admiration, his
verse shows the influence of Rubén Darío only after he had met the
great Modernist bard in person.[5] Is it, then, just coincidence, mere
chance, an influence absorbed through contact with the poetical
milieu? There is one certain piece of evidence: among the poems
Rubén Darío wrote in his adolescence, there is one in *romance* verse-
form[6] entitled "La niña de ojos azules" ('The Blue-eyed Girl'). Although the poem has no date, Méndez Plancarte places it with those
written between 1882 and 1884. The poem is divided into three parts.
It has an assonance in "i-a," is similar to a madrigal and is sentimental
in tone. The third of these parts opens with these four lines:

Cuando la hablé de mi amor
inclinó la frente tímida;
y como perlas, dos lágrimas
rodaron por sus mejillas.[7]

Juan Ramón, in a poem entitled "Adolescencia" ('Adolescence'), says the following:

> No se atrevía a mirarme;
> le dije que éramos novios,
> . . . y sus lágrimas rodaron
> de sus ojos melancólicos.[8]

Is it not a fact that there exists a real resemblance of tone and even of vocabulary? "Two tears rolled" in the first of the poems, and "the tears rolled" in the second. Both feminine figures are timid young girls. But what emerges as something out of the ordinary in Darío, yet still surrounded with pleonastic padding, is already well established in Juan Ramón, and the poet, in our opinion, is master of his word and tone. Credit for this is due in part to the selective criteria used in the preparation of the Hispanic Society's edition of *Poesías escojidas* ('Selected poems').[9] The editor had the good taste to eliminate those poems of inferior quality which appear in Juan Ramón's first two books, *Almas de violeta* ('Souls of Violet') and *Ninfeas* ('Water Lilies') (1900). But, I insist that it is curious how both poets, separated by a distance of twenty years, somehow end up offering each other a handshake that was wet with the tears of a girl in their youth. There also exists another example of a similar close resemblance in Darío's *Romance*, which for some unknown reason is excluded from Méndez Plancarte's edition:

> Era una tarde de enero;
> el sol casi se ocultaba,
> y las brisas dulcemente
> gemían entre las ramas. . . [10]

Another *romance*, the second of the poems in *Rimas* ('Rhymes') (1887), may also serve to point out those echoes of Rubén Darío in Juan Ramón Jiménez. It begins this way:

> Amada, la noche llega;
> las ramas que se columpian
> hablan de las hojas secas
> y de las flores difuntas.[11]

And it ends in this exquisite manner:

> En tanto los aires vuelan
> y los aromas ondulan;
> se inclinan las ramas trémulas

> y parece que murmuran
> algo de las hojas secas
> y de las flores difuntas.[12]

Undoubtedly, this is a foretaste of some of the early Juan Ramón *romances*, found in his "Rimas de sombra" ('Rhymes from the Shade') and *Arias tristes* ('Sad Arias').

As far as José Martí is concerned, Max Henríquez Ureña says in his *Breve historia del Modernismo*: "The influence of Martí, to whom Darío devoted several articles of remarkable criticism, beginning with the one that appears in *Los raros*, is already seeping through to aspects of his prose style. In 1891 Martí published *Versos sencillos*, and some of the turns of phrase and lyrical tendencies of these poems found an echo in later compositions of Rubén Darío. For instance, in his "Elogio a Don Vicente Navas" (1893), Darío models verses that imitate Martí's 'manner,' as Regino Boti has remarked."[13] Indeed, Boti, the Cuban poet and critic, has managed to isolate some of the lines or verses in Rubén Darío that are very close to the Martí of *Versos sencillos*.[14] He highlights these *redondillas*:[15]

ELOGIO A DON VICENTE NAVAS

> Tejo mi corona, llévola
> para honrar al ciudadano
> que hubiera puesto su mano
> sobre las brasas de Escévola. . . . ;
> a quien, por firme y leal,
> el deber bronce daría;
> a quien el alma tenía
> fundida en bronce moral.
>
> Loor, pues, a quien fue noble,
> honrado, viril, sin tacha
> El leñador movió el hacha;
> cayó el varón como un roble.[16]

In this instance, it can be clearly seen that Darío had read not only Martí's prose, about which so many good studies have been done, but also his poetry. Nevertheless, it happens that if we examine the work done by Rubén Darío prior to 1891, the date of publication of the already mentioned *Versos sencillos*, we discover many instances reminiscent of Martí's octosyllabic combinations. In fact, I have a special interest in these "instances." They first attracted my attention in 1962. Indeed, I did, in passing, point them out at that time in my study

of Martí's verse.[17] I believe that the first example of *redondilla* octo-
syllables to be found in the Cuban poet's work is the delightful poem
"Dormida" ('Asleep') (1878), which, however, was not published
until many years after Martí's death, and therefore could not have
been known by Darío in 1880. After this, we have to wait until 1889
when he writes "Los zapaticos de rosa" ('The Little Pink Shoes') for
his review, *La Edad de Oro*. Then we have the whole gamut of various
octosyllablic combinations in *Versos sencillos*. As far as Rubén Darío
is concerned, the *redondillas* appear even in his first collection, to
which the poet himself gave the title "Sollozos del laúd" ('Sobs from
the Lute'), but which never appeared in print as such. There is, for
example, the poem "Desengaño" ('Disillusion'), probably written in
June 1880, some of whose verses are more than adequate to illustrate
this point. He writes:

> De la fuente las espumas
> se miraban blanquear,
> y en los espacios cruzar
> pájaros de airosas plumas.[18]

A poem that does resemble Martí, though unwittingly, such as the
one entitled "Cámara obscura" ('Dark Chamber'), should be situated
chronologically, as don Alfonso Méndez Plancarte has done, in or
around 1882. We should read it all, because within these verses we
shall find the characteristic style, that particular vein of *Versos sencillos*. It reads as follows:

> La calle de la Amargura
> nos ve llevar nuestra cruz;
> pero en la cámara obscura
> penetra un rayo de luz.
>
> En la mía, no da el cielo
> un solo rayo feliz;
> la mía tiene un tapiz
> de fúnebre terciopelo.
>
> Tiene la tuya del día
> el espléndido irradiar;
> de la noche el sollozar
> es lo que tiene la mía.
>
> Bajo mi cámara obscura
> Cristo gime en un madero;

bajo ella, un sepulturero
cava una honda sepultura.

Bajo la tuya, su historia
pintó el ángel del trabajo;
y las coronas que trajo
muestra el ángel de la gloria.

Neurótico y visionario
gózome yo en tu labor:
cuando vas a tu Tabor,
voy subiendo mi calvario.

Ve cómo es la suerte rara:
juntas dicha y desventura;
la tuya, cámara clara;
la mía, cámara obscura.[19]

This poem, especially the first stanza, the third and fourth lines of the
second, and the whole of the fourth, has the very rhythm, the very
manner, the same characteristics, the same spirit of Martí's *Versos
sencillos*. Yet another example: "El organillo" ('The Little Organ'),
of 1881, which belongs to the series of poems dedicated to the Central
American patriot, Máximo Jerez. Here are three quatrains:

Busca y pide; la doblez
recoge por lo que quiere:
al fin, Máximo Jerez
deja el organillo y muere.

. . .

Sí, otro anciano marcha ahora
con el organillo; ha de ir,
camino del porvenir,
por la calle de la aurora.

Y el viejo y pobre instrumento
de la canción de la Unión
ha de poner su canción
sobre las alas del viento.[20]

Another example is found in "A unos ojos" ('To a Girl's Eyes')
(1884) of which the first verse reads:

El sol con sus rayos rojos
ya no brilla, ya no arde;

> que está dormida la tarde
> y está dormida en tus ojos.[21]

In another poem, of about the same year, which is entitled 'Introducción a "La Aurora" de Joaquín Méndez' ('Introduction to "The
Dawn" by Joaquín Méndez'), we read

> . . . color rosado en las nubes
> que se mecen con donaire,
> ruidos de alas en el aire,
> como que vuelan querubes;
>
> en redes de flores, presos,
> gorriones y mariposas,
> y los lirios y las rosas
> como si se dieran besos;
>
> estremecimientos vagos
> en las hojas y en las brisas;
> por todas partes sonrisas,
> aquí un eco, allí un halago;
>
> el césped, de olor cubierto,
> junto al riachuelo sonoro,
> y un ave con pluma de oro
> sobre un capullo entreabierto;
>
> una bella que camina
> junto a un joven trovador;
> él le habla cosas de amor,
> y ella la cabeza inclina;
>
> y mientras el aire deslíe
> recio, tenue y liviano,
> él la toma de la mano,
> y ella le mira y sonríe.[22]

Another Martí 'instance' appears in 1888, "La lira de las siete cuerdas"
('The Seven Stringed Lyre'), written by Darío in January of that year
in Santiago de Chile for Elisa Balmaceda y Toro's album. The poem is
divided in seven parts or 'strings'. Each part has a different structure;
the length of the lines and of the stanzas varies. It is only the first part
that is of interest to us:

> ¿Cantar a la dama? Bien
> está, por belleza y fama,

y es muy justo que a la dama
galanterías se den.

¿Cantar a la niña? Es cosa
que más mi lira prefiere.
Soy un loco que se muere
por los botones de rosa.

Tú, ni dama ni niña eres,
porque estás en el divino
crepúsculo matutino
en que nacen las mujeres.

Luz y gloria son tus galas,
ángel eres y en Dios sueñas:
tú debes tener las señas
donde tuviste las alas.[23]

This brings us up to the prologue of *Abrojos* ('Thorns') (1887)
which is written in *redondillas*. The book is dedicated to Manuel Rodríguez Mendoza to whom this initial poem is addressed. It contains
verses of a similar tone to those already mentioned. Here are a few
random examples:

Juntos hemos visto el mal
y, en el mundano bullicio,
cómo para cada vicio
se eleva un arco triunfal.

· · ·

Vimos perlas en el lodo,
burla y baldón a destajo,
el delito por debajo
y la hipocresía en todo.

· · ·

Mucho tigre carnicero,
bien enguantadas las uñas,
y muchísimas garduñas
con máscaras de cordero.

· · ·

La envidia que desenrosca
su cuerpo y muerde con maña;
y en la tela de la araña
a cada paso la mosca. . .[24]

Had Martí read any of these verses? It is possible only if they were published in reviews, or if the Cuban poet possessed a copy of *Abrojos* or of *Rimas*. But let the patient scholar answer such questions, for I neither am nor claim to be one. Rather, while reading these poems, so valuable in themselves, I have been interested only in noting that re- semblance of tono, of expression, of vocabulary, and even the volun- tary repetition of interior rhymes, as in the case of the composition written for the album of Elisa Balmaceda y Toro. They present us with a Rubén Darío who, around the year 1882, when Martí was publishing his famous free hendecasyllables, was already writing such extraor- dinary poems as one we have recently quoted, "Cámara obscura." This poem is a direct antecedent, although Darío did not know it, of what Martí himself was going to say eleven years later.

As we are dealing with relations and antecedents, I should like in a quick parenthesis to refer to a case of 'echo-ism' which I have found in one of Rubén's famous poems, and in one by José Eusebio Caro. In this case, I believe there is no doubt that the poet from Nicaragua read the poet from Colombia. Caro's verses were published in 1885 in Madrid, and "Canción de otoño en primavera" ('Song of Autumn in Springtime'), dedicated to Gregorio Martínez Sierra, appeared in *Cantos de vida y esperanza* ('Songs of Life and Hope') in 1905, when Rubén himself was living in Madrid. It is rather interesting to note the form of both poems: quatrains with lines of nine syllables, ending with consonant rhyme, masculine in the odd-numbered ones. Darío's poem is longer: seventeen quatrains and a final line of either eight or nine syllables, depending on how you make the synalephas. Caro's poem has ten stanzas. In place of the melancholy sensualism of the first, there is a tone of serenity and a predominance of nostalgia in the sec- ond. In "Estar contigo" ('To Be With You'), Caro writes:

> ¡Oh! ¡ya de orgullo estoy cansado,
> ya estoy cansado de razón;
> déjame en fin, hable a tu lado
> cual habla sólo el corazón!
>
> ¡No te hablaré de grandes cosas;
> quiero más bien verte y callar,
> no contar las horas odiosas,
> y reír oyéndote hablar!
>
> Quiero una vez estar contigo,
> cual Dios el alma te formó;

> tratarte cual a un viejo amigo
> que en nuestra infancia nos amó;
>
> volver a mi vida pasada,
> olvidar todo lo que sé,
> extasiarme en una nada,
> ¡y llorar sin saber por qué!

The last line reminds us of Rubén's line "a veces lloro sin querer" ("at times I weep without wanting to"). The poem continues:

> ¡Ah! ¡para amar Dios hizo al hombre!
> ¿Quién un hado no da feliz
> por esos instantes sin nombre
> de la vida del infeliz,
>
> cuando, con la larga desgracia
> de amar, doblado su poder,
> toda su alma ardiendo sacia
> en el alma de una mujer?
>
> ¡Oh padre Adán! ¡Qué error tan triste
> cometió en ti la humanidad,
> cuando a la dicha preferiste
> de la ciencia la vanidad!
>
> ¿Qué es lo que dicha aquí se llama
> sino no conocer temor,
> y con la Eva que se ama,
> vivir de ignorancia y de amor?
>
> ¡Ay! ¡mas con todo así nos pasa;
> con la Patria y la juventud,
> con nuestro hogar y antigua casa,
> con la inocencia y la virtud!
>
> Mientras tenemos despreciamos,
> sentimos después de perder;
> ¡y entonces aquel bien lloramos
> que se fué para no volver![25]

This final line is parallel to Darío's "te fuiste para no volver" ("you left, never to return") and its variant that is more often repeated "¡ya te vas para no volver!" ("you leave, never to return"). Is it not a fact, that in meter, accentuation, rhyme and even in that refrain, Rubén's song persistently brings to mind Caro's, or vice versa? This is just another curious point that I bring forward, in case nobody has noticed it before.

Now, I shall discuss something that I consider to be more important. I tried to find among Rubén Darío's initial poetical output some lines, verses or 'moments' in which the poet strides ahead of himself. That is to say, when his poetical language seems to be cutting a path for itself from among all the jaded foliage of useless verse. I expressed this once in a sort of aphorism: "How much useless verse before getting to the poetry, if one ever can get there!" Obviously, Rubén did; but arduously, by wrestling against his innate facility to versify, and against that essential impatience with living that led him along so many and such varied paths, until he eventually found his real self. Julio Saavedra Molina in his article on Rubén Darío's first book, *Epístolas y poemas* ('Epistles and Poems') or *Primeras notas* ('First Notes'), sketches a guideline which will help us glimpse what really interests us. He says: "As is to be expected, there are also in *Epístolas y poemas* of Managua (1885)—or rather, as Méndez Plancarte has observed: the *Primeras notas* of the false cover of 1888, —some foreshadowings that are rather typically Rubén Darío, —I mean, some heralding of what this poet's Modernism will later be."[26] He also quotes an example which we shall stop to examine later. But let us continue at a measured pace to examine the texts in the order in which they appear in Méndez Plancarte's edition. It is my opinion that this is a good edition to follow because it is complete and well arranged. However, I take exception to some of the titles that are given to different sections prior to *Epístolas y poemas* and after *Canto a la Argentina y otros poemas* ('Song to the Argentine and Other Poems') (1914). Such titles as "Iniciación melódica" ('Melodic Initiation') and "Del chorro de la fuente" ('From the Fount's Flow'), borrowed by the compiler from the final sonnet of *Prosas profanas*, strike me as rather unnatural, because they are taken out of context. With all due respect to Méndez Plancarte, I prefer the previously used titles:[27] "Poemas de adolescencia" ('Adolescent Poems'), "Poemas de juventud" ('Poems of Youth') and "Lira póstuma" ('Posthumous Lyre'). It is a pity that more care was not taken to arrange the chronological order of the poems grouped under these titles. In Méndez Plancarte's edition, on the other hand, the order has been carefully determined.

In the first place, we must remember, as Ernesto Mejía Sánchez says in his study of the classic humanities in Rubén Darío,[28] that from

an early age our poet mentions the names of Greek and Latin writers
and mythological characters that he had acquired through reading.
He never ceased to draw on classical antiquity and to treat it in his
poems. At times, we find, of course, that this antiquity has apparently
been transformed by his knowledge of French poets. ("More than the
Greece of the Greeks, I love the Greece of France," he says in *Prosas
profanas*.) This fondness comes to him very early, as does his interest
in civic and political matters. Such themes fill his first work, and they
reappear in some of his most powerful poems in *Cantos de vida y
esperanza*. On the other hand, there is his taste for the sumptuous and
the decorative, which makes its triumphal entry with the "Serenata"
('Serenade') of 1882. This poem opens with a series of fourteen-
syllable quatrains with masculine rhymes (or *rime riche*) in the
alternate lines. These are the alexandrines that he surely worked on
while in the company of Francisco Gavidia:

> Señora: allá en la tierra del sándalo y la goma,
> bajo el hermoso cielo de Arabia la Oriental,
> do bullen embriagantes la mirra y el aroma,
> y lucen sus colores la perla y el coral. . . .[29]

The dodecasyllabic line, comprising two units of seven and five syllables respectively,[30] in rhyming couplets makes its appearance in
1886. In "Cantilena", a ballad, the poet begins with some rather bad
quintillas[31] and then suddenly changes the form of the verse. He is
certainly inspired as, injecting impulse, rhythm and cadence into the
lines, he exclaims:

> Virgen ardiente y pura de Nicaragua,
> tierna como la silfa reina del agua:
> de tus labios de rosa mana ambrosía,
> y de tus negros ojos, la luz del día.[32]

Here is the artist who is master of his palette. A little later on he writes:

> allí, en tus negros ojos irresistibles,
> he comprendido cosas incomprensibles;
> el fuego de tu mente que te ilumina,
> algo es como un destello de luz divina;
> y en el fondo de tu alma de soñadora,
> luce, en fuego apacible, plácida aurora.[33]

Among these poems written between 1882 and 1886, among the commonplace themes and long stretches of verse that say nothing, there

are to be found many drops of honey that gradually grow in size. This is what happens with some of the hendecasyllabic lines of "El poeta y las musas" ('The Poet to the Muses'). The following comes from his first book of poems, *Epístolas y poemas:*

> Batió el Pegaso el ala voladora,
> irguió la crin, y del Olimpo heleno
> hirió la cumbre con el leve casco;
> y el poeta preludió su hosanna eterno.
>
> El padre Apolo derramó su gracia,
> el padre Apolo del talento regio,
> aquel del verso rítmico y sonante
> que llenaba el abismo de los cielos.[34]

The poet is now twenty years old, and he is already familiar with the rhythms of poetry. However, time must pass before he will direct the flight of his Pegasus, even though the magnificent alexandrines of "Víctor Hugo y la tumba" ('Victor Hugo and the Tomb') are already apparent. These alexandrines are certainly prolix, perhaps too prolix, but they contain some first-class verses, such as these:

> Soplaron los tritones su caracol marino;
> las sirenas, veladas en un tul argentino,
> a flor de agua entonaron una vaga canción,
> y se unieron al coro de las ondas sonantes;
> y el mar tenía entonces convulsiones gigantes
> y latidos profundos como de corazón.[35]

This is the verse form and the meter of the "Sonatina," though in major key. In "Ecce Homo," a long poem with philosophical tendencies, there suddenly appears this exclamation:

> ¡Ah, los astros, los astros!
> ¡Ah, carbunclos y perlas y alabastros!
> ¡Infinito joyel; grandiosa altura. . . .[36]

an exclamation that springs with transcendental impetus like a cross or fountain from the middle of a rather mediocre, prosaic and vulgar poem.

In 1889, in San Salvador, he composed a "rhymed chronicle," entitled "Tres horas en el cielo" ('Three Hours in Heaven') about a school function. It is deliberately prosaic in nature, not lacking in wit. At one stage in a conversation he has with a friend, he points out one of the ladies at the gathering and says about her:

> Sí; la que tiene sus cabellos de oro
> como espigas mojadas por la lluvia.[37]

Once again there is poetry in the simplest and briefest of words. And a little further on there is suddenly a "flow" of purest lyricism in a most astounding expression:

> Entró una turba de lirios,
> una insurrección de rosas,
> un gran batallón de hermosas
> y un diluvio de delirios.[38]

Just like that! Then, the "chronicle" continues, and nothing else occurs; only that *redondilla* which, nobody can deny, is a real gem. However, there is this which appears a little earlier in the same poem:

> Abilia Flores, niña süave,
> lanzó una ráfaga de melodía,
> cual si muriendo cantara un ave
> cuando desmaya la luz del día.[39]

A year later, there is "Laetitia," a hymn to happiness which ends with two splendid lines that are so distinctly Darío:

> y se enciende la vida de la tierra
> con la llama invisible del amor.[40]

There are also these two isolated hendecasyllables of "A una estrella" ('To A Star') which recall his lines to "Venus," of which they seem to be the prelude:

> Princesa del divino imperio azul,
> ¡quién besara tus labios luminosos! . . .[41]

And the beautiful "Lied" (whose date Méndez Plancarte suggests is possibly 1890):

> Mirad ¡qué delicia! . . .
> La aurora triunfal,
> su pelo de oro
> y el cesto de rosas que riega en la tierra y el mar.
>
> ¡Y luego, una estrella
> y el rayo de luz
> por donde camina, volando a la estrella que adora
> un pájaro azul!

To this we could add the eighth poem of "El salmo de la pluma" ('The Pen's Psalm'), which is supposed to have been written between 1888 and 1889, and which, in my opinion, is a magnificent prefigurement of his "Responso a Verlaine":

> Pan vive; nunca ha muerto. Las selvas primitivas
> dan cañas a sus manos velludas, siempre activas
> siempre llenas de ardor.
> ¿Dónde no se oye mágico su armónico instrumento,
> del árbol regocijo, delectación del viento,
> delicia de la flor?[42]

I said 'prefigurement' because throughout this composition Darío uses a six-line stanza. Structurally, there are two rhyming alexandrine couplets, each followed by a line of six syllables. In his "Responso a Verlaine," he uses the same type of structure. The six-syllable lines are, admittedly, replaced by nine-syllable ones, but they, like the short lines of the "Salmo," end with an oxytonic rhyme.

In the same way, the Versailles described in "Era un aire suave . . ." is already prefigured, although in a different form, in the first sonnet of a series of four entitled "La revolución francesa" ('The French Revolution'). These were written in San Salvador on the fourteenth of July, 1889. Here are two parts from the first sonnet; the first quatrain:

> De raso azul vestidas están las bellas damas,
> Entre tapices llenos de asuntos de Watteau;
> la reina danza alegre, sus ojos son dos llamas;
> habrá lirios como ella, pero más blancos, no.

And the first tercet:

> Gentil el paso mide, su cuello real erguido,
> sonriente y desdeñosa su linda boca en flor;
> paloma de alabastro que tiene de oro el nido . . .[43]

Let that suffice.

We can already see how Rubén Darío's lyrical spirit was gradually trained in these exercises. The last samples are, admittedly, taken from work later than the first edition of *Azul*, but they might easily have been included in that book without discrediting the other poems. I have not been able to resist the temptation to transcribe them. Why? Because they are so little known and because they contain so much of what is purely poetic in Rubén Darío, he who was able to pursue with speed and without respite the ascent of the luminous ladder of poetry.

NOTES

[1] See the latest editions of his complete poems published by Aguilar: *Rubén Darío: Obras poéticas completas,* ed. Federico Sainz de Robles (Madrid, 1945); *Rubén Darío: Poesías completas,* ed. Alfonso Méndez Plancarte (Madrid, 1961); all references in this article are to the 1961 edition by Méndez Plancarte (hereinafter called P.C.) unless otherwise stated.

[2] See E. Anderson-Imbert, "Voluntad de Innovación en Rubén Darío," *La Nación,* (Buenos Aires, March 4, 1951), and *Rubén Darío; Poesía,* ed. Ernesto Mejía Sánchez, Fondo de Cultura Económica (Mexico, 1952).

[3] Mejía Sánchez, *Ibid.,* p. xi.

[4] P.C., p. 699.

[5] *Vida y Obra de Juan Ramón Jiménez* (Madrid, 1957).

[6] Octosyllabic verse with second and fourth lines in assonance.

[7] P.C., p. 168.

[8] Juan Ramón Jiménez: *Pájinas Escojidas,* ed. Ricardo Gullón, Editorial Gredos (Madrid, 1958), p. 21. This book has been translated into English by Eloïse Roach and published by the University of Texas Press (Austin, 1962).

[9] New York, 1917.

[10] Sainz de Robles, *op. cit.,* p. 59.

[11] P.C., pp. 561–562.

[12] *Ibid.,* p. 562.

[13] Quoted by Max Henríquez Ureña, *Breve historia del Modernismo,* Mexico, 1962, p. 94.

[14] See "Martí en Darío", in *Cuba Contemporánea,* January 1925.

[15] Eight-syllable quatrain with rhyme abba or abab.

[16] P.C., pp. 1071–1072.

[17] *José Martí, Versos* (New York, 1962).

[18] P.C., p. 8.

[19] *Ibid.,* pp. 17–18.

[20] *Ibid.,* p. 69.

[21] *Ibid.,* p. 176.

[22] *Ibid.,* pp. 195–196.

[23] *Ibid.,* p. 99.

[24] *Ibid.,* pp. 512–513.

[25] *Poesías,* Madrid, 1885.

[26] Santiago de Chile, 1938.

[27] See the Sainz de Robles' edition of *Obras poéticas completas* (Madrid: 1945).

[28] "Las humanidades de Rubén Darío. Años de aprendizaje", in *Libro Jubilar de Alfonso Reyes* (Mexico, 1956).

[29] P.C., p. 123.

[30] In Spanish: *dodecasílabo de seguidilla.*

[31] A stanza composed of five eight-syllable lines and employing two rhymes.

[32] P.C., p. 137.

[33] *Ibid.,* p. 138.

[34] *Ibid.,* p. 374.

[35] *Ibid.,* p. 439.

[36] *Ibid.*, p. 447.
[37] *Ibid.*, p. 1036.
[38] *Ibid.*, p. 1039.
[39] *Ibid.*
[40] *Ibid.*, p. 1044.
[41] *Ibid.*, p. 1045.
[42] *Ibid.*, p. 1024.
[43] *Ibid.*, p. 1028.

Director artístico : LEO MERELO ❧ Administradores : ALFRED & ARMAND GUID

MUNDIAL
MAGAZINE

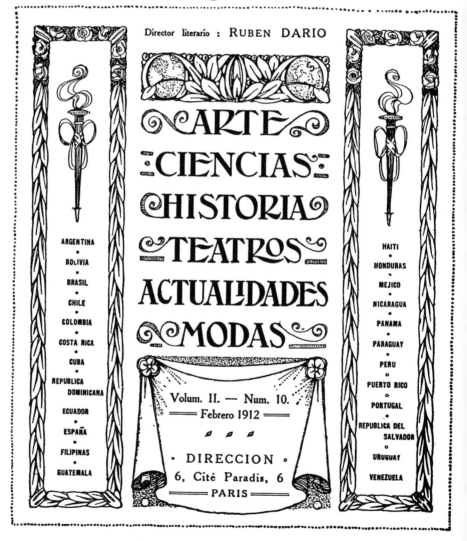

Director literario : RUBEN DARIO

ARTE
CIENCIAS
HISTORIA
TEATROS
ACTUALIDADES
MODAS

ARGENTINA
•
BOLIVIA
•
BRASIL
•
CHILE
•
COLOMBIA
•
COSTA RICA
•
CUBA
•
REPUBLICA
DOMINICANA
•
ECUADOR
•
ESPAÑA
•
FILIPINAS
•
GUATEMALA

HAITI
•
HONDURAS
•
MEJICO
•
NICARAGUA
•
PANAMA
•
PARAGUAY
•
PERU
o
PUERTO RICO
o
PORTUGAL
•
REPUBLICA DEL
SALVADOR
o
URUGUAY
•
VENEZUELA

Volum. II. — Num. 10.
Febrero 1912

• DIRECCION •
6, Cité Paradis, 6
PARIS

[Sample cover of the review edited in Paris by Darío.]

ALLEN W. PHILLIPS

RUBÉN DARÍO AND VALLE-INCLÁN: THE STORY OF A LITERARY FRIENDSHIP

translated by Esther W. Phillips

ON THE OCCASION OF THE DOUBLE centenary of Rubén Darío and Valle-Inclán, we propose in this study to offer a few considerations about the firm friendship, literary and personal, which existed between the two writers from the moment of their first meetings in Spain in 1899 to 1914, when Darío left for America on his last and final journey. Up to now, whatever has been said about this deep friendship, well known to everyone, does not go beyond generalities, and we hope therefore to indicate here, with greater exactitude and on the basis of appropriate documentation, the extent of their mutual admiration, manifest, as we shall see later, in many forms.*

* After this lecture had been translated, I received further information concerning the literary friendship between Darío and Valle-Inclán. Antonio Odriozola kindly sent me his article "Una desconocida dedicatoria de Valle-Inclán a Rubén Darío," published in *ABC*, July 11, 1967, reproducing the inscription borne by the second edition of *Sonata de estío* (Madrid, 1906). The inscription, later deleted, reads as follows: "A Rubén Darío: con toda mi admiración y mi amistad." Odriozola points out that this was Valle's way of reciprocating since the Nicaraguan had sent him from Paris his "Soneto autumnal al Marqués de Bradomín," which appeared as frontispiece to the second edition of *Sonata de otoño* (1905).

More important, though almost unknown, are some lines written by Darío apparently between 1899 and 1900, in which he refers to his Spanish friend. There is no doubt that they precede the well-known commentary entitled "Algunas notas sobre Valle Inclán" and yet, in them, Darío not only recreates Valle's personality but also reveals interesting insights about the novel esthetic prose-style of works such as *Epitalamio* (". . . a precious little book [*librito bijou*] whose only blemish might be the excessive emulation of Gabriele D'Annunzio and its exaggeration of the delicate") and *Femeninas* ("This is the first instance in which over a correctly written Spanish narrative passes the shadow of French birds in flight"). The text also includes allusions to two other works then in progress: *Tierra caliente* ("reminiscences of travels in [Spanish] America") and *Adega*, in the first chapters of which, already published in journals, Darío finds ". . . the same mannered qualities, the same concerns with plasticity and rhythm, the recognizable devices and the artfulness of D'Annunzio." These lines have been published by Dionisio Gamallo Fierros in *Revista de Occidente*, IV, 44–45 (Nov.–Dec. 1966), pp. 362–363.

Closely united by their devotion to art and by the same aesthetic preoccupations, Darío and Valle are both essentially creators of an individual style. It is true that the Spanish writer came relatively late to literature and that he elaborated part of his early work under the obvious influence of the renovation wrought by Modernism. Soon and progressively, however, he withdrew from a style really foreign to him, passing beyond the aristocratic exquisiteness inherited from Darío and other models of the epoch, to forge his own manner, the style of the later *esperpentos*, which belong to his last and most characteristic period. And it is precisely writers like Unamuno, Juan Ramón Jiménez and Alfonso Reyes who recognize Valle-Inclán's linguistic creativeness. To say that he begins a part of his work with a clearly modernist imprint is not to deny the great originality of his talent, apparent in his first books and carried thence, incorporated with new qualities, into an art that is personal and modernist at the same time. In spite of this filial tie, Valle later departed from the modernist inheritance, as far as outer manifestation is concerned, to enter the regional, time-honored territory of his own tradition. We are well aware of the difficulty of synthesizing adequately the aesthetic trajectory of a writer as complex as Valle-Inclán. Only as an approximation is the habitual formula valid: from *modernismo* to *esperpentismo*. Or this other: from impressionism to expressionism. That is to say, an evolution which starts from an aristocratic aesthetic and the exquisite preciosity of a literature finding inspiration more in art than in life (the *Sonatas*), to reach later on a more transcendent human expression, less gratuitous and less frivolous (the *esperpentos*). Keeping strictly to these two simplifying formulas would mean passing over significant intermediate stages: the pastoral *Flor de santidad* (1904) and *Aromas de leyenda* (1907); the stage of the first *Comedias bárbaras* (*Aguila de blasón* 1907, *Romance de lobos* 1908); that of the three historical novels of the Carlist cycle whose main interest lies in their being an antecedent of those of *Ruedo ibérico*; and lastly certain stories of varying dates, related either to his legendary and mystical style or to the more violent and barbaric one. Nor should we forget new excursions into a scene, still modernist and Versaillesque, in *Cuento de abril* (1909) and *La marquesa Rosalinda* (1913). This last is a transitional work which, with its burlesque tone, anticipates the new attitudes that are to appear very clearly in 1919 with the publication of *La pipa de kif*, a book which is, in turn, an unmistakable forerunner of Valle's modes of expression and thematic preoccupation in his final period. On the other hand there are those who see the work of the Spanish writer as merely a progressive *esperpentización* of reality, discerning from an earlier time scattered elements which will later coagulate and take first place in the genre of the *esperpentos*.

However, through the years and despite many changes in his work, Valle-Inclán always remains true to his profound literary friendship with Darío, who died precisely at the moment when the course of his Spanish friend's writing was about to change. We should like to bring up here a testimony which proves the continuing respect and admiration that Valle felt for the American poet. Angel Lázaro remembers how he and Rivas Cherif used to accompany Valle back to his house in the early hours of the morning. When asked if he still admired Darío in spite of poetic evolution from Modernism to the present, he answered: [1]

Rubén Darío is our great lyric poet. Before him we had none, none in our language. We had, yes, great dramatic poets in Calderón and Lope; but a lyric poet of this dimension, a lyric poet like Petrarch or Dante, this we did not have until Rubén Darío appeared with his great orchestration. Darío—he said it himself—is the complete lyre.

Let us now go on to observe the beginnings of this intimate personal and literary friendship.

Meetings: testimony and anecdotes

Rubén Darío arrived in Spain for the second time on the first of January 1899, commissioned by *La Nación* of Buenos Aires to comment in his chronicles, later collected in the volume *España contemporánea* (1901), on the situation of the country directly after the national disaster of 1898. Let us think for a moment about the date of his arrival in the Peninsula. The triumph of Modernism had been consolidated: Darío himself had published three brilliant books and American youth had rallied to him almost unconditionally. He was, then, at that moment, a consecrated figure of the new literature, and his supremacy was soon acknowledged by the Spanish writers who, in their turn and in their own way, were only a little later to revolutionize Peninsular letters.

Another great friend of Darío and Valle, Juan Ramón Jiménez, who it might be said in passing has written some of the most penetrating pages known about the American master, remembers the time of Darío's second residence in Spain in this way: [2]

But Rubén Darío, synthesis of all this new French poetry, loved Spain like a child, and came to Spain loaded with what he could give her: poetry . . . Rubén Darío lives on in Madrid with the same rank of journalist as Martí, his predecessor on *La Nación* and in Spain; a new Martí, another in love with Spain, in revolt body and soul against injustice. Rubén Darío was considered friend and master by a part of the generation of '98, influenced as they were by some of *los raros*, by Rubén Darío and other rare souls: Ibsen, Nietzsche, Maeterlinck . . . Jacinto Benevente, then chief of the renascence, admired him frankly; Ramón del Valle-Inclán read him, re-read him, quoted and then copied him; others including cognate painters, surrounded him, spoiled him, loved him, treated him like a big child with genius. The youngest aspiring poets sought him out. Villaespesa served him as page, and I observed him from a little further off. Rubén Darío himself kept giving us books received from his Modernist friends in America. . . .

The critic Fernández Almagro, biographer of Valle, does not himself hesitate to point out the importance of Darío's presence in Madrid, and shows the relation of the Nicaraguan poet to Valle much as Juan Ramón Jiménez did in the fragment quoted above:[3]

Present at all the conversations of writers who, in flying patrol, formed the *tertulias* of the Café de Madrid or of the Inglés, or of the Horchatería de Candela, was inevitably Rubén Darío. His *Prosas profanas* arrived from Buenos Aires in waves of extraordinary sound. There are some who have known him personally ever since his first journey to Madrid, in 1892, for the ceremonies commemorating the discovery of America. And they will all know him when he returns to Madrid in the early days of 1899 . . . Happy for Valle-Inclán the revelation of this pilgrim friend. They recognize in each other mutual aesthetic tendencies, while in the impassible simplicity of the Spaniard from Nicaragua the impulsive Spaniard of Galicia finds a healthy counterpart.

In his long years of residence in Europe, Darío had made many Spanish friends,[4] and among them perhaps none closer and more brotherly than Valle, who so much admired the American poet. They surely met in 1899, the year in which the Galician writer lost his arm, and it is very possible that they were brought together by another common friend, the unfortunate writer, the picturesque figure of *fin-de-siècle* Bohemia, Alejandro Sawa, then recently returned to Spain from several years' residence in France. Sawa, friend of Verlaine and the symbolist poets, had been, with Gómez Carrillo, the assiduous companion of Darío on his nocturnal adventures in the

Latin Quarter during his first Parisian journey in 1893.[5] Darío, at first disillusioned by the lamentable condition of Spanish literature, speaks years later in his autobiography of the first days spent in the *corte* and calls to mind former companions and new friends, singling out Benavente, Baroja, Maeztu, Ruiz Contreras and, among the young, the Machado brothers, Palomero, Villaespesa, Juan Ramón Jiménez, et cetera.[6] It is perhaps surprising that Valle was not mentioned in his first list, but after evoking Campoamor, Pardo Bazán, Valera and others he had known earlier, he says, a little further on: "We had indescribable culinary sessions, of ambrosia and above all nectar, with the great Ramón María del Valle Inclán, Palomero, Bueno . . ."[7] Nor is it superfluous to mention here, that, walking with Valle in the surroundings of the Casa de Campo of Madrid in the spring of 1899, Darío met for the first time Francisca Sánchez, the humble peasant girl who was to be the distinguished poet's faithful companion for so many years. And once his apartment was established in Marqués de Santa Ana street, Valle came regularly to the house.[8]

In spite of frequent absences of both Darío and Valle from the city, at different times, there must have been many meetings in the Madrid cafés, where literary reunions had their great influence, long since recognized, on the development of Spanish letters of the twentieth century. These took place no doubt in the *Café de Madrid*, in the *Nuevo Café de Levante*, in *El Colonial* and in many others not mentioned here. Both writers, as is well known, were especially devoted to café life: one silent and drinking deep, the other rather more aggressive and exaggerated in speech and gesture. By means of the recollections of other *contertulianos* it is relatively easy to document the encounters of Darío and Valle on the café benches, but we will be satisfied with indicating a few trustworthy testimonials to prove these friendly contacts. From Juan Ramón Jiménez, whose pages of memorabilia about the period must again be emphasized, we have an important piece of prose, never sufficiently praised, not only as a precious document of the time but also for its great beauty of style. We are referring, of course, to "Castillo de quema," that impressive lyric portrait of Valle, published by the poet of Moguer in 1936, the year of his friend's death. Let us look at a few fragments from this substantive and beautiful prose. First, Juan Ramón recreates a characteristic reunion of writers about 1899, at which the principal actors are Darío and Valle:[9]

Valle . . . was reading, declaiming, from a number of *La Ilustración Española y Americana*, the Parnassian alexandrines of *Cosas del Cid* by Rubén Darío. . . . All that matters is alcohol whatever the distillations and labels. Rubén Darío asks again and again for "whiskey and soda" or three star Martel cognac. Everyone here undoubtedly a personality, but J.R.J. concentrates only on Rubén Darío listening ecstatically and on Valle reciting . . . Rubén Darío . . . say only "admirable" and smiles a little with contracted lips. Valle simple, plain, resonant, upright, reads, smiles openly, speaks, smiles, calls out, shouts, smiles, exaggerates, smiles, gets up, smiles, comes and goes, smiles, enters and exits. They go out. The others repeat, "admirable, admirable," in various tones. "Admirable" is the high word of the epoch, "imbecile" the low. With "admirable" and "imbecile" Modernist criticism is constructed. Rubén Darío, for example, admirable; Echegaray, imbecile.

Juan Ramón then refers to the years 1901–1902 when he was in the *Sanatorio del Rosario* and to the writers, Darío and Valle among them, who visited him there, incorporating in this prose important literary considerations about his book *Rimas*, published in 1902, and the aesthetic change it represented. He affirms again the ascendancy of Rubén Darío and Valle, saying: ". . . And Valle influences everyone, like Rubén Darío and with Rubén Darío, who influenced him so greatly, and whom he respects, makes known, celebrates and talks about so contagiously . . ."[10]

And the occasion described by Juan Ramón Jiménez was not by any means the only one when Valle declaimed the master's verses. It has been recorded that at a later date, autumn of 1905, Darío used to attend the *tertulia* at the *Café Colonial*, where he joined old friends, among them the unrepentant dipsomaniac Sawa, and how once again Valle gave a recital, this time directly from the galley proofs of *Cantos de vida y esperanza*, which were just being corrected at the café table, of stanzas of "Canción de otoño en primavera" and "Marcha triunfal."[11] One more bit of evidence will serve to complete the theme of Darío and Valle in the café. It comes from Ricardo Baroja. Although he seems to have made a slight mistake in the date, Baroja has recreated a typical scene in the *Café de Madrid* with the following words:[12]

—And all the people arriving, are they poets?
—All of them. Some of them write on the table covers, others invent novels and stories. In short . . . poets—and the waiter, after a pronouncement,

comes up to the person with the long beard who summoned him by striking with his cane on the marble table, at the risk of scarring it.

The young man with the Merovingian hair was, as I learned later, Ramón del Valle-Inclán.

A few young men had entered the café and sat down near the poet at nearby tables.

. . . .

Another gentleman, a little older, enters and, walking with that springy roll characteristic of people born in a tropical climate, approaches the group. He is corpulent, with a large head. His black hair has a slight tendency to be kinky. Short arms, small hands and feet. He sits down in the chief place. From my seat opposite the newcomer I observe him. In his olive skin the little eyes open only slightly, very black, veiled by that vague nostalgia lent by equatorial sun to men of the Negroid race. His gestures are slow; he seems to be paralyzed by the waistcoat and jacket squeezing his torso. He hardly speaks, hardly seems to listen either; but when Palomero shouts some sarcasm in his cavernous voice, when Benavente makes an epigram and Valle-Inclán a pronouncement, the paralyzed personage murmurs:

—Admirable! admirable!—and changes his Buddha-like immobility to ecstasy.

Past the thick lips of his silent mouth flow rivers of beer, and as the table fills with empty bottles the drinker's eyes grow more opaque.

The indefatigable drinker is the poet Rubén Darío.

If indeed poetic tributes and Valle's correspondence, matters shortly to be explored, give further proof of the sustained mutual admiration of the two writers, we do not want to close this section without emphasizing other facts which of themselves are useful for measuring the extent of this literary and friendly relationship. For example, Francisco Contreras, friend and biographer of the American poet, speaks of his calls on Darío in Madrid somewhere around 1910, and then states:[13]

. . . One afternoon when I went again to see him, accompanied by Valle-Inclán, he was more animated. . . . There was a moment of very agreeable talk, but certainly dominated by the Spanish eloquence of the Marqués de Bradomín. I remember that, as we were leaving, in the green half light of early evening, Valle-Inclán said: Rubén is a genius. His observation has nothing to do with that of common writers, like Blasco Ibáñez, for instance. He perceives the mysterious interrelation of things. . . .

For reasons to be seen later on, we should like to underline the phrase
in which Valle alludes to his friend's extraordinary capacity to perceive *the mysterious interrelation of things*. Other words also of the
Galician writer reaffirm and insist upon this exceptional quality in
Darío for penetrating the mysterious: [14]

Darío was a child. Immensely good. He lived in a kind of blessed religious
dread. He saw things of the other world continuously. Even better, there
were no objects not projected thither. I repeat that he was a child. Not
proud, nor spiteful, nor ambitious. He had none of the angelic sins. Further
removed than anyone from satanic sin, he knew only the sins of the flesh.
His soul was pure—completely, utterly pure.

In this connection certain observations of Valle's, made immediately
after the Nicaraguan's death and collected by Sassone, are interesting
in themselves: [15]

Have you read of it? Poor Rubén!
Don Ramón del Valle-Inclán gave me the sad news, his wizard eyes
reddened with weeping.
Horrible! With whom now shall I discuss my *Lámpara maravillosa?*
Rubén would have had his whiskey, I my hashish, and we would have
plunged deep into mystery. He was a man in contact with the mysterious.
And while the master of the *Sonatas* spoke thus, a few tears shone on the
crystals of his eyeglasses and his beard trembled beneath his sorrowful
voice.

There can be no doubt that the death of Rubén Darío was a profound
grief to Valle-Inclán. Melchor Fernández Almagro recalls how he
came to know Valle personally on February 7, 1916, and how in his
tertulia at the *Café del Gato Negro* he paid tribute to the poet so
recently vanished: "Valle-Inclán turned the whole conversation into
the most fiery encomiums of the person and work of Rubén Darío, expressed . . . in terms of great emotion; and nothing impressed me more
in all that Don Ramón said than the deeply sincere grief-stricken
tone and the fine declamatory art with which he recited the 'Responso
a Verlaine' . . ."[16] In the year of Rubén Darío's death, Valle went to
Paris. As a guide he had Pedro Salinas, and we know that he insisted
on being taken to see the house where Darío lived in the rue
d'Herschelle, thus to pay homage posthumously to the memory of his
dear friend.[17]

Poetic tributes

On more than one occasion Rubén Darío revealed his great talent for painting in verse the portrait of a poet. We all remember, for instance, the wonderful verses that succeed in expressing with singular skill the intimate essence of Antonio Machado, a poet more and more admired every day, and we cannot resist the temptation to quote a fragment from the beginning of the poem:

> Misterioso y silencioso
> iba una y otra vez.
> Su mirada era tan profunda
> que apenas se podía ver.

And let us not forget that the Spanish poet in turn wrote two poems to the Nicaraguan.

To Darío we owe also three sincere tributes in verse to Valle-Inclán, which not only treat with authority certain aspects of his work but show as well profound admiration for the man and his writing. Very famous is the "Soneto autumnal al Marqués de Bradomín" (1904) collected in *Cantos de vida y esperanza*, admirable verses which really deserve complete quotation here. In them, from Paris, Rubén accompanies his friend in his development as a writer and affirms aesthetic solidarity with him. This is the poem in which Darío, as he said years later, extols the aristocratic thought of a great talent of the Spanish world.[18]

The second sonnet for Valle-Inclán, the one sometimes called "iconographic" and which appears in *El canto errante* (1907), seems to us less successful, but here are a few significant lines:

> Tengo la sensación de que siento y que vivo
> a su lado una vida más intensa y más dura.

> Este gran don Ramón del Valle-Inclán me inquieta,
> y a través del zodíaco de mis versos actuales
> se me esfuma en radiosas visiones de poeta,

> O se me rompe en un fracaso de cristales.

In Darío's own opinion,[19] this poem for don Ramón del Valle-Inclán does not succeed in expressing the complexity of the personality, but it does appear in Valle's first book of verse, *Aromas de leyenda* (1907). This latter work is intimately related to *Flor de santidad* which prolongs, on a mystical and legendary base, Christian and pastoral, certain Galician motifs already present in Valle's earlier prose. Because of its musicality and the vague lyric suggestiveness, more symbolist than Parnassian, as well as for its careful formal elaboration, the verse

of *Aromas* evinces an assimilated and very personal Modernism, far
from mere exotic and ornamental externals. Furthermore, Valle uses
metric and stanzaic forms made fashionable by Modernism: verses of
nine syllables, for instance, and tercets on a single rhyme. Here is revealed the age-old soul of Galicia insofar as pertains to poetic mystery.
Valle perceives sensuously, and through all the senses, the native landscape; he shows his sympathy for the humble and destitute people of
Galicia; and in this simple poetry, in minor mode, he gathers vernacu-
lar materials and displays a Franciscan attitude. Gentle poetry, without violence, composed on a nostalgic note, it is regional in the best
sense of the term, while Valle does not ever abandon his position as an
artist. When Darío writes his "Notas sobre Valle-Inclán" he gives us
the following version of his friend's whole work: [20]

Whatever in the poetic work of Valle-Inclán seems most fantastic and
obscure, has a basis of reality. Life stands before the poet, and the poet
transforms it, subtilizes, elevates, multiplies it; in a word, deifies it with all
its inward power and music. He who has no *daimon* cannot do this; and
for this reason I have maintained the superiority of Unamuno to other men
who write purely formal and skillful lyrics.

In the same pages, which reveal great sympathy for Valle and his artistic expression, Darío comments in very favorable terms on the
poetry of *Aromas*, noting their exquisite softness and rhythmic movement.

Later, in 1911, when Rubén was editor of *El Mundial*, and in sad
circumstances of which we shall speak later, the Nicaraguan poet,
again in Paris, sent the often-requested prologue in verse to Valle's
Voces de gesta, the "Balada laudatoria a don Ramón del Valle-Inclán,"
a poem which appears, with its title slightly changed, in modern editions of the aforementioned poetic drama. It is significant that in the
poem the author emphasizes themes and tones characteristic of the
work of his friend, to whom he was united, as he says here, by the
sacred influence of Apollo and the Moon. For the sake of its value as
characterization let us give here the first stanzas:

> Del país de sueño, tinieblas, brillos,
> donde crecen plantas, flores extrañas,
> entre los escombros de los castillos,
> junto a las laderas de las montañas
> donde los pastores en sus cabañas
> rezan, cuando al fuego dormita el can,
> y donde las sombras antiguas van

por cuevas de lobos y de raposas,
ha traído cosas muy misteriosas
DON RAMON MARIA DEL VALLE INCLAN.

Cosas misteriosas, trágicas, raras,
de cuentos obscuros de los antaños,
de amores terribles, crímenes, daños,
como entre vapores de solfataras,
caras sanguinarias, pálidas caras,
gritos ululantes, pena y afán,
infaustos hechizos, aves que van
bajo la amenaza del gerifalte,
dice en versos ricos de oro y esmalte
DON RAMON MARIA DEL VALLE INCLAN.

After Rubén Darío's death, Valle published in 1919 *La pipa de kif*,
a revolutionary book and a significant landmark in his literary development. Here it is that he speaks for the first time of the "musa
moderna", the new aesthetic of distortion and caricature, which is to
predominate in all his later work. With his notorious capacity for re-
newal, Valle demands for himself new standards: he penetrates the
street scene and creates a motley setting of circus and fair populated
by strolling players, thieves and other popular types. Left behind are
the sumptuous linguistics; the language becomes strident, picturesque
and plebeian. The tone is ironic and clever and the poet takes up a
position facing the dissonance of the world. It is, besides, a work pointing toward the avant-garde and to the poetic games played in the years
after 1920. In spite of such great changes of theme and tone, it is significant that Valle does not forget Rubén Darío, naming him directly
in two poems of the book.[21] In the composition "¡Aleluya!", the writer
makes fun of the academicians and the purists who are about to be
terrified by his acrobatic verses and lyric capers. At this very moment
he in turn salutes Rubén Darío, saying:

Darío me alarga en la sombra
Una mano, y a Poe me nombra.

Maga estrella de pentarquía
Sobre su pecho anuncia el día.

Su blanca túnica de Esenio
Tiene las luces del selenio.

¡Sombra de misterioso delta
Vibra en tu honor mi gaita celta!

¡Tu amabas las rosas, el vino
y los amores del camino!

Cantor de Vida y Esperanza,
Para ti toda mi loanza.

Por el alba de oro, que es tuya,
¡Aleluya! ¡Aleluya! ¡Aleluya!

Of course in the transcribed verses are encased various textual quotations from Darío. In parenthesis, we should like to point out that also in *La pipa de kif* Valle incorporates his own "sinfonía en gris mayor",[22] arranged for the modern muse. We refer to the composition entitled "Marina norteña," which includes the following illustrative verses:

Escruta el mar con la mirada quieta
Un marinero desde el muelle. Brilla
Con el traje de aguas su silueta
Entre la boina gris, toda amarilla.

Viento y lluvia de mar. La luna flota
Tras el nublado. Apenas se presiente,
Lejana, la goleta que derrota
Cortando el arco de la luz poniente.

Se ilumina el cuartel. Vagas siluetas
Cruzan tras las ventanas enrejadas,
Y en el gris de la tarde las cornetas
Dan su voz como rojas llamaradas.

. . . .

Las olas rompen con crestón de espuma
Bajo el muelle. Los barcos cabecean
Y agigantados en el caos de bruma
Sus jarcias y sus cruces fantasean.

La triste sinfonía de las cosas
Tiene en la tarde un grito futurista:
De una nueva emoción y nuevas glosas
Estéticas, se anuncia la conquista.

Letters of Valle-Inclán to Rubén Darío

In this section we shall concern ourselves rather summarily with what has so far been published of Valle's correspondence with Darío, letters confirming once more the cordiality that always characterized the personal relationship of the two writers. As we shall see, one of these communications goes beyond the mere theme of friendship, since in it is given some precious information concerning the real genesis of Valle's *Luces de bohemia*. In 1943 Alberto Ghiraldo published four letters written by Valle to Darío,[23] and more recently Dictino Alvarez Hernández, who had at his disposal the documents belonging to the Seminario-Archivo Rubén Darío in Madrid, has enriched this correspondence by bringing to light seven other Valle letters and four of his wife's, Josefina Blanco, all of them addressed to the Nicaraguan poet.[24] At the same time it is well to note here that the archives mentioned, very rich in letters *to* Darío, are on the other hand relatively poor as regards letters from the poet himself.

Most of the letters making up this short correspondence are concerned with editorial matters. The first, undated, reproduced by Ghiraldo, treats of an introduction in behalf of M. Chaumier, translator of *Romance de lobos* and Consul General of France in Spain. Apparently, at an earlier date, Valle had written to Darío asking him to influence Rémy de Gourmont so as to assure publication of the work in *Le Mercure de France*. And actually, a few years later, in 1914, under the title of *La geste des loups: Comédie barbare en trois journées*, it appeared in the French review. It is worth mentioning that, in introducing M. Chaumier, Valle wrote: ". . . in whom you will find a true connoisseur of our literature, who knows how to look even into the esoteric depth of your verses that seem so arcane to many of our academics, critics and poets."[25] Two communications of 1907[26] reveal to what extent Valle tried to intervene in the publication of *El canto errante*. From a letter of the publisher, Gregorio Pueyo, dated August 10, 1907, and collected by Ghiraldo,[27] we learn that Darío himself had written Valle about this matter. In his efforts Valle took great pains to place the original of the book with Pueyo, and even thought of taking charge himself of the proposed edition. It turned out, nevertheless, that Darío's new work was published ultimately by the firm of Pérez Villavivencio, which Valle, on a postcard dated later, described as "a collection of thieves", who had cheated him of a thousand pesetas.[28]

In 1911 began the publication of the *Mundial Magazine*, an undertaking destined to bring painful problems to Darío in his position as director of such a sumptuous review. Two letters copied by Ghiraldo[29] and various others published by Alvarez[30] treat precisely of the insertion of *Voces de gesta* in *Mundial* and the payment thereof, the price being left by the author for Darío to determine. The three acts of the work were, in effect, printed in that review, published in Paris. In the correspondence Valle asks Darío urgently, over and over again, for the promised prologue in verse for his books. For a time the printing of the *de luxe* edition intended by Valle was held up because the invocation to go in the first pages did not come. Although it has not been possible to authenticate the fact, we suspect that the first edition of *Voces de gesta* (1911) appeared without Darío's verses, but in the second, published the next year, the "Balada laudatoria que envía al autor el alto poeta Rubén" was included.

Of greater literary interest and truly sensational for reasons to be shown later, is a letter written by Valle to Darío in 1909. The first to reproduce it was Oliver Belmás[31] and it was later published in the book, already quoted, of Dictino Alvarez.[32] The most eloquent passage is the following:

Dear Darío:

I come to you after having been at the house of our poor Alejandro Sawa. I wept over the dead man, for him, for myself and for all poor poets. I can do nothing; nor can you; but if a few of us join together we could do something.

Alejandro leaves an unfinished book. The best he ever wrote. A journal of hopes and tribulations.

The frustration of his desire to publish it and a letter cancelling a contract of sixty pesetas for contributions to *El Liberal* drove him mad these last days. Madness of despair. He wanted to kill himself. His was the end of a king of tragedy: mad, blind and raging.

Now, neither Oliver nor Alvarez seems to have remarked on the literary importance of these honest lines, motivated by the sad circumstances of Sawa's death, a friend, as already indicated, of both writers. Here, then, is the true genesis, in 1909, of *Luces de bohemia*, an *esperpentic* work published years later, in 1920, created out of authentic reality and inspired by a concrete painful event that in fact moved Valle quite deeply.[33]

Let us see, very briefly, how certain details of such a lamentable event and the reaction Valle felt at Sawa's tragic end, passed with time into his creative work. As is well known, the character of Max Estrella, protagonist of *Luces de bohemia*, is none other than Sawa, who wrote several naturalistic novels and a volume of short pieces, published posthumously with the significant title: *Iluminaciones en la sombra* (1910). This is a miscellaneous collection of pieces, compositions of different dates, which serve to complete the intimate portrait of the unhappy Sawa. The book is, as Valle said in the letter already quoted, "a diary of hopes and tribulations." Mostly, we here add, tribulations of the blind, impoverished writer.

In *Luces de bohemia* Valle calls up the bitter reality described in his letter of 1909: in the first scene we learn that Max, the blind poet with the classic profile, has received a letter from the *Buey Apis* dismissing him. He even thinks, talking with his French wife, of mutual suicide because of having lost the twenty *duros* paid him for his articles. The picture of Sawa which Valle gives us here is essentially accurate, and even in some small details concerning his family situation, the author makes use of what we know of Sawa. In other details, however, the apparent suicide of the wife and daughter after Max's death, for instance, historic truth does not seem to interest the author. In *Luces de bohemia*, then, we not only accompany the unrepentant Bohemian, gesturing wildly, in his eternal wandering through the streets and taverns of Madrid, but witness also the strange circumstances of his death, the same that Pío Baroja, surely not favorable in general to Sawa, evoked in *El árbol de la ciencia*. Thus we come to know the desperate blind poet, Max Estrella, in the last hours of his life, accompanied always by his dog-friend Don Latino, (is Valle perhaps remembering here León, Sawa's real dog, who used to follow him through the streets of Madrid?), the same Don Latino who would take charge, as he said, of publishing the writings of his dead master.

The action of the piece takes place in "an absurd Madrid, brilliant and starving", and Valle gives us with consummate skill the chronicle of this whole motley literary world he knew so well, naturally allowing himself great liberty in regard to dates and outward events. With very few exceptions,[34] critics have not concerned themselves with the artistic value of such an accomplished book, but preferred to call attention to the important conversation on aesthetic theory in the twelfth scene, in which the reader attends the baptismal ceremonies of certain artistic procedures, some of them already long present in Valle's work and now openly solidified in the *esperpento*. In *Luces de bohemia* we see, in one form or another, many qualities of style which characterize the aesthetic predominant in his last works: the bitter attitude and the resentment produced by the farce of the actual Spain, the technique of caricature and systematic distortion of people and things, and the violent popular language of the lower classes. Even the blind classic poet, bearing an echo of Homer and Oedipus, is caught in a deforming mirror, contorting and degrading himself in one unworthy posture after another. This work, merciless in its biting satire, had its true origin in personal grief, in an attitude towards incongruities in the world, and Valle has wept, as he says, "for him, for myself and for all miserable poets." In the theatrical spectacle Max Estrella keeps something of his tragic grandeur, but little by little outside circumstances destroy his dignity, and in the end he remains irremediably humiliated by a cruel reality. Nevertheless let us remember Valle's words in the letter quoted: "His was the end of a king of tragedy: mad, blind and raging." All this is true, but the tragic implications of the life and death of the unfortunate poet, drunken and rejected by almost all, tends to be "diluted" to a point by the grotesque vision Valle offers us of Max Estrella and the absurd world in which he moves. It would not be pointless to quote two sentences of Valle's referring to his protagonist: "Blindness is beautiful and noble in Homer. But in *Luces de bohemia* this very blindness is sad and lamentable because it is a question of a Bohemian poet, of Máximo Estrella."[35]

Luces de bohemia is enriched also by the most varied literary themes. A whole gallery of faces (writers, journalists, booksellers and publishers), some recognizable and some not, figure in the main body of the work. No less frequent are allusions to writers not directly actors in the play, and Valle intentionally incorporates in the dialogue aesthetic judgments and textual quotations.[36] Within the theme concerning us now, we need only call attention to the active role of Rubén Darío in a few scenes. As a character he appears in the ninth scene, taking place in the *Café Colón*, and talks with Max and Don Latino on literary matters, especially about celestial mathematics and theosophy. The following words are important:

RUBEN: I, too, am studying celestial mathematics.
DON LATINO: Excuse me then! Since, señor, even I am reduced to the extreme point of selling in instalments I am none the less an initiate of Gnosis and Magic.
RUBEN: I, too.
DON LATINO: I remember that you were getting somewhere.
RUBEN: I have sensed that Elementals are Consciences.

Later in the same scene he recites a few verses of "Peregrinaciones" (1915?), a poem never collected by Darío in book form and in which the Marqués de Bradomín appears. The Nicaraguan poet is presented again in the fourteenth scene of *Luces de bohemia*. It is a question of the funeral procession and Max's burial, and on this occasion he talks of death with the Marqués de Bradomín, already an old man. The portrait of Darío also is authentic: his silences and the laconic statements of "admirable," even to his "idol mask" and the "vast and sinister sadness sculptured in the likeness of Aztec idols." Significant, too, in its literary and personal context, is the noble letter already quoted that Vallo wrote Darío in 1909 about the pathetic death of Alejandro Sawa, whose figure, though partly legendary and on the outskirts of the literary revival, brought to a head by writers of greater talent, is still not devoid of interest.[37]

Traces of Darío in the work of Valle-Inclán

Looking back over the long road travelled up to now at the many evidences, some merely anecdotal and others more literary, that are useful in indicating the extent of literary and friendly relations between Darío and Valle-Inclán, there is definite interest in pointing out how different, concrete recollections of the Nicaraguan's work served Valle in the enrichment of his own writing. Verbal traces are innumerable and even thematic ones offer abundant harvest.[38] In showing some of these reminiscences, we are not unaware of the possibility of mutual influence, but for the moment let us limit ourselves to examining a few passages that seem derived from the influence Darío had on the Spanish writer.[39] We are definitely not proposing here a traditional study of literary sources, but for the moment merely wish to isolate a method of composition in Valle and the legitimate means by which an author inspires an initiated reader offering him an opportunity to be an accomplice of the creator himself. As is well known, Valle used to embroider his work with intentional and voluntary textual memories of other writers. Sometimes he did this to achieve a more biting satire, as in *Los cuernos de don Friolera, Las galas del difunto* and *Tirano Banderas*. At other times he did it for atmosphere and to offer authentic documentation for unfamiliar epochs. Of such is, of course, the already familiar case of accusation of plagiarism brought by Casares,[40] who found in the *Sonata de primavera* fragments taken directly from the memoirs of Casanova, a source admitted by Valle himself in the text of the work.[41] On the other hand, it is legitimate to believe, as stated by Emma Susana Speratti Piñero, who has so subtly studied particular sources and Valle's use of them, that he delighted also in mocking the learned and putting off the scent those near-sighted critics who jealously dedicated themselves to discovering immediate sources.[42] That is to say that on more than one occasion Valle intentionally made literature out of literature, often confessing by artful indications the paternity of the alien texts used in the great mosaic of his work.

As has been already said, certain works of Valle's first period, above all the *Sonatas*, show without obscuring the individuality of the author, a clear and decided Modernist influence. This juxtaposition persists, although with an important change of attitude, in later works like *Cuento de abril, La cabeza del dragón, La marquesa Rosalinda* and many others. In Valle's stories antedating the *Sonatas*, with their complicated elaboration, as is confirmed by Speratti Piñero in the case of the *Sonata de otoño*,[43] the one nearest to the same sensual and voluptuous style is "Augusta," collected later in *Corte de amor*.

No one can forget the refined and courtly ambience in which the characters of the *Sonatas* languidly move. To delightful frivolity and great elegance are added typical examples of *fin-de-siècle* decadence, as well as the constant search for rare and exquisite sensations. Valle cultivates the characteristic mixture of the profane and the sacred, a motif so dear to the Modernists, the two extremes being present in compositions like "El reino interior" and "Ite missa est" by Darío. And lastly, reality is embellished by many aesthetical procedures. As we all know, around this literature inspired more by art than life, gather many decorative materials of Modernism—swans and peacocks—and it would not be superfluous to mention here that concerning this precious style, essentially poetic and musical, Darío once wrote: "Valle-Inclán is called decadent because he writes a worked and polished prose of the finest formal excellence . . ."[44] All the same, the *Sonatas* are small masterpieces written in a manner now somewhat out of fashion, of which years later Valle himself made fun, and in which the author perhaps paid excessive tribute to the formalist literature of the age. It is not surprising, then, that much is owed to the ascendancy of Darío and to the many French authors they both knew. Many images seem to have a more or less direct reminiscence of Darío. For example, Valle writes in the *Sonata de invierno*: "With the warm chorus of the trumpets rose shrill neighing, and in the street resounded, valiant and martial, the clang of horses' hooves, that noble sound of arms and paladins belonging to the old romances." It is immediately clear how this synaesthetic image, several times elaborated in the same work and in later ones,[45] is related to certain verses of Darío's poem "Marcha triunfal".[46] Other fragments bear no less an echo of Darío and of the

Modernist motifs put in circulation by the American poet. Let us look at a few of the many that might be cited:[47]

(1) ... From the drawing room could be glimpsed the garden, motionless beneath the moon, which veiled in a pale clarity the languid tops of the cypresses and the balconies of the terrace, where in other days the peacock opened its chimeric and storied fan. (*Sonata de primavera*)

(2) The soft and gentle air, an air to conjure sighs, passed murmuring, and far away among the motionless myrtles, stirred the wavelets of a pool ... (*Sonata de primavera*)

(3) ... The salon was gilded in the French style, feminine and luxurious. Garlanded cupids, nymphs in lace, gallant hunters and stags with branching antlers peopled the tapestry on the wall, and on the consoles graceful groups in porcelain, pastoral dukes enlacing the flower-decked waists of peasant marquesses ... (*Sonata de primavera*)

(4) ... That night she howled in my arms like a faun of olden days ... (*Sonata de invierno*)

Furthermore, in the *Sonata de estío*, where there are clear allusions to Bécquer and Silva, Valle writes: "... with that smile which a poet of today would have called a winged strophe of snow and roses." Is this a definite reminiscence of Darío?

In 1904 Valle publishes *Flor de santidad*. He is quite conscious of having done something different and explains it in a letter to his friend Torcuato Ulloa.[48] The aristocratic world of the *Sonatas* has disappeared, and another has been substituted for it: primitive, elemental, age-old, popular. The background is Galician, a landscape nearly always sombre; the motifs are consistently superstitious and supernatural; the regionalism artistic and evocative, not descriptive; the structural axis of the short novel is the contrast established between the pious soul of Adega and the more sensual and vengeful one of the pilgrim. Although in *Flor de santidad* the merely literary and Parnassian element recedes, there is no doubt that Darío's prose is still influencing Valle's, as Raimundo Lida saw clearly.[49] In this work, more poem than novel, the same ideal of stylistic perfection persists, now at the service of a Galician theme, and an essential Modernism in process of transformation is revealed especially in the sustained lyrical beautifying of the landscape and the figure of Adega. In this accomplished work occurs one short passage which interests us here because it seems to carry an echo of Darío's "Sinfonía en gris mayor":

They went on in silence. The path was full of cloudy pools, reflecting the moon, and the frogs, chanting in that silver light their monotonous senile song at the brink, leapt into the water as soon as footsteps came near. . . .

The style in the three novels of the Carlist wars (1908–1909) wherein the main interest consists in their being a first step leading, years later, to the great novels of the *Ruedo Ibérico*,[50] does not in general continue the Modernism of earlier and later works. The exigencies of the subject are simply different. We should like, however, to call attention now to an interesting reminiscence of Darío which appears first in *El resplandor de la hoguera* and again in *Gerifaltes de antaño*, the last volume of the trilogy with a title taken directly from a verse of Darío.[51] In the first novel mentioned, the Field Marshall, Don Enrique España, moves with his staff to the palace of Redín, the property of an aged countess of the same name. In a few pages, slightly more Modernist in tone, Valle introduces us to the interior of the palace and to Eulalia, the granddaughter, companion to her venerable grandmother. This name does not appear here for the first time in Valle's work, but the following words are interesting:

Eulalia, if at any moment she was unobserved, would look at herself in the mirror, put a flower on her breast and, on her grandmother's clavichord play the waltz to which in other days she had so often danced when her parents gave parties at their palace in Madrid. . . .

And then a little further on:

O gay music scattered by that ancient clavichord full of sorrows! Eulalia had forgotten it, and suddenly thought she could hear it very far away, with the vagueness of a dream, under the glance of a hussar bearing on his dolman the cross of Santiago . . . without finishing the waltz she leans her forehead on the ivories of the clavichord which gives out a deep groan:
  —How mad! how mad! . . . and he married!

The traces of Darío are obvious: the poem "El Clavicordio de la abuela," a composition not included in *Prosas profanas*, where because of date and tone it might belong, but collected in *Poema del otoño y otros poemas* (1910) the heroine of which, the marquesita Rosalinda, gave Valle at a later time the title of his eighteenth-century farce. And, so the crossing of reminiscences may not elude us, in the last work of the series the Duke of Ordax calls the granddaughter "divine Eulalia," an epithet carrying us back again to "Era un aire suave."[52]

Between 1909 and 1914 Valle-Inclán published a series of books independent yet related, being works for the theatre in verse. If *Voces de gesta* (1912) is somewhat solemn in purpose, with tragic and epic overtones, the other pieces (*Cuento de abril*, 1909, and *La marquesa Rosalinda*, 1912) of that intermediate period show, in various degrees and intent, a certain Modernist residue, especially as regards their decorative background. In the delightful *Cuento de abril*, for instance, there is manifest a whole refined and courtly atmosphere: Provençal gardens propitious for love, fountains around which peacocks spread their tails, the chorus of *azafatas* (ladies-in-waiting) that play in this exotic and artificial world. Although the principal dramatic motive, surely very weak, is the opposition quickly established between the ascetic customs of Castile and the sensuality of the Court of Love presided over by the Princess Imberal, of greater interest is the fine and elegant atmosphere of affected discretion and gallantry, where the relation to aspects of *Prosas profanas* is clear. The following stanzas of "Preludio," for example, anticipate the tonality of this light and graceful theatrical work:[53]

La divina puerta dorada
del jardín azul de ensueño
os abre mi vara encantada
por deciros un cuento abrileño.

. . . .

Bajo un vuelo de abejas de oro,
las gentiles rosas de Francia,
al jardín azul y sonoro,
dan el tesoro de su fragancia.

Fragancia de labios en flor,
que al reír modulan un trino,
labios que besa el ruiseñor
con la luz de su trino divino.

¡Oh, la fragancia de la risa
fragante escala musical,
que al alma leve la brisa,
le brinda su verso de coral!

¡Oh, rosa de la risa loca,
que rima el teclado de su son

con la púrpura de la boca
y las fugas del Ave-Ilusión!

At this transitional stage there emerge two of Valle's works that must be judged supremely important, although in fact they have been very little studied: *La marquesa Rosalinda* and *La cabeza del dragón*, the latter written in prose in 1909 although not collected in book form until 1914 with a slight change of title.[54] The interesting thing, for purposes of this article, is to point out that in both farces persists the Modernist décor which Valle-Inclán is soon to abandon forever. The thing that differentiates these works from earlier ones is the author's new posture. A definitely humorous and scoffing attitude tinges the Modernism of *La marquesa Rosalinda*. The viewpoint, grotesque and jovial at the same time, will change in time to sarcasm and grimace of the later years. Even earlier, in *La cabeza del dragón*, a *farsa infantil* as the author later baptised it, there are perceptible indications of new stylistic modes, in bits turned frankly towards caricature, although there is still lacking the moralistic dimension that will appear later. Nor is this farce out of tune, delicious satire as it is on fairy tales and novels of chivalry, in the volume *Tablado de marionetas*, the subtitle of which, "for the education of princes," is also meaningful. And if in *La cabeza del dragón* some aspects of the style of the *esperpentos* are anticipated and the Vallesque sense of humour is shown in high relief somewhere between comic and grotesque, yet the Versailles décor still appears. A great part of the action takes place in the fantastic kingdom of King Micomicón, and certain stage directions recall closely, even verbally, Rubén Darío:

. . . Rose garden and marble stairway, where peacocks spread their tails. A lake and two harmonious swans. . . .

In the royal gardens. The peacock, with tail always spread like a fabulous rainbow fan, stands on the marble stairway trimmed with roses. At its foot, the silver gondola with ivory canopy. And the fair swans sailing at the prow, like music in their lyric curve. . . .

Of capital importance in all this intermediate stage is, as said before, *La marquesa Rosalinda,* presented in 1912 and first published in book form a year after. The verse of this charming farce is clearly Modernist, both in form and in decorative background. The Darío contagion is decisive, in the sense that no aspect of the refined Versailles ambience is lacking, and all the characters, typical of balls and gallantry, move with steps of a minuet. The note of idle frivolity and courtly discretion is presented with mastery. It is easy to appreciate how Valle has incorporated in his "sentimental and grotesque" farce all the familiar fauna and flora of Modernism, but the most important thing is that at the same time he departs from this frequented path with tonality openly burlesque. The nine syllable verses of the prelude, dated 1911 when they were published in Darío's *Mundial*, show an intentional departure from Modernist solemnity. Of course, echoes of de Banville are not hard to find in Darío and other Modernists, particularly in Lugones, but let us see how, with tinkling rhymes, Valle tells us his little story:

> Y sollocen otros poetas
> sobre los cuernos de la lira,
> con el ritmo de las piruetas
>
> . . . .
>
> Por el sendero la vestía
> la noche, de niebla y armiños
> y la luciérnaga seguía
> en su falda, haciéndome guiños.
>
> . . . .
>
> Enlazaré las rosas frescas
> con que se viste el vaudeville
> y las rimas funambulescas
> a la manera de Banville.
>
> . . . .
>
> Versalles pone sus empaques,
> Aranjuez, sus albas rientes,
> y un grotesco de miriñaques
> don Francisco Goya y Lucientes.

This lightness being noted, *La marquesa Rosalinda* is also a seedbed of suggestions which Valle will take possession of later: the theme of honor in the theater of Calderón, as well as the conventional personages of the *commedia dell'arte* and their masks, which had been revived also in Modernism. Even in the moon motif rises an echo of Laforgue's irony and of Lugones, the much admired author of *Lunario sentimental*. Verses spoken by Arlequín in *La Marquesa Rosalinda* are pertinent to this:

> ¡Oh, luna de poetas y de orates,
> por tu estela argentina

mi alma peregrina
con un ansia ideal de disparates!

. . . .

¿Quién el poder a descubrir acierta
de tu cara de plata,
de tus ojos de muerta
y tu nariz chata?

. . . .

¡Hilandera divina de sonetos!
El barro de mi alma se aureola
con tu luz enigmática,
y te saluda con la cabriola
de una bruja sabática:
Luna que de soñar guardas las huellas,
cabalística luna de marfil,
tú escribes en lo azul moviendo estrellas:
¡Nihil!

It would be truly unproductive to collect the infinite number of echoes,
even verbal ones, of Darío in this work, but it should at least be mentioned that Doña Estrella, Rosalinda's beautiful daughter, was locked
up in a convent lest she overshadow her mother. On one occasion the
butterfly escapes, although soon forced to return to her *cage* to sigh
over her troubles and die with her *head under her wing*. She even
exclaims, "Oh, to be a bird in the sky/ to fly, fly, fly!" And the charm
is that Valle, point counterpoint, mingles with Doña Estrella's lyric
raptures the ironic commentaries of the Dueña and the Marquis. Nor
is the lovelorn page omitted. As in *Cuento de abril* the motif is repeated
of a young girl waiting, and the opposition between Versailles and
Spain appears again because in Spain the Marquis is given the evil
eye, he who earlier smiled at the blunders of husbands in the Spanish
theater. This change into a heroic Castilian Rosalinda attributes to
the *autos de fe* and the plays of Calderón.

Also with eighteenth-century surrounding in which Italian notes
are combined with the more classic Spanish, cultured as well as
popular, is the successful and complex *Farsa italiana de la enamorada
del rey* (1920). This is a work constructed predominantly out of literature, especially that of Cervantes, in which standards of poetry and
fantasy finally triumph. The literary satire is truly witty; various
planes of reality and illusion cross one another; again Versailles is

contrasted with Spanish usage ("This Spanish race loves only realities;/For the native Iberian, and more and more hirsute,/to name the Absolute is to name his mother"). Guillermo Díaz-Plaja has intelligently noted[55] how the imprint of Darío persists in this farce, particularly as regards the parody of "Sonatina" in the verses of Maese Lotario, which recount the loves of Mari-Justina, whose dreams "are clothed/in the sad blue of the ideal." Because of its French novelties and its *"pies excomulgados,"* the alexandrines of the puppet-master did not, of course, escape censure from the learned and rhetorical Don Furibundo, who for his part pretends to an academic chair.

In the new direction taken by his work from here on, Valle naturally abandons the sumptuous and exotic motifs derived from Darío and the Modernist school. Let us remember, however, that in *La pipa de kif* he respectfully salutes the American poet who in key scenes of *Luces de bohemia* even figures in person. It is worth noting moreover how Valle, in his great *esperpentic* novel *Tirano Banderas* (1926) sounds intentional echoes of Darío's poetry. The illustrious Spaniard Don Celes, baroque and pompous, flatters the tyrant and calls him by way of encomium: "Professor of energy, as they say in our Diario!" The pointed ironic intention stands out in relief if we recall Darío's poem, "A Roosevelt," which appears in *Cantos de vida y esperanza.* Again, to characterize the fatuity of this same Don Celes, Valle has very closely in mind some verses of "Pórtico" when he writes:

The Spaniard experienced breath-taking conceit, an overwhelming sensation of pride and reverence. The bluster of famous sonorous names clattered like hames upon his chest. . . .

and in another later visit to the grotesque Minister of Spain: ". . . he spread himself like a peacock with marvelous tail." In the tremendous passages where Valle satirizes the diplomatic corps, direct quotations from Darío can be found. First, Aníbal Roncalí, Minister of Ecuador, recommends a meeting under the presidency of the Minister of Spain, saying: "The young eagles which spread their wings for heroic flight, grouped around the maternal eagle;" then to top it all, the Spanish diplomat, who has developed an anything but healthy passion for the representative of the Ecuadorian government, calling forth the following observation from another colleague: "Lyrical, sentimental, sensitive, emotional, exclaims the Swan of Nicaragua! Because of this you will not be able to separate diplomatic action from the Spanish

Minister's flirtation." Thus it is that even in his eagerness to mock the tragic reality of America, Valle again adapts the verses of Rubén Darío, now in an ironic context.[56]

Some final observations

In the preceding pages we have seen only a few reminiscences, thematic and verbal, of Darío in various works of Valle-Inclán. The Spanish writer's profound admiration for the Nicaraguan poet actually goes much deeper and widens to embrace many attitudes towards the world and literature in general. That is to say, it is by no means limited to the use of the so-called decorative motifs of the Modernist school, those same aesthetic symbols that lose force in the hands of followers without true poetic talent. On the contrary, the harmonious swans and divine princesses are concentrated symbolic forms chosen in protest against the flat and shabby reality which both writers knew all too well. In the spiritual complexity implied in what we call Modernism, a movement of profound ideological content, there is always a desire to go above exterior circumstance, creating and affirming a world of eternal artistic beauty, uncontaminated by the bourgeois materialism of the times. Rubén and Valle, by rejecting in their work earlier well-trodden paths, reacted positively against a reality dominated by mediocrity, and defending themselves with these aesthetic weapons, fought the vulgarity of the moment. Thus it is that both are fundamentally rebellious and each in his way opposes the conventionalities of the epoch, declaring his personal disenchantment with the vulgar, common world surrounding him.[57] Once again it is the acute sensibility of Juan Ramón Jiménez that manages to visualize even in *Prosas profanas* a dimension often underrated in Darío. In his lyric portrait the Spanish poet says:[58]

Today, when [Darío] is back with his golden spear of harmony, with the same roses on his breast, everyone sings his triumphal march. Taking off the armour, we have seen the heart. I had already seen it when, drunk with melancholy, he sang his *Prosas profanas*. Few have said it, but Rubén is a man who feels; his verses have a celestial and sad depth, even among the reddest silks and bodies fragrant with sun.

In its most lasting aspects, as a fruitful lesson in aesthetics and a linguistic revitalization, Modernism was not merely a squandering of empty symbols, but a noble, passionate and selfless gesture to spread supreme artistic beauty and aristocracy of thought. It is true that Valle begins in the *Sonatas*, for instance, by stylizing the lovelier side of things, only later to rid himself of his complex of princesses—a phrase of Salinas[59]—and create a different beauty, more involved, if you like, and differently directed. It is worthwhile asking, however, if the method is not in essence the same, although around 1920 the weapons of protest used before no longer sufficed for Valle. What can be stated with confidence is that a poetic quality always characterized Valle's work, no matter whether beautiful princesses or deformed puppets peopled it, for in both instances he maintains a clear lyric tension. Ultimately, then, the thing that Valle-Inclán found in his friend Darío was a deep affinity in the conception of art as an absolute value, and a system of thought oriented towards the mysterious very like that which the Galician writer expounded in *La lámpara maravillosa*.

Like any conscientious poet, Rubén Darío had an aesthetic of words, that is, *del verbo*. It may perhaps not be idle to transcribe here a well-known passage from the "Palabras liminares" of *Prosas profanas*:

Since each word has a soul, in each verse besides the verbal harmony there is an ideal melody. Often the music is that of the idea alone.

The screaming of the three hundred geese, Silvano, will not keep you from playing your enchanting flute, provided that your friend, the nightingale is pleased with your melody. When she is not by to listen, close your eyes and play for those who dwell in your inner kingdom.

Resuming these same ideas in "Dilucidaciones," prologue to *El Canto errante*, Darío says: ". . . I have wanted to go towards the future, always under the divine rule of music—music of ideas, music of the word (*del verbo*)." In this context we may remember how Rubén Darío, with his sure criteria, saw the poet in Unamuno ("to be a poet is to look through the doors of mystery and come back with a glimmer of the unknown in the eyes"), and in these same prophetic pages the American poet said: "In Unamuno we see the necessity which requires the soul of the true poet to express itself rhythmically, to tell his thoughts and feelings in a musical mode." Having rejected the "legion of piano players" and with a mind open to all forms of beauty, Darío in his evaluation of Unamuno as a poet insists again on musicality as essential:[60]

The thing that stands out in this case is: the necessity of song. After wearying the arms and blunting axes in the flowering fields of lucubration, comes a moment when it is necessary to seek a peaceful corner of freshness

and green to rest in, where the limpid soul may listen to the nightingales'
song. These nightingales, like the bird of paradise the monk of the legend
heard sing, know of the eternal, of that which has nothing to do with the
changing and ephemeral in our earthly life or our rapid passage through
existence, which is that of a rainbow bubble.

The necessity of song: song is the single thing which frees us from what
Maeterlinck calls the tragic of every day. Insofar as time passes and in
spite of the triumphs of material advances, Orphic omnipotence grows and
becomes always more invincible. And the poet sees passing in triumph,
beside the aviator, the conquering flight of the ode.

Toward the end of his life Darío wrote his little-known autobiographical novel, *El oro de Mallorca*, in which the protagonist-mirror is a
famous musician. Baring his tormented spirit in this human document,
Benjamín Itaspes says to himself in one of his many introspective
moments:

Art, like his religious tendency, was another preserver of life. When he
submerged or let his soul float in it, he felt the emancipation of another
and higher world. Music was like an ocean in the waters of which, subtle
and spiritual essence as they were, he acquired the strength of immortality
and something like vibrations of eternal electricity. All the visible universe
and much of the invisible was shown in rhythmic sonority, like a perceptible angelic language, the absolute meaning of which we cannot embrace because of the weight of our material mechanism. The vast forest,
like the system of heavenly mechanics, possessed a melodic and harmonious
language that only demiurgic beings could perceive: Pythagoras and
Wagner were right. Music in its immense concept embraced all, material
and spiritual, and for this reason the Greeks also understood in these terms
sublime Poetry, *La Creadora*. . . .

The mention of Pythagoras and Wagner is not casual, and makes explicit the longing to be submerged in the cosmic harmony through a
series of magic correspondences and poetic associations. Another text,
in this case much earlier, found in the story "El velo de la reina Mab"
(*Azul* . . . .) confirms this same desire for absolute experience and
immersion in the great whole. Again it involves a musician:

. . . I listen to all harmonies, from the lyric of Terpander to the orchestral
fantasies of Wagner. My ideals shine in the midst of my audacities, those
of a man inspired. I have perception like the philosopher who heard the
music of the stars. All sounds can be imprisoned, all echoes are susceptible
to combination. Everything lies within the boundaries of my chromatic
scales.

The vibrating light is a hymn and the melody of the forest has an echo in my heart. From the roar of the tempest to the song of a bird, all is mingled and woven into infinite cadence.

And does not Valle surrender, from the beginning, to this mysterious power of the word, with all its musical and ultralogical radiations? Does he not long to pull the curtain back and approach the enigma of a world visible and invisible through a similar system of thought? In the Spanish writer this same passion for the musical and emotive word does indeed exist. These lines date from 1902: "According to Gautier, words acquire by their sound a value that dictionaries cannot determine. In sound some words are like diamonds, others gleam like phosphorus, others float like mist. . . ."[61] And in this connection will inevitably be remembered the short chapter of *La lámpara maravillosa* entitled, "El milagro musical." From the same book of aesthetics, a book full of verbal resonance from Darío and above all from the introduction in verse to *Cantos de vida y esperanza*, we quote two fragments where the clear meaning excuses us from further comment:

(1) The enchantment rests precisely on the mystery by which it is produced. Wherever the words cannot reach with their meanings, flow the waves of their music. . . . To the delight of their ideological essence is added the delight of their musical essence, numen of a higher category. . . .

(2) Let us seek out the mysterious and subtle allusion that shakes us like a breeze and lets us glimpse a secret meaning beyond human thought. . . . Let us make of all our life a sort of strophe, where the interior rhythm awakes indefinable sensations, wiping out the ideological significance of the words.

Moreover, in *La lámpara maravillosa*, the orthodox, neo-Platonic and above all Gnostic elements have been fully recognized. In this book Valle confesses to having given way to the temptation of practicing the occult sciences. It is worthwhile to remind ourselves again that Darío also was an initiate in the esoteric worlds of Spiritualism and the Cabala. At the news of the death of the American poet, as we have already mentioned, Valle lamented that he now had no one with whom to discuss his new book on aesthetics. In *Luces de bohemia*, furthermore, we find the conversation already alluded to, between Don Latino and Rubén Darío about their common theosophical studies and celestial mathematics. That is to say, both writers are related also, in a complex series of correspondences, by a current of thought that would permit them to penetrate the most arcane mysteries of the universe and achieve, by seeking the occult meaning in the whole of creation, a desired communion with the harmony of the Great Whole. Faced with the indecipherable, both were aroused and both tried, sometimes by the same road, to approach the secret and find the key to this mysterious harmony. Let us listen to the Valle of *La lámpara maravillosa:*

Knowledge of a grain of wheat, with all it evokes, would give us full knowledge of the universe. . . . Into this world of evocation only poets penetrate, because in their eyes everything has a religious significance, near to its unique significance. There where other men find only differences, poets discover the luminous interweaving of a secret harmony. The poet reduces the number of allusions without transcendence to a divine allusion loaded with meanings. A bee loaded with honey!

And a little further on he reaffirms: ". . . The thorn of the bramble and the venom of the serpent tell me a secret of harmony as surely as maiden, rose and star." For the rest, in the immense gallery of Vallesque personages, some professed theosophy and it is worth recalling here at least one of them, belonging to his last period. The antithesis to the dark dictator Santos Banderas is the illuminate, Don Roque de Cepeda, angelic figure and apostle of the redeeming light. Let us not forget that for the invention of this character, Valle was inspired to some extent by the figure of Francisco I. Madero, to whom theosophical or spiritualist ideas have been attributed. The author tells us of the man's profound religion, "forged of mystic and Hindu intuitions", and, resuming certain key ideas of *La lámpara maravillosa,* he then says: "An adept in theosophical doctrines, he sought in the furthest depths of his consciousness a relationship with the consciousness of the universe . . ." Thus, both Rubén Darío and Valle-Inclán, anxious to penetrate the occult meaning of things, turned towards the mysteries and sought exactly this unity between their own consciousness and that of the universe.[62]

In the preceding pages we believe to have offered ample proof, both in the form of concrete evidence and in quotations, of the mutual admiration that existed between Darío and Valle and the many ways in which each corresponded to the other. The two famous writers, united in a lasting friendship and in the supreme adventure of art, have achieved their portion of artistic immortality. Finally, an opportune epilogue to this modest tribute may be given in these verses of Rubén

Darío, where the inner meaning can be related equally well to the personality of the Spaniard:

¡Yo soy el amante de ensueños y formas
que viene de lejos y va al porvenir!
(*El canto errante*, "La canción de los pinos").

NOTES

[1] Angel Lázaro, *Semblanzas y ensayos* (Puerto Rico, 1963), p. 94.

[2] Juan Ramón Jiménez, *El trabajo gustoso* (México, 1961), pp. 227–228.

[3] Melchor Fernández Almagro, *Vida y literatura de Valle Inclán* (Madrid, 1943), pp.50–51.

[4] Concerning the theme of Rubén Darío and his Spanish friendships, the pages of Antonio Oliver Belmás are especially useful (*Este otro Rubén Darío* [Barcelona, 1960], pp. 141–194) and those of Dictino Alvarez Hernández (*Cartas de Rubén Darío* [Madrid, 1963], pp. 47–106.)

[5] Rubén Darío, "Autobiografía", *Obras Completas* (Madrid, 1950), I, pp. 102–104.

[6] *Ibid.*, pp. 141–142.

[7] *Ibid.*, p. 144.

[8] For more complete details about this significant encounter, see Carmen Conde, *Acompañando a Francisca Sánchez* (Managua, 1964), pp. 10–12.

[9] Juan Ramón Jiménez, "Ramón del Valle-Inclán (Castillo de quema)," *Pájinas escojidas. Prosa* (Madrid, 1958), pp. 133–134.

[10] *Ibid.*, p. 136.

These pages of Juan Ramón Jiménez are rich in literary and aesthetic intimacies, which have changed, with time, into literary history. In relation to the theme with which we are now concerned, we would not fail to mention the affection Valle felt for the work of Espronceda (no matter how pitilessly he satirizes him in *Tirano Banderas*), who, Valle proclaimed, saved him from d'Annunzio. Juan Ramón adds further that Galicia saved Valle from exotic Modernism. And lastly, how can one fail to remember the fine appreciation of Valle's style and language given by the poet of Moguer!

[11] Juan Antonio Cabezas, *Rubén Darío. Un poeta y una vida* (Madrid, 1944) pp. 235–236.

[12] Ricardo Baroja, *Gente de 98* (Madrid, 1952), p. 17 and p. 19.

[13] Francisco Contreras, *Rubén Darío. Su vida y su obra* (Santiago de Chile, 1937), p. 129.

[14] Francisco Madrid, *La vida altiva de Valle Inclán* (Buenos Aires, 1943), p. 292. For his part, Pedro Henríquez Ureña ("Don Ramón del Valle-Inclán", *Obra crítica* [México, 1960], p. 685) recalls the following words of Valle referring to Darío: "He was essentially good," said Don Ramón. "He had human failings. But no angelic sins: not anger, nor pride, nor envy."

[15] Felipe Sassone, "El lírico de la raza latina", *La ofrenda de España a Rubén*

Darío (Editorial América, 1916), p. 61. Juan José Llovet records the same reference, "Ha muerto el pontífice . . .", *Ibid.*, p. 114.

[16] Melchor Fernández Almagro, "Valle-Inclán, de cerca", *Indice*, IX (núms. 74–75, abril y mayo de 1954), p. 1 and p. 19.

[17] Fernández Almagro, *Vida y literatura de Valle Inclán*, p. 188. This same friend of Valle's has also said: ". . . Valle-Inclán feels wounded to the depths of his heart. No other writer of his time has he loved and admired so much. Federico Oliver, author of *La Niña*, and a young poet, Luis Fernández Ardavín, propose from the columns of *El liberal* a tribute to the memory of the 'magical poet and master' of so many; Valle-Inclán, jealous of his priority in the cult, hastens to reply to them, with his characteristic vivacity, stating in the same paper that appropriate commissions are already functioning in all the American Republics, in France and Spain. This last—he says—'consists of D. Enrique Gómez Carrillo, D. Rufino Blanco Fombona, D. Pedro Emilio Coll, D. Amado Nervo and another writer, myself, though unworthy.' 'Without doubt', he adds, 'in naming me they were considering, rather than my merits, the memory I have of the poet, the admiration I feel for his work and the friendship I had with that *gran niño* during his life.' . . . In effect, Rubén Darío and Valle-Inclán pass together and united into literary history, creators in collaboration of a poetic style, in prose or verse, which not only brought Modernism into existence but also shapes directly or indirectly, in large measure, the language written afterwards: a language which later came, in the mere imitators, to be frankly mannerist (pp. 178–179)".

[18] Rubén Darío, "Historia de mis libros", *Obras completas*, I, p. 222. It is curious to note that years later in *Los cuernos de don Friolera*, Valle obviously recalls a verse of this composition to incorporate it in the dialogue between Don Manolito and Don Estrafalario. The latter says, in the theoretical conversation in the prologue to this work: "Sentimentalists who at bullfights suffer for the agony of the horses, are incapable of the aesthetic emotion of the contest: their sensibility becomes the same as equine sensibility and, by *unconscious cerebration* they assume for the bulls a fate like that of the disemboweled nags . . ."

[19] Rubén Darío, "Algunas notas sobre Valle Inclán", *Obras completas*, II, pp. 578–579.

[20] *Ibid.*, p. 579.

[21] Besides "¡Aleluya!", a composition treated in the text, in the poem *"Clave V"*, called "Bestiary", are to be found the following verses referring to the elephant: "Meditaciones eruditas / Que oyó Rubén alguna vez: / Letras sánscritas / Y problemas de ajedrez."

[22] In his lecture on "The Art of Writing", given in Buenos Aires in 1910, Valle refers to this composition of Darío's and quotes a stanza from it, saying: "No one understood better than Zorrilla that there are words and constructions that have prestige because of their Greek, Latin, Gothic or Arabic value. And as his equal can be placed only Rubén Darío, who knew how to unite words of remote ancestry with new words from foreign languages . . ." Francisco Madrid has collected the reviews of these lectures, printed in *La Nación. Op. cit.*, pp. 184–201.

[23] Alberto Ghiraldo, *El archivo de Rubén Darío* (Buenos Aires, 1943), pp. 419–421.

[24] Dictino Alvarez Hernández, *Op. cit.*, pp. 70–71, 136–137, and 187–190.

[25] Ghiraldo, *Op. cit.*, p. 419.

[26] Alvarez, *Op. cit.*, pp. 136–137.

[27] Ghiraldo, *Op. cit.*, pp. 130–131.

[28] Alvarez, *Op. cit.*, p. 137.

[29] Ghiraldo, *Op. cit.*, pp. 420–421.

[30] Alvarez, *Op. cit.*, p. 187.

[31] Oliver Belmás, *Op. cit.*, p. 187.

[32] Alvarez, *Op. cit.*, pp. 70–71.

[33] We have already been concerned with this letter in an article entitled "Sobre la génesis de *Luces de bohemia*", (*Insula*, núms. 236–237, julio-agosto de 1966, p. 9) and, earlier, in some more extensive pages entitled "Las cartas de Valle Inclán a Rubén Darío" (*El Nacional*, núm. 1000, 29 de mayo de 1966). We have now seen that Guillermo Díaz-Plaja also has called attention to its importance in *Las estéticas de Valle Inclán* (Madrid, 1965), Nota 17, pp. 268–269.

[34] We should like to mention here two significant works of Anthony N. Zahareas: "La desvalorización del sentido trágico en el esperpento de Valle-Inclán", *Insula* (núm. 203, octubre de 1963) and "The Esperpento and Aesthetics of Commitment", *Modern Languages Notes* (Vol. 81, núm. 2, marzo de 1966), pp. 159–173. Lastly, we have read the article of Gonzalo Sobejano, "*Luces de Bohemia*, elegía y sátira", *Papeles de Son Armadans*, IX (núm. 127, octubre de 1966), pp. 89–106.

[35] Madrid, *Op. cit.*, p. 114.

[36] In addition to the allusion to certain of Darío's poems ("Canción de otoño en primavera", "Peregrinaciones"), we are interested in showing here another direct quotation from the American poet inlaid in the dialogue of *Luces*. Dorio de Gádez (Escena cuarta) greets Max Estrella with words taken from the first verse of the "Responso" for Verlaine, saying: "Padre y maestro mágico, salud!"

[37] Alvarez (*Op. cit.*, p. 198) reproduces a letter from Javier Bueno to Darío, dated March 9, 1912, with which he is sending the poet a eulogistic article by Valle. We do not know what text is meant.

[38] In his book, already mentioned, about Valle, Díaz-Plaja anticipated us in listing some of the same thematic and verbal reminiscenses collected here. *Op. cit.*, pp. 259–270.

[39] Arturo Marasso (*Rubén Darío y su creación poética* [La Plata, 1934], pp. 403–404), believes, for instance, that the archaisms of Darío's poem "Los motivos del lobo" come from the Galician writer's poetic drama *Voces de gesta*.

[40] For this characteristic procedure of Valle's it is indispensable to consult pages of Alfonso Reyes ("Las fuentes de Valle Inclán", *Simpatías y diferencias* [México, 1945], II, pp. 60–61) and those of Amado Alonso ("Estructura de las *Sonatas* de Valle-Inclán", *Materia y forma en poesía* [Madrid, 1955], pp. 292–293).

[41] In Valle's work there appears very frequently satire directed at the Academy and its members, but here we should like to mention only the burlesque portrait, presented in the *Farsa de la enamorada del Rey*, of the pompous and rhetorical Don Facundo (don Furibundo). Díaz-Plaja has seen in the aspect of this erudite personage unequivocal allusions to Julio Casares, recently, in 1919, elected to the Academy. *Op. cit.*, nota 28, p. 74.

[42] Emma Susana Speratti Piñero, *La elaboración artística en Tirano Banderas* (México, 1957), pp. 12–39 and pp. 136–137. For Valle's sources Joseph H. Silverman's article is also important: "Valle-Inclán and Ciro Bayo," *NRFH*, XIV (núm. 1–2, 1960).

[43] Emma Susana Speratti Piñero, "Génesis y evolución de *Sonata de otoño*," *RHM*,

XXV (núms. 1–2, enero-abril de 1959) pp. 57–80.

[44] Rubén Darío, "El modernismo," *Obras completas*, III, pp. 302–303. We allow ourselves to cite here a judgment of Valle's about prose and verse, dating from 1934, which is interesting particularly for the allusion to Darío. Valle-Inclán, talking with Gerardo Diego, says: "There is no essential difference between prose and verse. Every good writer, like any good poet, will know how to find number, rhythm and quantity for his style. In this way great poets eliminate empty terms, *appoggiaturas*, inexpressive particles, and keep to noble words, full, plastic and extended. Thus Rubén Darío: 'Ínclitas razas ubérrimas, sangre de Hispania fecunda,—espíritus fraternos, luminosas almas, ¡salve! . . .' " *Poesía española contemporánea* (Madrid, 1962), p. 85.

[45] The first to call attention to this verbal resemblance is César Barja ("Valle-Inclán," *Libros y autores contemporáneos* [Madrid, 1935], nota 7, p. 381), but the most interesting thing is to see how Valle is in love with this same image, re-elaborating it in various forms. We have noted the following examples: *Sonata de invierno* (Austral, 4a ed.), p. 104 and p. 149; *El resplandor de la hoguera* (Austral, 2a ed.) pp. 53, 117 and 123; and finally in *Tirano Banderas* Valle writes: " . . . encendían su roja llamarada las cornetas de los cuarteles."

[46] In "Marcha triunfal," these verses: "Los claros clarines de pronto levantan sus sones, / su canto sonoro / su cálido coro, / que envuelve en un trueno de oro / la augusta soberbia de los pabellones."

[47] Alonso Zamora Vicente has noted these and other examples of the contagion in his book *Las Sonatas de Ramón del Valle-Inclán* (Buenos Aires, 1951).

[48] For the genesis and elaboration of *Flor de santidad* this letter of Valle's is significant. In it he writes: "A few days ago I received a letter from you, here in this retreat of Aranjuez, when I came to write a novel five chapters of which I had had in hand for ten years. I finished it in twenty days . . . If I may be frank with you, this is the first time that I am in the least satisfied with my work. The title, *Flor de santidad*. It is a novel differing entirely in style and atmosphere and subject from the modern manner of writing novels. It resembles the books of the Bible rather than books of today; at other times it is Homeric, at others Gaelic . . ." *Indice*, IX (núms. 74–75, abril-mayo de 1954), p. 20.

[49] Raimundo Lida, "Cuentos de Rubén Darío," *Letras hispánicas* (México, 1958), pp. 233–234.

[50] Emma Susana Speratti Piñero, "Cómo nació y creció *El Ruedo Ibérico*," *Insula*, XXI (núms. 236–237, julio-agosto de 1966), p. 1 and p. 30.

[51] Darío wrote in "Los cisnes, I," a poem in *Cantos de vida y esperanza*: "Nos predican la fuerza con águilas feroces, / gerifaltes de antaño revienen a los puños . . ."

[52] In spite of a slight mechanical error, Díaz-Plaja has noted this same thematic trace, solely in respect to *El resplandor de la hoguera*. *Op. cit.*, p. 266, note 13.

[53] In an interesting work, perhaps still unpublished, which I have seen thanks to the author, Professor Gerard G. Flynn has compared "El palacio del sol," a story by Darío incorporated in *Azul . . .*, with Valle's *Cuento de abril*. Flynn finds gnostic traces in both works and concerns himself with the struggle between Christ and Cybele, pagan goddess of the earth, a struggle represented in *Cuento de abril* by the ascetic Infante de Castilla and the amorous princess Imberal de Provenza, azure country of art.

54 Professor Sumner Greenfield has seen clearly the importance of this epoch in Valle-Inclán's trajectory, and has written about it as follows: "The most significant innovations of the period are found in the farces *La cabeza del dragón* and *La marquesa Rosalinda*—a new genre for Don Ramón. Here are shown numerous shifts of orientation that will change into important characteristics of post bellum *valleinclanesque* literature. Satire, parody and humor are now added to irony as *materia prima* of the style of Valle-Inclán. Stylization of the human figure, a vital aspect of his art in every period, turns for the first time extensively and systematically towards physical deformation through a variety of dehumanized forms, notable among them puppets and grotesque elements. It is worth noting, indeed, that these physical stylizations are employed here principally for their picturesque and humorous value and not with the incisive moral intention with which they will be used later. Various types of persons from earlier works also are found in transition, showing the way to the final development some ten years later (Don Juans, old dueñas, ladies in love, cuckolds), and incipient new types appear, anticipating in the same way Valleinclanesque future: ruffians, soldiers, pompous ministers of state and other members of court and government . . ." "Valle Inclán en transición: una brujería dialogada," *La Torre*, XIII, núm. 51, (septiembre-octubre de 1965,) p. 177.

55 Díaz-Plaja, *op. cit.*, p. 225.

56 The quoted reverberations of Darío in *Tirano Banderas* have been collected also by Professor Speratti in her book already mentioned, *La elaboración artística en Tirano Banderas*. For our own part we should like to point out how in *Farsa y licencia de la reina castiza* Valle seems to recall Rubén Darío in an openly ironic context. Referring to the grotesque Rey Consorte, already *animalizado*, Valle writes: "La vágula libélula de la sonrisa bulle / sobre su boca belfa, pintada de carmín," verses that echo, now with a sarcastic tone, others in Darío's "Sonatina." Perhaps it is worthwhile quoting here the final distich of "¡Aleluya!," the second *clave* of *La pipa de kif:* "Llevo mi verso a la Farándula: / Anímula, Vágula, Blándula."

57 It is right to point out that the basis for these ideas is to be found in Ricardo Gullón, *Direcciones del modernismo* (Madrid, 1963), pp. 1–66, which, it is known, come from an immediate source, that is, Juan Ramón Jiménez, for whom Gullón has been and is chief literary executor.

58 Juan Ramón Jiménez, *Retratos líricos* (Madrid, 1965), p. 43. My friend and colleague Miguel Enguídanos called my attention to this important text.

59 Pedro Salinas, "Significación del esperpento o Valle Inclán, hijo pródigo del 98," *Literatura española. Siglo XX*, 2a ed. (México, 1949), p. 90.

60 Rubén Darío, "Unamuno, poeta," *Obras completas*, II, p. 791.

61 Quoted from the original text: "Modernismo," *La ilustración española y americana*, XLVI (núm. 7), 22 de febrero de 1902, p. 114.

62 Octavio Paz believes that a basic sentiment in Modernist poetry is precisely "nostalgia for cosmic unity" and "its fascination with the plurality in which it is manifested." Paz, surprised that the Modernist poets have been taxed with being superficial, resumes his critical thought saying: "Modernism rises as an aesthetic of rhythm and flows into a rhythmic vision of the universe." "El caracol y la sirena (Rubén Darío)," *Cuadrivio* (México, 1965), pp. 28–29.

RUBÉN DARÍO

CANTOS

DE VIDA Y ESPERANZA

LOS CISNES Y OTROS POEMAS

MADRID

ARTURO TORRES-RIOSECO

RUBÉN DARÍO: CLASSIC POET

translated by David Flory

FROM HIS EARLIEST YOUTH,
Rubén Darío acquired the aura of an exceptional poet, one already
marked out for a singular and prodigious destiny. At first the indications were vague and superficial, as for example his precocious anti-
clericalism, his infantile Voltairianism and his predilection for scientific problems. Later on we have evidence of his extraordinary facility
for versification in his thirty-page poems, his improvisations on out-
landish subjects and his versified journalism. His prolific output attracted attention even in his native tropics, where indeed it became
confused with poetic genius. This mechanical facility for expression,
on its own, would not have taken him anywhere, but the young man
possessed a keen sensibility for the language, and little by little new
and poetic words began to appear in these long and prosaic compositions: new poetic words which were to be the first manifestations of
exoticism. When these efforts became more numerous, when the ex-
perimental linguistic process became more precise, the value of exoticism was defined in the mind of the writer. Each thread in this evo-
lutionary process signifies a great victory for the poet, after an intense
struggle, and the victory can sometimes be considered as a loss. In this
case the exoticism of Darío leads him (at least in appearances) to
hermeticism. Now hermeticism can take many forms: that of Góngora
and of Mallarmé, that of Hopkins, or that of Eliot and Pound. The
hermeticism of Darío, however, is more apparent than real, because
his genius is actually that of simplicity and clarity. Such apparent
hermeticism is due to a certain level of difficulty in understanding the
mythological vocabulary of Rubén. This relative unintelligibility is
the fault not of the poet, but of the reader, especially the ignorant and
proud reader. The man who today has a great respect for science and
praises Einstein without understanding his theory will not do the
same for a great painter, a great composer, or a great poet. All art that
he cannot understand is absurd and bad. The worst thing is that this
man does not *want* to understand; he stubbornly persists in his ig-
norance and his pride.

In the case of Darío's work the resulting incomprehension was absolute and revealed a general lack of culture. Poems like "A Verlaine"
were classified as incomprehensible. Stanzas such as the following
were regarded as extravagantly silly:

> Padre y maestro mágico, liróforo celeste
> que al instrumento olímpico y a la siringa agreste
> diste tu acento encantador.
> Panida, Pan tú mismo, que coros condujiste
> hacia el propíleo sacro que amaba tu alma triste
> al son del sistro y del tambor.

How easy it would have been to find words like *liróforo, siringa,
panida, propíleo, sistro* in a good dictionary! Can we wonder, however,
that an uninitiated reader reacted against these words when Don
Miguel de Unamuno himself made fun of the word *"siringa?"*

The entire concept of poetry evolved with Darío and not even his
best friends in Chile could understand him. Perhaps the only exception is Pedro Balmaceda, although the character of his prose work lent
itself less to stylistic evolution. One has only to cast a glance at the
major themes of Darío's contemporaries to see a pseudo-philosophical,
pseudo-religious, pseudo-political and pseudo-moral poetry, all without artistic plan, without aesthetic radiations. Rubén Darío was suffo-
cating in this prosaic atmosphere of practical goings-on, politics, vulgar
bohemia, tariffs, commercial enterprise and provincial journalism. He
was predestined to be the exemplary author of his time, the synthesizer
of a poetical language and an extremely refined artistic sensibility.
For that reason he escapes from the real world to the world of imagination and daydreams, to the world of poetry. This was the magic universe of the French Parnassians, especially of Théophile Gautier. Darío
began to create a new language, and this language, because of the lack
of Spanish and Chilean literary models and because of the poverty of
the language spoken in a society of incipient culture, was to be of a
classical-mythological type. It is true that this style may be only somewhat genuine, and even a sort of classical *pastiche,* but over the years,
as Darío matures, we see his style also acquiring the perfection of
mature classicism.

After *Azul* Darío tends to *perfection of form,* to *spiritual maturity,*
and to a *consciousness of the history of the Latin language.* It seems
there may have been a certain contradiction at this period between
the poet's eccentricity and his maturity, but later we see the fusion of

all the creative elements. Being a poet of Greco-Latin tradition, Darío possessed a mental equilibrium which restrained the romantic impulses of his youth and thus enabled correct Spanish syntax to predominate in his writings; his images have a Renaissance precision and harmony, and his symbols are most properly those of a high Mediterranean culture. The proof of what I am saying is that the vulnerable point of his style, the only thing that betrays a weakness, is his well-known use of Gallicisms, a minor element in the Modernist form.

The first centennial of the birth of Rubén Darío makes us pause to think for a moment of the significance of his work and of his life, because Darío has become a miracle, poetry incarnate. At first he was considered a precocious child-poet, then a daring reformer of the poetry of his time, still later the master of his generation of writers, and finally the major figure of Spanish-American lyric poetry. I think all these opinions are just. His precocity is proverbial. His power of innovation took him quickly from *Abrojos* to *Azul* and from *Azul* to *Prosas Profanas*. No one has denied him the title of leader of Modernism, and today he is unanimously recognized as the great poet of Spanish America. It is true that precocity is not an absolute sign of future greatness, but in this case the augury was fulfilled. His spirit of renovation could have run its course in mid-youth but it lasted until the end of his life. He synthesized the most profound qualities and characteristics of the movement which he initiated, and since 1916 his name has been held in the highest reverence.

Sometimes the glory of an artist derives from circumstances. Mysterious reasons accelerate or retard the growth of his fame. Rubén Darío is an example of true glory, based on the firm foundation of real values, which with the passage of time tend to become permanent, eternal.

Rubén Darío's life was simple. He did not create a courtly, luxurious, dramatic or heroic environment with which to surround himself. His loves were unfortunate; his love affairs, vulgar. Poverty was much more a reality to him than was opulence. The drama of his life developed in derisive forms. What could have been heroic became reduced to no more than empty gestures. His fame then grew on its own, as a result of those authentic values of artistic creation. He put it this way himself: "My poetry is mine within myself." (*mi poesía es mía en mí.*) And thus it was, always: an extremely personal combination, organic product coupled with mental elaboration. Some artists create an artificial atmosphere in order to exist within it, and thus detract from their personalities either by inventing something false or expressing their thoughts and their dreams in a language foreign to their own experience. What long hours of labor Góngora must have spent in raising the scaffolding of his *Soledades* and what nightmares Sor Juana must have had when composing her *Primero Sueño*! On the other hand the pure aesthetic joy of San Juan is authentic in his *Cántico Espiritual* as is that of Garcilaso in his *Eglogas*.

The stylistic evolution of Rubén Darío goes hand in hand with his ever-increasing mental profundity and with the enriching of his thematic materials. Although he must have felt the fever of violent imaginative outbursts, he restrained his impulses and established the equilibrium of his classically conceived work. Many times I have been tempted to make the analysis of the creative mind of Rubén Darío: the struggle between the vital passion and the philosophical serenity of the mature man. In this essay, we will discuss some isolated characteristics of his creative processes, starting with his *simplicity*, an essential part of his classical attitude.

In the year of his poetic initiation (1880) Darío showed that simplicity is the dominant characteristic of his art. In one of the first poems of this period, he writes:

> Las aves sus dulces trinos
> iban alegres cantando.
> Y blandamente saltando
> de rama en rama, en los pinos. . . .

And in one of the last, in 1915, he says:

> A Amy V. Miles
> dedico este tomo
> de versos galantes
> muy siglo XVIII.

Darío follows his first lyric attempts with anti-clerical poems; later comes his poetry on political and didactic topics which requires nothing of exotic attitudes or complex rhetoric. Around the age of sixteen, the courtly theme begins to dominate his poetry, and it seems that a period of more difficult and *recherché* technique was initiated, but this in fact is nothing more than an enriching of oriental vocabulary. Any dictionary could have solved the most abstruse linguistic problem for the timorous reader. This is the period in which he employs words such as *ámbar, hastchis, sándalo, loto, cinamomo,* the

period in which his poetic geography became enriched with *Golconda,*
Alejandría, Bassora, the period of adjectives such as *marfileño* and
ebúrneo, and yet a period in which his syntax retains its accustomed
simplicity. Among the most frequent influences on the Darío of those
days we note the names of Campoamor, Reina, Núñez de Arce,
Bécquer and Martí, none of whom was given to stylistic extravagances
of any kind.

Darío's desire for clarity is evident in the poem "La Poesía Caste-
llana" of 1882 in which he praises "simple, harmonious, lusty" poets,
condemns *culteranismo* and criticizes Góngora, who, he says,

> con las ondas de su ingenio
> antes tranquilo manantial de amores,
> derramó de su mente los fulgores
> de la española musa en proscenio.
>
> Mas ¡ay! la ruda tempestad del genio
> con sus horrendos rayos vibradores
> de su alma en el vergel, tronchó las flores
> que aromaron su dulce primigenio. . . .

which brings to mind the fact that years later he was to repeat the
same thought in a masterful way, in the poem "A los poetas risueños,"
from *Prosas Profanas:*

> prefiero vuestra risa sonora, vuestra musa
> risueña, vuestros versos perfumados de vino
> a los versos de sombra y a la canción confusa
> que opone el numen bárbaro al resplandor latino:
> y ante la fiera máscara de la fatal Medusa
> medrosa huye mi alondra de canto cristalino.

Around 1887 a desire for style (*voluntad de estilo*) manifests itself
in Darío. In *Azul* (1888) it is evident in the prose of his stories, and it
attracted the attention of the entire world. The fact that the simplicity
of the poems of *El año lírico* is maintained, indicates that essentially
the poet's talent seeks the most direct forms of expression, while the
prose writer is permitted the caprice of experimenting with new
elaborations of syntax, youthful artifices which do not complicate the
intention or disturb the measure of his composition. The novelty of
the prose of *Azul* is never based on mysterious complexities or strange
conceits. The verse (in the compositions added to the 1890 Guatemala
edition) becomes increasingly rich because of the vocabulary that

Darío was gathering along his poetic development and particularly because of the expert use of those words. Take, for example, his sonnet "Caupolicán." If we compare it with his "Central American" verses, we find an evident stylistic advancement. The harmonious quality of the composition is superior; the adjectives are chosen with exactness and propriety; the verses acquire a lightly symbolic sense; the historical references are more abundant. For the cultured reader there is no difficulty in understanding the meaning of the sonnet. In the remaining poems of this section the linguistic element livens the aesthetic, for example, in words such as *avatar, oarystis* and *cinegético*.

Darío arrived at the high point of his creative power in 1896, when his first great book, *Prosas Profanas*, appeared. His poetic language is now definitively formed. His inventions of syntax are unique in the history of Spanish literature; his vocabulary has a novelty and grace never before seen. It is not the formal syntactic richness of Góngora, mathematical and sometimes arbitrary, but rather a logical richness, with a sure movement toward excellence, with a high measure of reason, with the constant desire for perfection which always characterizes the work of the Nicaraguan poet. Darío had learned, assimilated, and improved. The superficially metaphoric became more profound and refined; it was transformed and became personal: "Most importantly, do not imitate anyone," declared the young master. With this, he created a cultured poetry of exemplary brilliance. And yet, he complained of the haste with which he wrote:

I have lacked the time and had too much weariness of heart and soul to make, like a good craftsman, my majuscules worthy of each page of the breviary. (*Prosas Profanas*)

Rubén penetrated this mythological artistic universe, assimilated it, and with his marvelous intuition turned it into something personal. In this way the ancient becomes modernized and that which was archeological is transformed into poetry.

In reviewing all the poems of *Prosas Profanas*, we find in "Era un aire suave," that marvelous example of euphony, of rhythmic grace, of word-discovery, such structural purity that at times a verse is composed of a simple succession of nouns, while at other times by a repetition of one verb in different forms. Some of the most famous poems of Rubén are included in this book: "Sonatina," a model of poetic elegance, so ingenuously conceived that today it appears in children's anthologies; "Margarita," in which the florescence of form gives way to the intensity of passion; "Heraldos," in which a chain of symbols is deciphered in natural form; "Coloquio de los Centauros," a simple yet philosophical explanation of the myth of the divine beasts, "Sinfonía en Gris Mayor," which presents a large quantity of new and strange images, difficult to interpret. In "El Reino Interior" Darío offers us one of his most beautiful allegories, in a perfect, transparent, classic structure.

It might be observed that Darío still favors the narrative form, the story-in-verse, which does not lend itself to the subtle distillation of style. In "Recreaciones arqueológicas" the greater or lesser capacity for comprehension corresponds once again to the proportional literary culture of the reader. This is due as much to the cultural geography of the poems as to their symbolism. It is apparent that Darío was familiar with René Ménard's *Mythologie dans l'art ancien et moderne* (1878) and that this book had a great influence on his style. To the knowledge of the Greek world through its poets, we must add what Darío obtains from the plastic arts, the painting of vases and bas-reliefs transmuted into lyric beauty by the words of the young poet.

In *Cantos de Vida y Esperanza* (1905) we find explicit statements concerning his manner of feeling and executing beauty. Everything within him is "anxiety, ardor, pure sensation and natural vigor"; there is in him no "falsehood, or make-believe, or literature." His soul is the essence of sincerity. There are in this work poems of such marvelous precision and simplicity, that Darío convinces us that this is indeed his most genuine creative vein. Consider, for example, "La dulzura del ángelus," "Canción de otoño en primavera," "Letanía de nuestro señor Don Quijote," "Lo fatal," and many others. In the *Cantos* there are tortured verses, philosophical verses, sensual and mystic verses, but there are never abstruse or *conceptista* verses. He sometimes comes in contact with Góngora, but he never lets himself be seduced by him. It seems that his own poetical profundity kept him away from a poetic structure which was more brilliant, but which was also of limited duration and vitality.

In his "Dilucidaciones" (explanatory writings) in *El Canto Errante* (1907), Rubén affirms his belief in sincerity and simplicity, and continues to put it into practice. He buries himself in his interior world, he contemplates the mysteries of life, the accelerated anarchy of his day, and he develops a more philosophical attitude. His style, however, is always careful and exact.

And so Darío's poetic gift culminates in *Poema de Otoño* (1910), a poem of synthesis, the happiest artistic expression of the poet, his definitive philosophy of Man, in which we see life, in perfect harmony, in all its purity and clarity:

> Y sentimos la vida pura,
> clara, real,
> cuando la envuelve la dulzura
> primaveral.

A man who had suffered; who had written once of anguish in lines such as "Que no hay dolor más grande que el dolor de ser vivo" (there is no greater pain than the pain of being alive); "La camisa de mil púas sangrientas," (the shirt of a thousand bloodstained thorns); "La vida es triste, amarga, y pesa" (life is sad, bitter, hard to bear); says here—facing the moment of truth, and affirming the exaltation of the individual:

> Gozad del sol, de la pagana
> luz de sus fuegos;
> gozad del sol, porque mañana
> estaréis ciegos.
>
> En nosotros la vida vierte
> fuerza y calor.
> Vamos al reino de la muerte
> ¡por el camino del Amor!

Even though many of the poems written after 1910 are of great human significance and philosophical inspiration, in which the thought of death makes the poet's voice tremble, it would be futile to look through them for "reconditeness," for the obscurity, or for the metaphysical orientation of other poets. Quite the contrary, Darío's last poem, "Divagaciones," shows us that his trajectory was unswerving:

> Mis ojos espantos han visto,
> tal ha sido mi triste suerte;
> cual la de mi Señor Jesucristo
> mi alma está triste hasta la muerte.
>
> Hombre malvado y hombre listo
> en mi enemigo se convierte;

> cual la de mi Señor Jesucristo
> mi alma está triste hasta la muerte.

The first poetic attempts of Rubén were imitative of the prosaic Campoamor (with a youthful and playful "bad taste") or of the exaggerated sentimentality of Bécquer's disciples or of the pseudophilosophical tirades of Núñez de Arce, and they persist thus until his arrival in Chile. Shortly thereafter, the Parnassian note is sounded, first in prose and then in poetic anticipation of *Azul*. His pure literary taste still predominates; sophisticated French models replace old Spanish mentors.

But soon uncomprehending critics began to protest. Valera himself, basically fair in his study of Rubén dwelt at too great a length on his "mental gallicism"; Clarín (Leopoldo Alas) revealed his inability to understand contemporary poetic techniques; later Unamuno did not seem to realize the transcendental value of the renovation that was taking place in Spanish literary style.

Darío, then, turns out to be a strange poet to those used to traditional Spanish poetry, and a misfit of a poet, surrounded by the versifiers of America, who were busy singing the praises of political "caudillos," celebrating the beauty of the wives of presidents, deifying ministers and dissatisfied patrons. These versifiers, who were the first to applaud Darío's early compositions on themes such as those just mentioned, were also the ones who later began to give him a reputation as a difficult poet. His literary enemies were of three kinds: the masters of traditional taste, those who confused poetry with patriotism, who accepted a single artistic norm; the writers who envied him because they feared that Darío's triumph would end their local success, and finally, the ignorant poetasters for whom poetry was merely a social activity.

We can be thankful that Darío understood his mission, that he knew how to liberate himself from his initial literary environment, from the mediocrity of his friends and protectors, and from the vulgar bohemia that could have destroyed him. This is what he understood and said in his great poem "Yo soy aquél":

> Mi intelecto libré de pensar bajo,
> bañó el agua castalia el alma mía,
> peregrinó mi corazón y trajo
> de la sagrada selva la armonía.

Today those to whom mythology and its vocabulary are unknown, whose knowledge of poetry is strictly limited, still speak of the complicated genius of the Nicaraguan poet. A basic lesson in good taste and a dictionary would be sufficient to show them their error.

I have tried to show that Rubén Darío is a classic poet, and I believe that he is just that. I see in him a case analogous to that of Lope de Vega, who, dazzled by the genius of Góngora, imitated him only to return to his own original simplicity. In the same way Darío imitated brilliant poets (although they were inferior to him) and later returned to his candor, to his sincerity, to his clear interpretation of the world and to his simple and perfect form.

Darío now ranks on the highest artistic level beside Garcilaso, because of his lyrical fluidity and his immense tenderness; beside San Juan de la Cruz, because of the psychological mastery with which he handles the poetic idiom; beside Quevedo, because of rigorous structure and formal perfection; beside Fray Luis de León, because of his serenity. In spite of the fact that the famous verses of Darío

> Amo más que la Grecia de los griegos
> La Grecia de la Francia, porque en Francia . . .
>
> Demuestran más encantos y perfidias
> las diosas de Clodión que las de Fidias . . .
>
> Verlaine es más que Sócrates y Arsenio
> Houssaye supera al viejo Anacreonte

seem to express a definitive predilection for modern French culture over the classical culture of the ancients, Vergil and Ovid dominate Rubén's aesthetic horizon during the epoch of *Prosas Profanas*, and Platonic sentiment is the essence of his feeling in the love poems. In all the work of the great Nicaraguan poet the intensity of his sense of classical beauty gives way only to the intensity of his fear of death.

OTOÑO

Los versos de Hugo, el son de flauta elegíaco de Millevoye, un grabado en madera de Narts, todas estas cosas y otras más surgieron en mi imaginación, como evocadas, delante de la palabra negra sobre la página blanca: *Otoño*....; pero más que todo, fuiste tú, Belisa, la que surgiste cual de una cripta, de mi alma, desolada bajo una lluvia de hojas pálidas, á la hora en que, después de mediodía, la tarde otoñal mira melancólicamente hacia el lado en que aparece el primer lucero de la noche. Porque tú simbolizas para mí la estación de la melancolía en que los árboles quedan sin las galas de su juventud y la fruta que no se ha cortado á tiempo cae y se pudre. ¿Recuerdas? Juntos nacimos á la vida, y la primavera nos saludó coronándonos de sendas coronas floridas. Nos criaron de modo que bien pudimos, al amor del trópico, en aquel país de fuego, jugar eficazmente á Pablo y Virginia. Fuiste tú la que por primera vez despertaste con la frescura floral y carnal de tu cuerpo maravilloso, la llama dormida de mi sangre ; y tus ojos azules, fijos en los míos, en el tiempo de nuestras dos adolescencias, y la roja calor que de cuando en cuando empurpuraba tus mejillas, y la palpitación columbina de tu naciente seno, me revelaban que en ti también nacía la gracia misteriosa del deseo. Ese era el momento, Belisa, ése era el instante sagrado ; pero no supimos tender la mano y cortar la rosa. La manzana quedó en el árbol y la primavera pasó, con su cortejo pomposo. Yo partí á lejanos países, pues mi alma de Simbad tiende á buscar siempre horizontes y paisajes nuevos, así fuese fuera del mundo: *anywhere out of the world*.... ; pero en todos lugares, desde aquellos días de llamas, cuando el sueño me conduce á su imperio, he ahí que tú apareces tal con el encanto de tu dominadora hermosura sensual ; y tú eras la amada, la querida de los ensueños. Lo eres aún. Pues aunque te haya vuelto á ver, vestida de negro, simbólica imagen del otoño, marchita ya bajo tu rubia cabellera, gastada, ajada, semejante á un árbol que deja caer sus hojas de oro enfermo, en el mundo de los ensueños renace intacta para el deseo. Las rosas de tu rostro son las mismas ; tu perfume es el mismo ; tus labios, tus senos, son los mismos ; y así, en una rabia de amor, caes bajo la tiranía de mis besos, bajo la locura de mis caricias. Y es porque, ¡ oh Belisa, triste imagen otoñal ! el deseo que no tuvo en sus labios la copa ardientemente aspirada, quedó en el fondo de mi alma, en donde, al amparo de la noche y del sueño, me rehace una adolescencia, y del real otoño, de la lamentación de las hojas caídas y de la tristeza del árbol marchito, forma una alegría de abril, un canto de gracia erótica, una primavera, que, como la del supremo Sandro, va tejiendo guirnaldas, rítmica, en un paso armonioso *incensu patuit Dea*.

RUBÉN DARÍO.

[A contribution of Rubén Darío to *Caras y Caretas*, Buenos Aires.]

ENRIQUE ANDERSON-IMBERT

RUBÉN DARÍO AND THE FANTASTIC ELEMENT IN LITERATURE

translated by Anne Bonner

I TRUST MY READERS WILL ALLOW me to start from the premise that literature is, ultimately, a means of escape from reality; not only from the physical reality around us but also from our own psychic reality that overwhelms us with emotions, impulses and ideas. The writer discovers that certain very personal experiences provide him with a peculiar esthetic delight. What interests him as a source of creativity is not reality but rather this new revelation, whose value is primarily artistic. He has moved reality into the distance leaving a void which, in turn, is filled by an image wrapped in symbols. It is as if in the space left behind, a figure had come forth and said: "Here I am" (literally "I appear"), which is precisely what the word *phantasia* means in Greek.

To the extent it replaces a reality already moved aside, all literature is fantastic. But even so, there is some fiction that is especially concerned with creating believable yet autonomous worlds. This is the case in fantastic literature. With the power of his imagination, the writer renders helpless the norms that had ruled our minds before, suggesting instead the possibility of other norms as yet unknown.

Among the various types of stories Rubén Darío wrote,[1] there were some that fit this description of "fantastic" or supernatural tales based on mystical experiences, on dreams, on states of mind bordering on insanity. These metaphysical, metapsychical, mythological, allegorical stories, fairy tales and lives of saints tell of imaginary happenings Darío did not always invent. But even when he chose to work with actual occurrences, he would either make them unbelievable, disfigure them with extravagant interpretations, or otherwise alter them by providing a mysterious setting. Somehow his use of language enabled him to dislodge events from the hold of empirical reality, elevating them to the realm of fantasy. Through his skillful selection of words, his choice of rhythms appropriate to the movement of his lyrical metaphors, the use of synesthesia and the transposition of techniques from music and the plastic arts, Darío managed to "unrealize" reality.[2]

The verbal texture of a story helps to intensify the symbolic transformation of facts. In addition, a story is composed of certain structural elements: the more form given by such elements, the more the work distinguishes itself from reality which is amorphous. The writer's imagination is not only evident in his stylistic traits, but also on higher levels; in ideas that emanate from the text and register with our minds and our memories. There is form to be found, for example, in the way action is woven into a plot and given a certain design.[3] There is also form in narrative sequence,[4] in points of view,[5] in interior duplication,[6] in the utilization of other literary genres within the story.[7] For the present I will be concerned with only one of these structural elements: the surprise ending. This particular device can make any given narrative situation, no matter how realistic, seem the contrary. Life is, of course, full of surprises, but they follow no plan. In a story, however, unexpected turns imply a strategy of deliberate concealment. Darío keeps us deceived so he can shock us with his ending. He does this often[8] but, in my mind, the two best examples are "Un sermón" and "Respecto a Horacio." The device is even more effective because in both stories the author is playing boldly with the element of time.

As Darío wrote "Un sermón" in 1892, he projected himself into the future and, from that imaginary point of time, evoked a scene that supposedly took place the first day of January, 1900. This is a paradoxical resurrection: not of the past, but of the future. With verbs in the past tense Darío pretends to record the sermon he said he heard Fray Pablo deliver in St. Peter's basilica at the inauguration of the twentieth century, a term which for Darío and his readers involved a vague conception of future time. There is yet another surprise.

Upon leaving, still under the magic spell cast by the monk's sermon, I inquired of a French journalist who was assigned to the event:
"Who is that great man? Why, he's another St. John Chrysostom!"
"As you probably know," he replied, "this is his first sermon. He's almost seventy and was born in Spain. His name is Fray Pablo de la Anunciación and he is one of the true geniuses of the 19th century. His secular name was Emilio Castelar."

The shock of discovering, in a story written in 1892, this anachronistic apostasy that in 1900 the impetuous liberal, Emilio Castelar, will become a monk (or *has* become a monk, if we adopt the narrator's point of view) was strengthened even more by a coincidence Darío did not count on. As it turned out, that same Castelar whom we see in a fictional 1900 in the mysterious habit of an Augustinian monk, had actually died in 1899. If to begin with, his story had been just a playful joke, afterward Darío must have felt that it had been some kind of a premonition.

In "Respecto a Horacio" Darío set a trap that goes off only if the reader is familiar with Horace's Ode XIII, Book II. The slave, Lucio Galo, had confessed (in writing) that out of resentment, he had arranged for a tree to fall and crush Horace. Five years later, Galo adds a few lines to his confession: he is pleased with his criminal attempt because as Horace barely escaped the tree falling toward him he was able to write "the beautiful verses that begin: *ille et nefasto te posuit die. . . .*" Darío's text ends here but the reader who knows that once a tree actually did fall on Horace and almost killed him, is left with the remaining lines of the ode echoing in his mind. It is as if Horace himself were continuing the narration with his own words:

> On an ill-omened day, accursed tree,
> Did your first planter plant you, and profane
> The hand that reared you to the infamy
> Of country-side, and to descendants' bane.[9]

If the style used to transform language into poetry together with the structural forms that make up a story in themselves are able to attenuate real anecdotes, it is clear their effect will be even more powerful on material which, to begin with, is unreal.

What does it mean to say that certain material for a story is "unreal?" This is surely the most difficult problem in the analysis of fantastic literature.

The material for any narration is traditional in the sense that the number of possible situations is, of course, very limited and the writer has no choice but to repeat them. It is interesting to see what Darío did with old themes and, more important, what he felt to be the fantastic as opposed to the "real" elements in each one of them. Just as in the most realistic story the narrator's fantasy intervenes, in the most unrealistic narration there will always be a minimum of reality.

We have seen that a fantastic story rejects empirical reality to put in its place the image of a reality freed from psychological and physical laws. Obviously this freedom cannot be complete. If the work were to obey restrictions imposed on the real world it would no longer be literature. But if it could totally escape psychological and physical nature it would cease to be intelligible. Invention will always build upon realistic elements. So it is that the critic is first tempted to distinguish fantastic literature on the basis of its subject-matter; he would measure the angle of deviation between the content of a story and reality as we know it, setting up categories ranging from the probable to the possible, from the possible to the improbable, from the improbable to the impossible.

According to these divisions, there would be stories with probable situations like "El fardo." A man is crushed to death while unloading a ship on a wharf in Chile. Any insurance salesman could calculate the possibilities of such an accident on the job. There would be stories with possible situations like, for example, "La ninfa." At a party given by an actress in her mansion, a poet dares to doubt the existence of nymphs. The following day as he is walking through the park, the actress appears before him naked: now he knows he has seen a nymph. Although it may not seem probable that a hostess would undress for her guests, still it is possible. So much so, in fact, that years after having written this story (1887) something very similar happened to Darío himself. While in Hamburg in 1911, he and Fabio Fiallo paid a visit to a distinguished woman who was known to entertain prominent artists and writers in her salon. That afternoon the three of them were alone. Darío and Fiallo recited poetry. Their hostess, out of sheer gratitude, undressed and allowed the men to admire her beauty. Darío was convinced he had seen a nymph.[10]

"La muerte de Salomé" would be classified as an improbable story, although Darío presents it as an historical document. It is, however, improbable that Salome's head, severed by a gold serpent she wore at her neck, would have rolled next to John the Baptist's, which she herself had had cut off shortly before.

The events of "La pesca" would be labeled impossible. The chances that a fisherman, having thrown his nets into the sea where the stars were reflected, could catch the planet Saturn, and that his son could eat the star, then play with its huge rings as with the bones of a fish are, I believe, not very good.

Obviously this method of tabulating the realistic elements of a story is not valid. If such things can be measured and weighed it is because they are no longer in the story, but only in the mind of the critic. The temptation, then, to arrange stories along a probability scale should be resisted. Such scientific classification is not compatible with literature. The critic's criterion should be literary: not to focus on the nature of things, but rather on their function. After all, the same applies to the short story as to the metaphor. One might ask if a metaphor is new and alive or if it has been used over and again, if it has been fossilized in the language and reduced to a cliché. To answer this question we have to consider whether the speaker was conscious of having united two logical meanings in a lyrical synthesis. In the same way we ask if a fantastic story is new. Do the things related in it, however absurd, pass for the truth? Again we must discern whether or not the metaphor was aware of referring to a dual reality. What the author does is to establish tangential contact between a reality common to all men and an extremely personal reality of his own. Once there on the faint border line between two worlds, does he distinguish what exists only for him and what also exists for the rest of us? We can say that a story is fantastic if it can be substantiated from the text that the author's intention is to credit as the only explanation for the events he narrates, the one he himself has chosen to give. This explanation can be arbitrary and independent of rational causes that might apply to analogous situations outside of fiction. To study Darío's fantastic stories we must first understand what his intention was.

When I speak of intention, of course, I am not referring to the psychological motivation of Darío the man. This does not concern the critic and, even if it did, he could not pretend to psychoanalyze his subject. He should limit himself to the artistic intention of the author such as it is expressed in each story. When dealing with truly great writers, it is easy enough to put aside consideration of psychological experience and dedicate oneself instead to the description and evaluation of the work. But Darío, a pure poet, was impure as a writer of short stories. His fantastic tales are so much colored by obscure emotions that we cannot help but relate them to personal psychological sources beginning with his first disquieting experiences as a child.

Fears arising from superstition, beliefs imparted by the Church, repeated readings of *A Thousand and One Nights*, ghost stories, horror novels: all these left an indelible mark on an already nervous and impressionable Darío. For a short time as an adolescent, he demonstrated anti-clerical attitudes, but almost immediately came back to the Church; at least, that is, he declared himself respectful toward her mysteries and sacraments. He did not, however, take part in the rituals or the moral teachings of Catholicism. From 1890 on he professed a kind of religious syncretism that combined and confused bits of Catholic theology with oriental cosmogonies, the cabala with Masonry, the theories of Pythagoras with mesmerism, and esoteric doctrines with the occult sciences. At this same time, he was introduced to theosophy and the books of Madame H. P. Blavatsky, among others.

When he wrote stories of fantasy, Darío let himself be influenced by these beliefs. He would tell of things that had no logical explanation, that could not be substantiated by the natural sciences, but that, nonetheless, he believed took place. He seemed to be stimulated by the kind of literature that emphasized the improbable or even the impossible. Such writing has a long tradition. It was known to Antiquity, to the Middle Ages and to the Renaissance. But the history of fantastic literature, as we understand it today, dates back only to the end of the 18th century. After the Industrial Revolution, the critical scientific mind discarded the old phantasms and turned to the art of inventing new ones. Like Coleridge said, one had to "procure for these shadows of imagination that willing suspension of disbelief which constitutes poetic faith."[11] At the same time the new critical spirit was provoking a reaction, a return to the oriental, medieval tradition. There was a little of everything: skeptical writers who amused themselves with extravagant notions, fanatics taken in by the supernatural, etc. From it all a new kind of story was emerging; a story designed to excite the reader with its atmosphere of terror and suspense and to shock him with an unexpected ending. It was this fantastic literature, a product of the period during the 19th century between Romanticism and Symbolism, that Darío saw subsumed and given new life.

The relationship between Darío's vague religiosity and his also vague symbolism can be documented. His initiation into theosophy in 1890 had an immediate effect on stories written during the same period. Between 1893 and 1894, he not only wrote the majority of his stories, but in them appear his most novel thematic content: mysteries, magic, miracles, ghosts, psychic anomalies, and experiments in time. Two of his essays, both published in Buenos Aires, are helpful as clues to the influence that theosophy and so-called decadent literature had on the material of these stories. In "Onofroffismo: La comedia psíquica" (1895), he speaks of the poetic inspiration he got from his readings in theosophy. He says that in spite of the well-founded attacks against the "psychic comedy" of the theosophists and occultists, he, Darío, because of his credulity as a poet and his fondness for the supernatural, continues to believe, at least, as long as "he does not leave the realm of his dreams," in the "magical powers of a Madame Blavatsky," "surrounded by her subjects like the queen of a fairy tale." In the essay on "Richard Le Gallienne," we find his conviction that literary symbolism was an invitation to tales of mystery:[12]

The so-called decadents have searched everywhere for deep manifestations of the world-soul. They have found in Eastern cultures a world of exotic practices . . . They have removed all obstacles from the way of the psyche . . . Who better than Poe and his followers has explored the dark realm of Death?

Interestingly, Darío calls Poe the father of the decadents. The fascination the French symbolists felt for him is, of course, well-known. There were also other important names in the formation of Darío, the story writer, but since this is not the place to go into them all,[13] I would like to examine the case of Poe because it is especially revealing. In Darío's attitude toward this writer we find the key for understanding his artistic intent.

In his chapter on Poe in *Los Raros*, Darío expressed amazement that one who had created such strange worlds had not been a believer: "Philosophical speculation stood between him and the faith he should have had as a great poet. . . . He did not believe in the supernatural." It did not occur to Darío that perhaps the strangeness of the world envisioned by Poe may have benefited from that very philosophical detachment with respect to his fantasies. Poe was, in fact, a declared materialist. He reduced the psychic to the physical; for him spirituality was either material or it did not exist. The supernatural element in his stories was gratuitous; the note of gloom was owing more to a morbid curiosity about death than to religious or metaphysical concepts of reality. If Darío was surprised to find that Poe was imaginative at the same time that he was skeptic, it was because in his own case imagination was inseparable from religious beliefs. Darío found metaphysical concepts in "Mesmeric Revelation" but he apparently did not know that in "Marginalia," Poe had mocked the Swedenborgians who took him seriously: "This story," he had said, "is a pure fiction from beginning to end."

In an article on H. G. Wells,[14] Darío seems to contradict what he had said with respect to Poe, though here again his reasoning betrays the same desire to associate whims of fantasy with magical explanations. If before he found it hard to believe that Poe should write "extraterrestrial fantasies" in spite of his skepticism, now he assumes that Wells' "extraordinary fantasies" are in some way involved with the occult sciences. He is seemingly unwilling to accept that these writers, famous for their imaginations, would invent situations they did not believe in. His comments on "The Plattner Story" are typical. Mr. Plattner, a chemist, is hurled from the earth by an explosion and returns days later with his anatomy reversed: his heart on the right side, etc. In 1897 Wells was sophistically playing with physical-mathematical speculations on the plurality of spatial dimensions. Confronted with this example of science-fiction, Darío does not stop to consider Wells' mischief in speaking of something so strange as if it were an ordinary occurrence. Instead he takes seriously what, in the story, is nothing more than a possible hallucination of the protagonist: that Plattner says he saw dead people watching over us in outer space. In spite of the fact that Wells was an atheist and did not believe in life after death, or in the transmigration of the soul, Darío, rather than include him among the physical-mathematicians, considers him a spiritualist like Annie Bessant:

"The Plattner Story" takes on a level which undoubtedly enhanced the author's particular talent. I mean the hereafter, the other life, whatever conscious part remains of the human being after death . . . It would seem that Wells was either a member of select groups or a successful researcher of occult practices. This would not be surprising in the land of Annie Bessant, so often visited by Hindu theologians and masters of the occult.

Apparently what motivated Darío in the writing of certain fantastic stories was a very personal combination of psychological forces—superstition, anxiety about the mysterious, fear of death—the same forces operative in his verse as well. In some of his stories the unbelievable occurrences stemmed from non-artistic preoccupations. Instead of contemplating the figures of his imagination at a suitable distance, that is, from an esthetic perspective, Darío was unable to separate them from his own feelings. In this sense we can say that his belief in the supernatural, after inciting his imagination, deterred it and forbid it to go any farther. It was both a stimulus and an obstruction.

Darío's success or lack of it in the fantastic genre depends on whether or not he can liberate himself from theology, theosophy, oneiromancy and occultism. Such "liberation" does not mean his "ceasing to believe" but only his being able to see those beliefs in an esthetic light and to understand that they cannot be valid as true explanations but merely as incitement to artistic creation. Religion, as a system of beliefs established by a church and accepted by a community, does not always allow for the free play of imagination. Fantasy is more effective artistically the more it risks caprice, even heresy. Let us compare two of Darío's religious allegories that take place during the life of Christ.

The first is conventional: "Historia prodigiosa de la princesa Psiquia." Psiquia, the soul, is unhappy because she cannot be satisfied possessing love, or glory, or strength, or science but only the secret of Death. When the resuscitated Lazarus whispers this secret in her ear, she falls into eternal sleep.

The other allegory, "Las tres Reinas Magas," is the Christ story with the sexes changed. The one who is born in a manger is Crista, the daughter of a virgin and a worker. Three queens visit her and offer her the choice—after her martyrdom on the cross—of one of three paradises. Crista, who is a symbol of the poet's soul, chooses the paradise of myrrh.

This is the land of woman; the land where marvelous feminine flesh, displayed in its pagan, natural nudity casts a rosy hue upon the trembling twilights. Under the azure canopy turtledoves fly, and now and then the green thickets reveal flitting white shapes pursued by hairy creatures with cleft hooves.

In my opinion, the story of a Psiquia who longs to unveil the mystery of death and does so only by dying herself, since it does not avoid the commonplace, is artistically weak. On the other hand, the story of a female Christ who prefers a paradise of satyrs is so unexpected that it frees itself from the religious theme and, once outside the reach of orthodoxy, soars freely.

Darío's stories of miracles further demonstrate that fantasy suffers when not divorced from religious belief. The fantastic element here is not the miraculous event itself, but the way in which it is presented. Someone can tell of a miracle that upset the entire natural order of the universe without exciting our imaginations in the least. If the reader is a believer, theological explanations have influenced him beforehand and save him from that perplexed state so familiar to devotés of fantastic literature.

In "Cuento de Noche Buena," a monk goes back in time so that he is present at the birth of Christ. While he is adoring the Child, the organ he used to play in his monastery rings out with celestial music.

The material was most fitting for a fantastic tale: two occurrences—the friar's adoration and the music from his organ—separated by centuries and yet simultaneous! But Darío, more religious than imaginative, preferred to give to his work the tone of an ordinary hagiography rather than present in a flash the paradox of time and eternity.

In another of these stories, there is a monk who practices the occult sciences. With a camera given him by the Devil, he photographs Christ's face in the sacred host. The first version (1896) was called "Verónica," the second (1913) "La extraña muerte de fray Pedro." An excessive religious piety in his last years affected Darío in such a way that his artistic liberty suffered. In the 1896 version, Christ, surprised by the click of the shutter, naturally appears in the picture with a horrified expression: *Terrible*, says Darío. By 1913, the look, unfortunately, from an esthetic point of view, has become sweet. Obviously Darío, more attentive to the conventions of a religious tale than to the demands of a fantastic one, forgot that, if there are looks that kill, the one that killed Fray Pedro must have been "terrible," not sweet. He thought more of the image of the smiling Christ children carry engraved on their medallions than of the image of a Christ who intimidates us from atop Byzantine altars. The first title was also better: "Verónica," the name of the Roman woman who wiped Christ's bleeding face and carried away its imprint on her cloth, was an ingenious if not somewhat irreverent title for the photograph.

In short, a miracle excites our imaginations the more distant it is, not only from the natural laws governing reality but also from the conventions of a cosmogony founded on the supernatural.

The same is true of the dreams Darío used in some of his stories. He also believed in oneiromancy. In a group of articles written in 1911—collected after his death and entitled *El mundo de los sueños*—Darío said that for him dreams were not merely a psychological phenomenon but that they represented a supernatural reality. "There is much truth," he added, "to the ancient belief among occultists that everything we imagine, no matter how marvelous and strange, does exist." This idea that dream-images correspond to real things entered into the composition of some of Darío's stories. To see just how this happened, let us look at the genesis of "La larva."

For a time, Darío was obsessed with a nightmare in which he saw a cadaver coming toward him. During the discussion of a macabre painting by Gauguin in an article included in *Los raros* ("Rachilde"), he alluded to this dream without revealing that it was his own.

. . . the experience elicited by nightmares in which walking corpses approach the dreamer, touch him, embrace him and, in spite of being only a dream, he actually feels the contact of waxen skin and perceives the peculiar and frightful odor of dead flesh.

But elsewhere—in *El mundo de los sueños*—he does claim the dream.

I cannot find a way to describe the sensation I have in dreams when *something*, an unknown being who in that realm of darkness takes the shape of a spectre, a human-like monster, or a walking corpse touches me, takes my hand or simply brushes past me. There are countless descriptions that come to mind. It is something like an electric shock, at once painful and horrifying. But it is more than that. It is something that I just cannot put into words.

In *La vida de Rubén Darío escrita por él mismo* (1912), he makes a slip that is very significant to our knowledge about the evolution of the story "La larva." Inadvertently Darío repeats the same scene: once as a nightmare brought on by nervous tension and again as a true supernatural apparition. In chapter IX, he remembers his first frightening dream when he was 14 years old:

I had a dream in which I sat reading near a table at home, by the light of a kerosene lamp . . . In the dark frame of the door I saw a whitish shape like that of a human being wrapped in linen cloth. I became terror-stricken because I noticed that it moved toward me without walking . . . I felt utterly helpless as "the thing" came near me. I tried to run but I could not move. And the sepulchral materialization came closer, filling me with such indescribable fear that my whole body was paralyzed. That thing had no face and yet it had a human body. That thing had no arms and yet I knew it was going to embrace me. That thing had no feet and yet it was already close to me. Then came my greatest horror—the hideous odor of dead flesh. Something like an arm touched me, and I felt shocked as if by electricity. Realizing that I had to defend myself, I bit the "thing" and it was exactly as if I had sunk my teeth into a candle of oil wax. Then I woke up sweating and with a feeling of dread.

In chapter XLVI, recalling that same year of his youth, what was a nightmare in chapter IX is a real experience:

. . . one night just before dawn, in the square in front of the cathedral of León, Nicaragua, while in complete possession of my senses, I saw and touched a larva, a horrible sepulchral materialization.

Why is it that Darío would confuse dreams with fantasies? Like the theosophists, he seemed convinced that everything he saw really existed. A person who is sleeping, drunk or delirious may not have the control of a medium, theosophists conceded, but because his mind is relaxed he is susceptible to "waves of Astral Light." So it was that Darío believed the larvae and pupae he saw in his dreams were real. In *Viaje a Nicaragua* (1909), he said:

When I was 14, in front of the cathedral I saw a larva, or what the theosophists call an elemental. What I saw was true and really there. However, I will not insist upon it, for I'm afraid that my wise friend José Ingenieros might become interested in the account and look upon it as those who deal with science and have no faith look upon such matters.

"La larva" was published the following year in *Caras y Caretas*. The narrator, Isaac Codomano—an obvious Hebrew-Persian pseudonym for Rubén Darío, also a Hebrew-Persian name—swears he saw the larva:

The shape turned toward me and uncovered its face. Horror of horrors! The face was viscous and decomposed; one eye hung over a bony and oozy cheek. Then I perceived the smell of putrefaction.

What these quotes indicate is that, in the genesis of "La larva," there was non-literary interference. A recurring nightmare, reinforced by theosophical beliefs, became a story the author tried to pass off not as a fantastic creation but as an autobiographical document. In "La larva" Darío let himself become involved with his own beliefs. On other occasions he was able to escape them.

In "Thanathopía" (1893), the first in this series of macabre tales, the vision of a walking cadaver was the product of pure imagination. A magician's son leaves his boarding house in Oxford and goes to London to meet his new stepmother. When he sees her, he realizes that his father has married a vampire: "All of a sudden a smell, a smell, *that* smell." In occultist terminology a vampire was a pupa or an evil spirit given a new form, a larva or animal soul grown out of a person. Darío had followed closely the stories about Katie King whom the English occultist William Crookes had said was a dead woman among the living. He did not get carried away with morbidity, but structured his story skillfully with two points of view (his and Mr. Leen's), in two cities (Buenos Aires and London) and gave two solutions, madness or black magic.

Darío also made use of another kind of nightmare in his stories.

I cannot find words to describe the hypnagogic visions I so often have. They border on what might be called mathematical fantasies and are intimately associated with my preoccupations with the occult.

He goes on to give examples of nightmares in which an infinite number of fragments combine to form total images or, on the contrary, in which these images dissolve into thousands of geometrical figures like the decorative arabesques of oriental art. He surely was thinking of Poe when he called them "mathematical fantasies." In an article in *Los raros*, Darío associates imagination with madness, showing amazement at Poe's "mathematical momentum:"

... his fantasy is full of chimeras and ciphers like an astrologer's chart ... The algebraic nature of his imagination produces melancholy effects when he takes us to the brink of the unknown.

He must have also been thinking of the "cabalistic Mallarmé," as Darío called him. In an essay published in *La Nación* (Buenos Aires), he attributed to Mallarmé the same characteristics the French poet had seen in William Beckford, author of *Vathek*,[15] a pseudo-oriental novel.

No one else could have so dedicated himself to the mathematical formulation of nightmarish effects: 'the melancholy produced by huge and monumental perspectives' . . . 'the dizziness (caused) by the oriental propensity for numbers.' Is it that we are overcome by a whirlwind of hypnological remembrances? For my part, I keep a fluttering memory of all such things as of a far-off world in which I once lived.

He could have possibly been thinking of Thomas De Quincey, whose *Confessions of an English Opium-Eater*, were familiar to him. Since these writings of Darío betray unconscious recollections of various authors, it is not surprising to find echoes of Poe, Mallarmé and De Quincey together on the same page.

In "La pesadilla de Honorio" (1894), Darío refers to De Quincey. Honorio remembers, without identifying it, the sentence: "that affection which I have called the tyranny of the human face"; and sees the face of the Malayan who visited De Quincey. Outside time and space, Honorio, alone and anguished, sees "in the distance the overwhelming, monumental perspective of strange architectures, visionary arrangements, styles of an unbridled, prodigious orientalism." (These words not only recall Beckford, Poe and Mallarmé, but also De Quincey's association of Piranesi's style of architecture with his own dreams: "with the same power of endless growth and self-reproduction did my architecture proceed in dreams . . . ; the splendours of my dreams were indeed chiefly architectural; dreams of oriental imagery . . . multiplied into ten thousand repetitions," etc.) Honorio foresees a universal cataclysm—the city disintegrates heralding the End of the World—then turns to watch a horrifying parade: "Before him had appeared the infinite legion of Faces and the innumerable army of Gestures. The images dissolve into an inferno of prisms and mirrors, finally becoming "the seven capital sins multiplied by seventy times seven." The story ends with the suggestion that this march of faces and masks entered the sleeping man's mind with the sounds of a carnaval that was passing through the street.

In "Cuento de Pascuas" (1911), the narrator, thanks to a drug, is able to perceive forms that ordinarily are invisible, but that he sees reproduce and change into others; the air, like a many-sided crystal, refracts light and a woman's head becomes the guillotined head of Marie Antoinette. In the frightening atmosphere of the French Revolution, under the light of a head-shaped moon, characters stumble on streets paved with heads, walk among trees whose fruits are heads, hear heads moaning . . . "And the heads multiply in groups, in gruesome heaps, in Paris, nerve center of the world."

One of Darío's best fantastic stories is "El caso de la señorita Amelia." In it, all the characters grow old with the exception of a twelve-year old girl. For her alone, time has stopped. Amelia, like Wendy who would be another Peter Pan, is the child who does not want to grow up. The difference is that James Barrie created a magical world while Darío—through his narrator Doctor Z, occultist, cabalist, student of oriental culture and black magic—presents an enigma that he believes will someday be solved by Theosophy. Incidentally this Doctor Z really lived. A few years later he appears in *Les Mystères de la Kabbale* by Eliphas Lévi. In Darío's story, Doctor Z corresponded with Madame H. P. Blavatsky, who in 1875 founded the Theosophic Society in New York. Before telling his story, the gnostic Doctor Z hesitates: he is afraid no one will believe him. Then Darío (or, at least, the first person narrator) encourages him with these words: " 'I believe,' I answered with a firm, calm voice, 'in God and in His Church. I believe in miracles. I believe in the supernatural.' " In this way Darío reconciled, as indeed he did in his own mind, Catholic theology and occultist theosophy.

Trusting in this religious syncretism, Darío believed in the reincarnation of the soul. This belief, one of whose first sources was Pythagoras, was his inspiration for many poems. It was less productive in his stories, in spite of the fact that Darío was familiar with excellent models. For one thing, he had read tales by Poe and Villiers de l'Isle Adam. Poe had treated the theme of reincarnation with glacial impartiality; Villiers de l'Isle Adam, an imitator of Poe, with transparent faith. As an unbeliever, Poe's stories were far superior, but Darío did not learn from his reading. Instead of writing stories of death with a free imagination, he let his knowledge of the occult sciences infect him. In poetry he intimated the theme of metempsychosis; in prose he hardly dared to. There was, however, one aspect of the belief in reincarnation that tempted him in his prose writings. He called it "euhemerism in reverse."

Euhemerus, who lived during the time of Alexander, had proposed the theory that gods and heroes were mythological figures derived from real men who had been benefactors of the people and, for that reason, had been turned into deities by posterity. According to Euhemerus, Zeus had once been a king of Crete, and Aphrodite a courtesan. In his essay, "Stéphane Mallarmé" (1898), Darío admires the idea of "earlier existences" and submits the theory of euhemerism in reverse, according to which it is possible to see incarnations of heroes in men today.[16] Much fantastic literature has been written around this theme; Darío even used it in some of his poems. He imagines that a certain friend had lived centuries before and that he, the poet, who had also had a previous existence, had known him then. The following example is from "Máximo Soto Hall," written in 1890, the year Darío was initiated into theosophy.

> I have seen you in a Florentine painting:
> You have been a sculptor, an artist, and a poet;
> . . . . .
> We have met somewhere along the way,
> And now, quite indiscreetly, I write about you.

José León Pagano ("Rubén Darío en mis recuerdos") cites an "Epístola" dedicated to Díaz Romero during Darío's years in Buenos Aires that begins:

> Pagano, being a pagan painter and a poet,
> Was in the Renaissance my friend and brother.
>
> During the Italian Renaissance I saw
> Someone who loved me and was just like you;
> . . . . .

You looked proud, strong, overpowering, profound,
As if you ruled the whole world.

It is not surprising that a poet should allude to magic in verse without rationalizing it. It is in prose, however, a medium used to express the writer's thought, to inform and to explain, where we can best see what was happening to Darío. He would think of a magical situation, but rather than tell it as pure invention, he preferred to substantiate it with occult science. The result was not a story, but an essay with a narrative structure. If he did come out with a story, it was burdened with elements that lacked any artistic form. When he was playing the occultist he was distracted and could not produce pure literature. Because he was too involved with his own beliefs and doubts, he did not elaborate some of his fantasies—the one of reincarnation, among others. *Tierras solares* is an example of how Darío simply failed to make the most of his material. He imagines a jump in time from the twentieth century to the sixteenth and a meeting with Blanco Fombona in Benvenuto Cellini's workshop.[17]

This morning, after reading some poems by R. Blanco Fombona, a fiery young poet, I had a strange feeling. It consisted of the following . . . :
Blanco Fombona is an old acquaintance of mine. I first met him at the home of the Cardinal of Ferrara, in Rome, where we were cordially introduced by *messer* Gabriel Cesano. Together we often visited the illustrious Benvenuto Cellini while he worked and later accompanied him during four days of escapades in Florence . . . We talked idly in the moonlight by the bans of the Arno . . . One night at an inn he beat a servant-boy. As a brawl ensued, he drew his sword and, when the constables were called in, I slipped away . . . Blanco Fombona was an avid supporter of the Medicis and was particularly fond of Lorenzo "the Magnificent" because he was a poet . . . Then he went to Flanders. In Paris he won the favor of King Francis. He quarrelled with the Primatrice because of Cellini and seriously wounded one of his worst enemies, an act for which he was put in prison . . . Being separated, I knew no more about him for a long time. A mutual friend from Rome told me he heard that he had gone to a far-off land, had taken part in a war, and had been made king. Another told me he had been killed. And still another that he had become a monk.

Behind all this there are the makings of a good story. Why didn't Darío write it? Here are his own reflections that round out the unsuccessful narration:

Today, on a hot morning of the May calends, in the year 1904, I have written, in the city of Florence, the preceding lines which I have since read several times carefully and reflectively. What do they represent: the product of imagination, the indelible recollection of a past existence, or the remainder of a dream? Let's go on to something else . . . A bit of cheap Alcanian wisdom wouldn't be bad, or some of the Hindu's and H.P.B.'s theosophy. Such means do not appeal to me. He who has eves should see. For the rest, all is useless!

This extra-literary observation is a symptom by which to diagnose what afflicted Darío at this time. The free flight of his imagination was deterred, he abandoned his theme, called on the credulity of others with like spiritual tendencies, and presented the "case" of his wanderings with Blanco Fombona through Benvenuto Cellini's Florence as something whose explanation could be found in the books of Felix Alban's library, in Hindu theosophy, or the writings of Madame H. P. Blavatsky.

When, on one occasion, the esoteric theme of pre-existence cedes to the theme of heroic madness, Darío, relieved from his fear of death, produces one of his best stories. The action takes place in the same year he had first spoken of euhemerism in reverse. The narrator relates an episode from his own experience during the Spanish American war. He describes a soldier he had seen in Santiago, Cuba: He was different from all the others; "he looked to be about fifty years old, but he might even have been three hundred. His sad gaze seemed to penetrate to the depth of our souls and tell us things of long ago." He is the standard bearer. He speaks very little, and then it is about dreams that could never come true. "He believes that shortly we will be in Washington and our flag will be flying over the Capitol." They all laugh at him: "They say that under his uniform he wears an old suit of armor." No one knows his name but his knapsack is stamped with two letters: D. Q. Suddenly the news is out: the Americans have won, "now Spain has nothing left of the world she discovered." They would have to surrender to the enemy.

When the time came to hand over the flag, something incredible happened that inspired awe in all those present. That strange man, whose eyes were as deep as the centuries, still carrying the red and yellow flag, gave us a look of bitter farewell and, as no one dared to touch him, slowly walked toward the cliff and jumped off. For what seemed a long time, we heard the sound of metal against rocks from the darkness of the precipice.

Then—euhemerism in reverse—everyone discovers in the soldier of 1898 none other than Don Quixote. The story is called "D. Q."[18]

Reality has been supplanted by an enigmatic and disturbing series of events with no more explanation than the one fantasy would provide. Darío wrote few fantastic stories of this type and quality. The lofty position he holds in literary history is due to his poetry, not to his fiction. But in a few cases he was also a master of the short story. Thus he was actually twice a master, the master-builder of an ivory tower as well as of a wind-swept tower of fantasy.

NOTES

[1] *Cuentos completos.* Edition and notes by E. Mejía Sánchez, Mexico, 1950. The fine study by Raimundo Lida that appears here as a prologue—"Los cuentos de Rubén Darío"—was revised, enlarged and published later in *Letras hispánicas,* Mexico, 1958.

[2] Two examples of verbal magic will suffice. In "La muerte de la emperatriz de la China", the situation is real. Darío took it from something a friend told him when he was in Chile. Pedro Balmaceda said he had fallen in love with a terra-cotta bust. Darío sets his story in Paris where two lovers quarrel because she, Suzette, is jealous of the affection Recaredo feels for the porcelain statue of a Chinese empress. In this woman's jealousy, no matter how contrived, we recognize very real human emotions. But Darío, through the use of poetic prose, gradually replaces this reality with an imaginary world. The story begins with a metaphor that strips Suzette of her human characteristics: she is a woman-jewel-bird who lives in a house-box-cage. The idealizing function of Darío's language is reinforced by a leitmotif of estheticism: the conflict between life and art. When Suzette, out of jealousy, breaks the porcelain bust, she repents and admits the superiority of art over life. Such anti-realism is even more evident in "Mi tía Rosa." The story is based on Darío's first encounter with love, an adolescent romance with his cousin whom he had mentioned in "Palomas blancas y garzas morenas" (*Azul*), and again in the fifth chapter of *La vida de Rubén Darío escrita por él mismo.* The evocation begins in the heavy style of a memoir. Suddenly it becomes a poem, ending with his aunt, transformed into a naked Venus, urging the youth to persevere in his love affair. If style is capable of changing real incidents like these, it seems valid to insist on its power to undo reality when from within historical circumstances it can suggest magical atmospheres—like in "Huitzilopoxtli"—or idylic atmospheres—"Historia de un 25 de mayo"—or when the very material for a story is fictitious—"El linchamiento de Puck." Often poetic style turns a story into a poem in prose: "Luz de luna," "Este es el cuento de la sonrisa de la Princesa Diamantina"; or the series of variations on the theme of the rose: "La resurrección de la rosa," "Preludio a Primavera," "El nacimiento de la col," "En la batalla de las flores." In the story "Por el Rhin" the delicate line of action is seen against the light inside a crystal ball and, there, is confused with multi-colored figures taken from *Faust* and other German sources. I might also add to what I have said the observations Raimundo Lida makes in his

study already cited, and what Rudolf Kochler says in "La actitud impresionista en los cuentos de Rubén Darío.", *Eco*, Bogotá, XIV, 84 (April 1967).

[3] Some of the designs of Darío's stories are very ingenious. If I had more time, and the means, I could diagram them with geometric or even topological clarity. In the place of diagrams, metaphors are handy. I would say, metaphorically, that there are some stories Darío decorated with the design of a fan, others with a pearl necklace, others with an hour glass. This is not the place to develop these metaphors either, but to demonstrate what I mean, I suggest that "Palimpsesto II" is an example of the hour glass design. We have to invert the story like we would an hour glass so that the action can continue. First position of the story-clock: a satyr and a centaur, although saddened by the death of the pagan gods, worship the God of the Christians. Second position: two hermits, Pablo and Antonio, announce that the satyr and the centaur will be rewarded for their conversion to the new faith. Think also of the pattern of a river that divides into two branches, and between islands and meanderings, finally disappears. In "Voz de lejos," the poet begins talking about the life of two saints, then his discourse breaks into fragments and falls apart. Or think of the design of a musical staff in "Las siete bastardas de Apolo," a verbal play on the names of notes and the double meaning of "sí" in the language of music and of women.

[4] A sequence that no sooner advances chronologically than it leaps back in time, then forward again. ("Voz de lejos").

[5] Narrative focuses according to the speaker's position outside of the story (perspectives of an omniscient author and of an observant author), or from within it (perspectives of the author-witness and the author-protagonist), with sudden changes when the point of view moves from that of the narrator to that of a character ("La pesca") or from one character to another ("Las razones de Ashavero").

[6] The story framed by words addressed to a friend which, in themselves, make up another story ("Un cuento para Jeanette"); the story with a "double" ("El Salomón negro"); the story that is interrupted when the narrator with deliberate irony begins to converse with an interlocutor or with the reader. In "Sor Filomela," for example, the author addresses himself to the reader: "And now, sir, I beg you to . . ." and an imaginary listener interrupts: "But doesn't what you're saying have to do with an actress?"

[7] Adaptions of hagiography ("La leyenda de San Martín, patrón de Buenos Aires"), apologues ("El nacimiento de la col"), theatrical dialogues ("Voz de lejos"), letters ("Carta del país azul"), memoirs ("Mi tía Rosa"), intimate diaries ("Esta era una reina"), allegories ("Cátedra y Tribuna"), etc.

[8] In "Un retrato de Watteau" from the series "En Chile" (*Azul*), it is suggested that an authentic marquise from the 18th century is making herself up in front of the mirrors in her rococo dressing room. In the end we find out that she is simply a woman from Santiago, Chile, getting ready for a masquerade ball. In "Por qué," there is a speech vibrant with moral indignation and revolutionary concern for justice. In the last lines of the story we learn that it has come from the mouth of a rogue. In his Epode II, Horace has the same kind of surprising twist. After an impressive description of the charms of rural life—"Beatus ille"—the speaker, Alfius, a money lender, returns to his anti-bucolic world. Using this same technique, Darío practically makes short stories of some of his chronicles. In *Todo al vuelo* there are pages where Darío describes the uneventful life of a run-of-the-mill

bureaucrat, then surprises us with the revelation that "he is the son of Paul Verlaine." The title of this selection is "El faunida"; that is, the son of the Faun, Verlaine.

[9] Horace, *Odes*, William Hawthorn Mills, trans., (Lederer Street and Zeus Company: Berkeley (1921). [Translator's note.]

[10] Fabio Fiallo, "El alma candorosa de Rubén Darío," *Rubén Darío y sus amigos dominicanos*. E. Rodríguez Demorizi (Bogotá, 1948).

[11] S. T. Coleridge, *Biographia literaria*, II, 6, Cambridge, 1920.

[12] "Onofroffismo. La comedia psíquica," *La Nación*, Buenos Aires, 1895, published in *Prosa dispersa*, Madrid, 1919. "Richard Le Gallienne," *Revista de América*, no. 2, 1894, included in *Obras completas*, vol. I, Madrid, Afrodisio Aguado, 1950–53. The information Darío had on spiritualism, esoteric sciences, demonology and theosophy is documented in "La Esfinge," a dialogue, yet to be published in book form, that appeared in *La Nación*, Buenos Aires, 16-III-1895 under the pseudonym "Misterium." In this dialogue, Alfa (who represents the skeptic side of Darío) converses with Omega (who represents his faith) about the magician Onofroff, a popular figure on the stage at that time in Buenos Aires.

[13] A list of names associated with fantastic literature and cited by Darío should be compiled and should include not only men of letters but also "delvers in the occult" and pictorial artists who left some mark on his imagination. One should begin, of course, with *A Thousand and One Nights*, a literary archtype with oriental setting, and the authors of "terror" novels Darío read as a child, such as Jean Baptiste Regnault-Warin (*La caverne de Strozzi*, 1798) and the English novelists of the late 18th-century "Gothic revival." One should probably close with the authors of pseudo-scientific novels which fascinated Darío (see "El pueblo del polo," *Letras*, Paris, 1911). The following list, though incomplete, should prove useful. English and American: William Beckford, Max Beerbohm, Thomas DeQuincey, Arthur Conan Doyle, H. Rider Haggard, Lafcadio Hearn, Rudyard Kipling, Matthew Gregory Lewis, Edward Bulwer Lytton, Edgar Allan Poe, Ann Radcliffe, Robert Louis Stevenson, Horace Walpole, H. G. Wells, Oscar Wilde. French: Paul Adam, Honoré de Balzac, Léon Bloy, Edouard Dubus, Erckmann-Chatrian (Emile Erckmann and Alexandre Chatrian), Nicolas Camille Flammarion, Anatole France, Théophile Gautier, Théodore Hannon, Ernest Hello, Joris Karl Huysmans, Alfred Jarry, Lautréamont (Isidore Lucien Ducasse), Jean Lorrain (Paul Duval), Maurice Maeterlinck, Guy de Maupassant, Catulle Mendès, Prosper Merimée, Octave Mirbeau, Jean Moréas, Charles Nodier, Gérard de Nerval, Rachilde (Marguerite Eymery Vallette), Henri F. J. de Régnier, Jean Richepin, Marcel Schwob, Jules Verne, and Auguste Villiers de l'Isle Adam. Italian: Fra Domenico Cavalca and Antonio Fogazzaro. Spanish: Gustavo Adolfo Bécquer and Juan Valera. Delvers in the occult: Apuleius, Helena Petrovna Blavatsky, Jean Bodin, Jules Bois, Jacques Cazotte, William Crookes, Gérard A. V. Encausse ("Papus"), Joseph von Görres, Stanislas de Guaita, Eliphas Lévi, Paracelsus, Sar Josephin Péladan, Edouard Schuré, and Emanuel Swedenborg. Pictorial artists: Aubrey Beardsley, William Blake, Hieronymus Bosch, Peter Brueghel "the Elder," Paul Gauguin, Grandville (Jean I. Gérard), Charles de Groux, Victor Hugo (his drawings), Edvard Munch, Giambattista Piranesi, Odilon Redon, Félicien Rops, and J. M. W. Turner.

[14] "Wells," in his *Obras Completas*. This was written after 1900.

[15] "Stéphane Mallarmé," *Escritos inéditos. Recogidos de periódicos de Buenos Aires y anotados por E. K. Mapes,* New York, 1938.

[16] *Ibid.*: "An euhemerism *à rebours.* Certain men living a temporary incarnation, having originally been gods, and presently maintaining a vague, clandestine relation with the Absolute. The suspicion or the certain knowledge of previous existences."

[17] The story of an encounter with Blanco Fombona and Benvonuto Cellini as Darío wrote it for *Todo al vuelo,* was published without the first lines, as "Prólogo para *Pequeña ópera lírica* de Rufino Blanco Fombona" (1904). On another occasion —"Primavera apolínea"—Darío again used fiction as the prologue to a book: a poet tells his life; he turns out to be Alejandro Sux, author of *La juventud intelectual de la América hispana,* (1911), the book Darío was introducing.

[18] "D.Q." appeared in Buenos Aires in the *Almanaque Péuser* around 1899. I thank E. H. Duffau for information on this date. Much later it was published in *Fray Mocho,* Buenos Aires, 13-I-1920. Ernesto Mejía Sánchez ("Un cuento desconocido de Rubén Darío," *Gaceta del Fondo de Cultura Económica,* México, XIII, 140, April 1966) took it from this source. Raimundo Lida tells me "D.Q." was reproduced in *Don Quijote,* Madrid, VIII, 8 (24-II-1899).

V.

Sabia de la Sofía que sabe antiguas ciencias
Te sumerges en reces entre imposibles muros,
Y más allá de todas las vulgares conciencias
Exploras los recodos ~~?~~ más terribles y obscuros.

~~Y nos encuentras~~
Y encuentras sombra y duelo. Que sombra y duelo encuentres
~~En la eterna [illegible] que~~

Bajo la viña en donde nace el vino del Diablo.
Te posas en los senos, te posas en los vientres
Que hicieron a Juan ~~e~~ loco e hicieron cuerdo a Pablo
A Juan virgen y a Pablo militar y violento.

[Fragment of Darío's autograph of *Divina Psiquis*]

BIBLIOGRAPHICAL NOTES
ON THE
CONTRIBUTORS

Enrique Anderson-Imbert is Victor S. Thomas Professor of Hispanic-American Literature at Harvard University. Among his works: *Estudios sobre escritores de América* (Buenos Aires: Editorial Raigal, 1954); *La crítica literaria contemporánea* (Buenos Aires: Gure, 1957); *El cuento español* (Buenos Aires: Columba, 1959); *Crítica interna* (Madrid: Taurus, 1961); *Los domingos del profesor* (México: Editorial Cultura, 1965); *El gato de Cheshire, narraciones* (Buenos Aires: Losada, 1965); *Spanish American Literature; a History;* translated from the Spanish by John V. Falconieri (Detroit: Wayne State University Press, 1963); *The Other Side of the Mirror (El grimorio)*; authorized translation by Isabel Reade (Carbondale: Southern Illinois University, 1966). Professor Anderson-Imbert is the author of a study on Darío's poetry, included in the edition prepared by Ernesto Mejía Sánchez (Mexico: Fondo de Cultura Económica, 1952). "Los cuentos fantásticos de Rubén Darío" was published by Harvard University in May, 1967.

Miguel Enguídanos is Professor of Spanish and Portuguese at Indiana University. His works include that of associate editor of *Image of Spain* (with Ramón Martínez-López and Miguel González-Gerth), a special issue of *The Texas Quarterly* (June, 1961). Also: *La poesía de Luis Palés Matos* (Río Piedras: Ediciones de la Universidad de Puerto Rico, 1961). Profesor Enguídanos is the author of a study of Jorge Luis Borges included in the Argentine writer's *Dreamtigers*; translated by Mildred Boyer and Harold Morland (Austin: University of Texas Press, 1964). He is also currently preparing a book on the work of Darío. "Tensiones interiores en la obra de Rubén Darío" appeared in *Papeles de Son Armadans* (Madrid-Palma de Mallorca) nos. CXXXIII-VIII (agosto-setiembre de 1967).

Eugenio Florit is Professor of Spanish at Barnard College, Columbia University. He is co-editor of *Literatura hispanoamericana, antología e introducción histórica* (with Enrique Anderson-Imbert; New York: Holt, Rinehart and Winston, 1960). His authorship includes a study of José Martí's poetry included in Prof. Florit's edition of *Versos* (New York: Las Americas Publishing Co., 1962). Also many books of original poems including *Hábito de esperanza* (Madrid: Insula, 1965).

Allen W. Phillips was Professor of Spanish and Portuguese at Indiana University when this symposium took place; he is now at the University of Texas at Austin. His works include the following: *Ramón López Velarde, el poeta y el prosista* (México: Instituto Nacional de Bellas Artes, 1962), *Francisco González León, el poeta de Lagos* (México: Instituto Nacional de Bellas Artes, 1964), *Estudios y notas sobre literatura hispanoamericana* (México: Editorial Cultura, 1965). At present he is preparing a book on Ramón del Valle-Inclán.

Arturo Torres-Rioseco is Professor Emeritus of Latin American Literature at the University of California, Berkeley. He is the author of several works on Darío: *Rubén Darío, casticismo y americanismo; estudio precedido de una biografía del poeta* (Cambridge; Harvard University Press; London: Oxford University Press, 1931); *Vida y poesía de Rubén Darío* (Buenos Aires: Emecé Editores, 1944); *Antología poética de Rubén Darío* (selección, estudio preliminar, cronología, notas y glosario de Arturo Torres-Rioseco; Guatemala: Ediciones del Gobierno de Guatemala, 1948; Berkeley: University of California Press, 1949). Also: *Precursores del modernismo* (Madrid: Calpe, 1925; New York: Las Americas Publishing Co., 1963), *The Epic of Latin American Literature* (London: Oxford University Press, 1942; Berkeley: University of California Press, 1959), *Ensayos sobre literatura latinoamericana* (México: Tezontle; 1953; Berkeley, University of California Press, 1953), *Aspects of Spanish-American Literature* (Seattle: University of Washington Press, 1963).

One Thousand Copies Printed
White Warren's Olde Style Sixty Pound Book
At
The University of Texas Printing Division,
Proof Having Been Read
By
The Editors
And
Mrs. Helen M. Barthelme
Dust Jacket and Title Page Design by David Price
Production Assistance by Linda Kennemer